Praise

Each day you have the choice to create a new beginning to your life story. You have a chance to create a whole new story if you wanted to; a story you want to remember on the roller coaster of life and say, "I had the time of my life." As you ride the highs and lows, remember to hang onto Dianna Bowes' book, The Fabulous at 50 Re-Experience, it reminds us all that it is never too late to create a life worth living and provides practical tips and tools to inspire and transform our lives. Get ready and enjoy the ride, it's going to be fabulous!

Debra Kasowski, Bestselling Author, Speaker,
and Certified Executive Coach
www.debrakasowski.com

"Dianna's book, "Fab@50 Re-Experience" is not only a compelling read; it's a step-by-step recipe for all women who desire to thrive. The stories shared by Dianna and her Fabulous at 50 community brought me to tears, yet I was so enthralled with the tenacity and determination of those women, despite daunting challenges. Whether you are approaching 50 or have traveled past it, if you hunger to have a better life, buy this book and immerse yourself in its content and exercises. Buy a second copy for another woman you care about. When we re-invent ourselves, we help re-invent the world!"

Sue Paulson, inspirational speaker and author of
"Magnificent Misery – From Adversity to Ecstasy"

The Fabulous@50 Re-Experience

It's never too late
to refresh your mind, body, and spirit,
and you don't have to do it alone.

Dianna Lee Bowes

Deborah L. Smith

Library and Archives Canada Cataloguing in Publication
Bowes, Dianna Lee, 1958-, author
The fabulous @ 50 re-experience : it's never too late to refresh your mind, body, and
spirit, and you don't have to do it alone / by Dianna Lee Bowes.

Issued in print and electronic formats.
ISBN 978-0-9917665-1-2 (paperback)
ISBN 978-0-9917665-2-9 (ebook)

1. Middle-aged women. 2. Self-realization in women.
3. Midlifecrisis. 4. Baby boom generation.
I. Title. II. Title: Fabulous at 50 re-experience. III. Title: Fabulous at fifty re-experience.
HQ1059.4.B68 2016 - 305.244'2 C2015-908796-1 - C2015-908797-X

Chapter Art by David Goertzen.
Cover Design by Dianna Bowes
Caricature by Cathy McMillan

CREATIVE
On The Move

For information about special discounts for
bulk purchase please contact publisher:
Creative On The Move
info@fabulousat50.com

To follow Dianna Bowes or Fabulous@50
www.fabulousat50.com   •   www.diannabowes.com

Fabat50   dianna.bowes   diannabowes   diannabowes

Foreward

Writing a book was something I never thought I would do. But I learned long ago to never limit or label myself. We are all limitless, if we choose to be.

This book is a result of so many people. First many thanks, Deborah Smith, who stepped forward to re-experience her life and present me with the idea for this book. Your courage is astounding and you will always be in my heart.

Second, so much gratitude to the circle of fabulous women who continually lift me up. Laurel Vespi, Sue Paulson, Bonita Lehman, Rae- Ann Wood-Schatz, Charmaine Hammond, Loretta Friedrich, Jo Dibblee, Sharon Pandza, Kyla Steinke, Jen Violi, Bonnie-Jean McAllister, Joanne Newenduk, Annie Pool, Pam Robertson and so many others. And to my husband John (lucky #3) who has never for a minute doubted me. His strong belief in me, is what keeps me moving ahead. A ginormous hug and smooches to my children Amber and David for trusting me to re-experience our lives even when situations looked dim. But most of all I want to dedicate this book to my Grandmother, Maxine Bowes. The woman who raised me from birth. The woman who raised many children (13+). The woman who felt she had no choices. The woman who was loved by so many. The most loving, gentle, humble woman I have ever known. The woman that is forever in my heart, encouraging me to create a legacy and to experience my life to the fullest.

Dianne Bowes

Contents

Savouring is a strategy that capitalizes
on redundancy rather than difference;
to multiply one's experience
is to double back, to re-experience
an experience.

—The Art of Creativity
- Ssu-k'ung T'u on the Art of Savouring

Introduction
If Not Now, When?

This is how my life began: my mother didn't want me.

As a child, I didn't much want myself either. I lacked confidence, I acted—or didn't—out of fear, and felt my life was over before it had even started. At twelve years old, I remember deciding not to take a dance class because I thought I was too old. Can you imagine?

Of course all of that changed because I was willing to change. I'm not sure that twelve-year old Dianna would recognize the one at fifty who started her own business and the one who now willingly steps on stage to speak to large crowds of women. This Dianna, the one I am now, knows something that my twelve-year old self didn't: it's not too late.

If you weren't going to read past this paragraph, and I had to get out the most important message I have right now, it would be this: it's not too late.

If you kept reading and weren't going to read past this paragraph, I'd add: you're not alone.

Of course I do hope you'll keep reading, because I have a lot to share about both of those things as well as the fabulous life that belongs to you now, no matter what you've experienced or how your life started.

As for me, my grandparents ended up being my parents, and the original plan for a short stay with them turned into nineteen years in a madhouse, with 13 older aunts and uncles growing up in various states of mild to severe addictions. My six half-siblings lived with my mom and stepdad and were virtual strangers. Small, quiet, and invisible I wondered if I'd ever belong anywhere.

As a child walking up to the door of our rental house, I never knew what I'd find. Depending on the day of the week or time of month or year, it could have been a peaceful scene: my grandparents quietly watching TV, or my grandfather working in the garden and my grandmother crocheting.

Or it could have been a household of my aunts and uncles partying, which would start nicely and end badly, with a fight over something ridiculous. I knew the pattern: first fun, laughing, and dancing; then loud talking; and before I knew it, that terrible uproar of fighting. Brothers against brothers, sisters against sisters, jealousy over girlfriends or anything that had been brewing. Blood, screaming, people being shoved out doorways, walls being damaged, and then finally the heavy quiet once they all left.

When the fighting started I would grab our cat, head to my room, and lay with my fingers pressed in my ears, jumping with fear that they would come to my room—even though they never did—and wondering if the police would come this time. Holidays, especially Christmas, were the worst, and for many years, until I met my first husband and we celebrated with his family, I'd get sick right around December 25. My body knew that chaos was imminent.

But when I walked through the doorway to that two-story house with the neatly trimmed hedge on 95th Street, I knew that if I caught the whiff of simmering soup, or sugar and butter baking, all was well. My grandparents cooked together and cooked well. I can still see my grandfather standing at the sink, with a towel at his waist, peeling potatoes. Good eating was important to them—everything slow-cooked and delicious. No fast food.

Every morning I awoke to the smell of coffee brewing and came downstairs to a wonderful breakfast, with my lunch packed for school. Food? That I could depend on.

And when my grandmother baked, Lord help us, the lemon meringue pies were heavenly. She was such a gentle woman, so loving, and it came through in her baking. Nothing rushed—every ingredient measured, every detail perfect.

There were not many spoken *I love yous* in our home, but the love came through the food, prepared with time, patience, and intention. As an adult when I would visit, I'd always find something delicious to nibble on no matter the time of day, and I never went home without a package of treats for later.

Since I was brought up by my grandparents after they'd raised thirteen of their own children, birthdays didn't seem to be a big deal. I can only remember having a birthday cake once. Of course my grandmother made it.

I can't recall who came to my birthday or what presents I received, but I sure can remember the beautiful chocolate cake. *Just for me!* No aunts and uncles pushing me to the side to have some.

I savour that memory, and in it is the heart of this book.

As a Baby Boomer woman between the age of forty-nine and sixty-four, you probably have some feelings when you hear the phrase: *just for me!* You might not be able to remember a single moment that has been *just for you*. You might have had a childhood like mine or one where you learned in subtler but still potent ways to feel insignificant or invisible. Likely, you've been so busy taking care of everyone around you, or making sure your kids or spouse or anyone in your vicinity had what they needed, that you're not sure what *just for me* would even look like. Or maybe you've learned, for various reasons, not to speak up for yourself, or receive deliciousness, or go after what you need and want.

However you got here, may this book be the first of many *just for me!* moments for you. It's not too late for you to have them, and getting them doesn't mean you have to be alone.

So please don't worry about being isolated, or selfish, or thoughtless. Because the truth is when you take care of yourself, you'll also be joyfully generous in ways you might never have imagined, and you'll inspire the women around you to do the same.

For starters you can apply this *just for me!* idea to how you use this book, because it is for you. You're welcome to jump ahead to any chapter that catches your attention. Or you can read in a linear fashion to follow the order I've suggested. However you do it, you can trust that you'll find yourself asking big questions, taking an honest and loving look at who you've considered yourself to be for the last fifty-some years, deciding who you want to be now, and how you'd like to re-experience your life.

What do I mean by re-experience? Well, at fifty we've lived a lot of life and had a lot of experiences, so it's easy to decide that we've done it all and ask: *why bother doing it again?* I say re-experience is worth the trouble. It's about slowing down to reframe what we think we know and savouring it with new awareness. As an example, I've been married three times. I lost one husband to death and one to gambling and alcohol. I could have stopped there and decided I knew everything there was to know about relationships, and I'm so glad I didn't. I would have missed my third marriage, one in which I've been able to find real contentment, delight, and an equal partnership, one in which I've reframed what marriage means to me and lived into it with a new grace and joy.

Re-experience doesn't have to be applied to everything, especially toxic or danger-ous choices we've made in the past. But it's magical when applied to the big and small things that enrich life, like engaging in relationships, cultivating fulfilling work, walking into a roomful of strangers, or feeding and nourishing ourselves. Instead of why bother? we have the opportunity to ask: how can this be better? There's power in a good question, and there's power in you when you ask it and act on it.

My grandmother isn't around anymore to bake a cake for me, but the good news is, I've learned how to bake for myself, how to find and be the nourishment I need. Throughout this book I'll invite you to consider the same, to look at where you are now and where you want to be. As you reflect, a little cake analogy might be helpful—a little actual cake might be helpful, too.

You might identify yourself as plain, white cake, even though you prefer devil's food. Perhaps you gave up on your rich chocolaty wishes and dreams. Or up until now you might have been an angel-food cake, existing to serve your family and community all your adult life and have yet to do something for yourself.

Whatever type of cake you choose to describe yourself, it is both your starting point and your turning point, the point from which you can choose to change and grow. This book is about learning how to re-experience life, and it's about turning points; that is, savouring the life you already have, enjoying the cake you already are, and taking bold new steps toward change.

Sometimes turning points are forced, like when the universe delivers a loss to your doorstep. Sometimes turning points involve hitting brick walls, figurative crashes that come after months or years of ignoring signs, gut feelings, and instincts that something isn't working and probably never will work. But my favourite kind of turning point is the conscious kind, the kind I like to call a *magical turning point*. A magical turning point comes when you have no idea what to do or how you'll get through, but you also know, with everything in your being, that you need to move forward. And you decide to do exactly that.

I'll bet you're perched on the tip of a magical turning point right now, feeling pricked by the challenge of this moment and having no idea how it's all going to turn out but committed to moving forward and ready to take action. I'm here to tell you, you don't have to go it alone.

Through these pages I'll offer you support to construct the recipe you need to transform, to release whatever role you've played to survive but no longer serves you, to concoct a truly fabulous life, to finally feel safe and supported. Consider: if you are the baker, what kind of cake do you want to make? If you are the cake, what kind of cake do you want to be?

In these pages you will meet other twenty-first century Boomer women who have the same concerns as yours. In these pages you'll find stories of women, shared to illustrate a variety of experiences and to highlight profound moments leading to transformation, wisdom, and determination to have meaningful re-experiences. These ladies that graciously consented to sharing their writings here get my deepest thanks and appreciation.

In these pages you'll find my delight (via artwork), a renewed pursuit for my own spiritual healing, and visual representations of some of the themes in this book. You'll find illustrations from my son and some paintings from me.

In these pages you'll find the tools and guidance for understanding how to jump in, when to hold back, and how to find the noble friend: that genuine, insightful person who wants you to win; who sometimes makes you cry or get damn angry because she sees you; who tells you the truth and helps get you back on track. If you don't have noble friends in your life and are ready to welcome some in, I will show you how to find them.

In these pages I will also remind you that change is hard and the work we do to facilitate it is even harder. I'm so weary of super-easy fixes or expensive, ready-in-an-instant self-help routines and practices. Sure, it can be easy to make a quick outfit change for a day, but I'm inviting you to strive for a constant, reliable, and comfortable fit designed for everything you're ready for, and for who you'll blossom into. I know that's a tall order, but I also know you are up for filling it, because I've been there and done it myself.

In these pages you'll also find this essential component: fun. I can't see anything worthwhile being all seriousness with no elements that make you laugh, allow you to be creative, or invite you to join a community where others gather to share, be supportive, and have a blast. Fabulous @ 50 and our community—one I'm proud to belong to—has had events that have saved many women from depression, loneliness, and stress. At our gatherings, fifty-plus women ready to re-experience their lives have found a place to do just that. If this book speaks to you, consider yourself invited to join us at the events. Whatever you choose to do, my sincere hope is that you find the clarity and support you need.

The year 2015 commemorates my fifty-seventh year as woman, one who has been daughter, granddaughter, wife, mother, and businessperson. I find myself at a moment when I feel it's time to share what I've lived and learned, who I was, who I wanted to be, and who I've become.

The best I can do and the most I can hope for is that anyone who reads this will see and honour the feelings and accomplishments of Boomer women who have faced so many challenges and turning points with courage and grace. In service to women approaching their prime years, I share my experiences, along with those of other women, to illustrate resiliency, optimism, and growth. Our forties, fifties, and beyond brim with challenge and hallmark profound changes in our bodies. Theses changes require us to evaluate and adapt our choices, while we continue to do everything else—working; perhaps returning to school after decades; managing various financial, medical, and emotional crises; and maintaining or guarding what we already have. We constantly face demands and tough decisions we don't feel prepared to make.

Sometimes our lives might be most accurately described as a fruit cake studded with nuts and all kinds of unexpected bits and bites and best soaked with rum.

I wrote this book for the woman who knows that her old ways of thinking, living, and planning doesn't fit; who knows that it might be time for an overhaul; and is ready to roll up her sleeves and work and play to reveal her best self. You deserve to live as the magnificent person you are; to remember all the skills, talents, and presence you can bring to the table; and to shine so brightly that people who haven't dared to shine themselves might have to look away.

You might be saying, *"I can't—at least not now."*

I say, *"If not now, when?"*

It's not too late.

When will you realize that as a Boomer woman like me, old experiences like a past failed marriage can be the launching pad for re-experiencing a relationship with more strength, love, and enjoyment? When are you going to change that dress code? Adding more colors to your wardrobe; trying out a new, vibrant hairstyle; or anything you do to take care of yourself—all of that also shows others how to treat you. I bring up physical appearances because we need to address what women can do to change how they see themselves to battle the serious influences of ageism and the flawed youth and beauty culture. Many Boomer women see that advertisers remain clueless to our needs, not just in terms of beauty but also in terms of lifestyle, health, and career. Most Boomer women have worked hard for what we have and have decades left to live, but we're not finding products and services appropriate for our tastes and requirements. Clearly I have some strong opinions on this matter, and you'll find more of them in the chapters ahead.

In these pages you'll find an opportunity to not only confront the you in the mirror but to also have a reckoning with your past; to consider, like I have, how you grew up and how that's impacted you, for better or worse. To this day I don't have contact with my half-siblings, and we don't take an active interest in each other's welfare. It's sad but true. Some families are dysfunctional and separated by the decisions and priorities of their caregivers, and children suffer from the dysfunction without having a say or the power to change it. As an adult I've reached some level of peace when I think about my relatives and how I feel about them.

I love and still miss my grandparents, who have both passed.

They were hard-working and lost to the ways their children were developing. The relationship with my mother is strained. Too often our conversations turn to her sadness and anger at how she sees things have turned out for her. For too many years I took the wrath of her guilt in giving me up, blaming me for just being me. My heart goes out to her, as it must be terrible to hold on to such negative feeling, but I choose to let that go and move forward, for my own peace of mind.

For those of you in the middle of re-learning how to deal with family after years of their mental health issues; drug addictions; or just plain, old-fashioned, toxic styles of relating, I hope this book offers some insight and compassion to you. I know we can carry shadow selves from childhood, and I say it's possible to balance those shadow selves with the light selves we also carry. We have the power to keep that light glowing.

As a child, I experienced teasing and ridicule daily. My aunts and uncles told me I was going to fail, get pregnant, or be a loser. It was everything I could do to keep my inner light burning. I persevered, pushing past all the negativity, but I learned to survive it all by being an invisible object, which meant allowing myself to be treated as less than human.

Objects are not human beings. They are vases, or spoons, or anything handled and placed according to the user's or admirer's or disposer's whims. I know I'm not the only Boomer woman who has felt objectified, for decades allowing everyone around me to gain from my efforts and then discard, shelf, or confine me.

Now I'm happy to report that I have a fantastic life with my husband, my adult children, and my work. My husband has my back. He works as hard as I do at this partnership thing. As with a healthy partnership, fabulous life results from long-term, daily effort and commitment.

Think of it this way: When you see an "overnight success" in the film or music industry, with few exceptions, don't you really believe that person has been years in the making? Has it really been that easy for them to step out on stage and belt out a beautiful melody? They haven't practiced at all? When you really listen to their stories, the majority admit to practicing, if only in the privacy of their bedrooms, for years. I know that my own experience has been decades in the making. I've spent the last eight years building the Fabulous @ 50 community, and I came to it through many tough lessons.

The first such lesson wasn't coming from a badly dysfunctional family who expected me to be a loser. It actually came when I was twenty years old, at the beginning of what I thought would be a grand and happy life with my new husband. The day I was told he had been killed and wasn't coming home I went into a paralyzing shock.

True to my family and their understanding of how I fit in with them, not one came forward with any kind of support or empathy. I felt alone. I did my best with what I had and—while dealing with the grief that hurt so deeply I wanted to die—redirected my energy to create a new life. I did receive support, and still do, from my late husband's family, who also suffered a great loss.

Eventually I remarried, and although that fifteen-year relationship ended in divorce, it also gave me two of the most beautiful gifts a woman can receive—my daughter, Amber, and my son, David.

Many Boomer women are mothers and grandmothers; some have also achieved great-grandmother status. Some have nurtured and created in other ways. Regardless, the generations preceding us have defined womanhood, and we need new, refined, and correct definitions for women and their experiences. We come from different cultures and economic backgrounds, and we have a host of wisdom, gifts, and talents that can make a significant contribution to the evolution of humanity—not to mention that we are the ones who have the babies who become future generations and have been the ones largely responsible for their welfare and development.

Our lives don't fit in narrow definitions, and they aren't easily divided into nice, neat, quaint little boxes with bows on top. We are not all surrounded by loving family and noble friends who provide a safe and caring environment. Sometimes things are messy. Chaos and confusion prevail. You look around and wonder: *Who are these people?!*

You ask yourself: *Why me? and Now what?*

If you are like me when I was widowed, reeling from a recent loss, you may wonder if anything is going to be good again.

You might expect that life is going to deliver another slew of bad things because that's what you deserve. You don't feel worthy of love and respect.

You may throw your hands up with a prayer you can't voice. *Oh Lord, to get some rest.* So how about that rest and relief? I say, if not now, when?

If you find yourself in a crisis or recovering from trauma right now, please stay with me and trust that you'll find a noble friend in me in these pages. If you're in physical danger, please know that there are people in every community ready to help you—like the kind people I've connected with at St. Albert Stop Abuse in Families (SAIF)—and reach out. Google your city and family violence help (or whatever issue you're facing), and reach out right away. I know crisis and trauma better than I'd like to. When I turned forty I was alone after an ugly divorce, with custody of my two children, and doctors had found a cyst on my spine. After surgery I was in a full body cast, about to lose my house, and financially in the doghouse. I managed but not to come out of that turning point with the same image of who Dianna was. Heck no. I was even more determined, clear, and prepared for the now what? I will show you how I engaged the now what? from what I learned along the way and the fantastic people that have guided and cared about me.

Know this: I am with you, and other Boomer women are with you in spirit.

You are not alone.

In working on this book, I thought about my grandmother, and I had one of those eye opening realizations. The kind that come with tears.

I realized that this book, and my life's work, is for my grandmother, the woman who raised me. So much of what I do is for her.

A woman who felt it was too late to do anything but keep house for her unpredictable and dysfunctional brood and alcoholic husband. A woman who wouldn't, or couldn't, do things for herself. A woman who was, in a house full of people, still alone. A woman who rarely went past her front door; in the nineteen years I lived with her, I only remember two times she wasn't at home.

I can still see her when I moved out: on the porch, wearing a simple housedress, facing out the old screen door. She looked so fragile and vulnerable. She was by herself, and I felt like I was leaving a bunny rabbit to the coyotes.

This book is for her and for all the women who feel isolated and inadequate in any way.

I know I couldn't rescue her and that I can't rescue anyone but myself. But I can share what I know to be true.

It's not too late.

You're not alone.

So please, read on. And before you turn the page, I encourage you to get a journal, if you haven't already started one, and a favourite pen. Sit back in a comfy chair with a glass of clean water, hot tea, or wine. Set yourself up well for some delicious *Just for me!* moments.

It has been a joy to bring this project to you. May the ideas within enlighten, inspire, and support you at your very own magical turning point. Welcome to your opportunity to refresh your mind, body, and spirit, and re-experience your fabulous life.

Dianna Bowes

Chapter 1
Now What?

We want women leaders today as never before.

Leaders who are not afraid to be called names and who

are willing to go out and fight. I think women can save civilization.

Emily Murphy

✍

When I stand before God at the end of my life,

I would hope that I would not have a single bit of talent left and could say,

I used everything you gave me.

Erma Bombeck

✍

Your birthday arrives. Fifty-plus candles blaze atop your favourite cake. Ready to blow out the almost alarming amount of fire, you mind the rule to make just one wish. With a big inhale, you hope you can safely extinguish all of the candles and guarantee your wish will come true.

A question for you, whether it's your birthday today or not: now that you're here, what is your wish? Or a shorter version: now what?

In seventeenth century Germany, large candles set in the center of cakes symbolized the *light of life*.[1] If anything matters on your birthday, it should be this: remember you are the true light of life—confident, secure, and ready for everything positive and negative midlife has to offer—and that whatever you wish honours your light. If you don't feel that way, on your birthday or otherwise, I can offer you hope that you can and you will.

First, let's talk straight for a minute.

We all know women in the enviable position of celebrating their fiftieth decade successfully and happily, prepared for a life of ease and enjoyment. At their own paces, they can afford to dedicate time to their families and altruism.

Then there's you.

You, on the other hand, are in the midst of puckering up at one sour flavour of crisis or another and asking yourself, *now what?* As in, *what else can go wrong?* A looming divorce, financial setbacks, unemployment, a devastating medical diagnosis, an empty nest, or any number of spiritual, emotional, and physical wants can converge. Your life plays out in a series of mini and major disasters and critical breaking points and as for the future—who knows?

Seriously, the concern of calories from the cake is the size of a pinhead compared to what you face. It bothers you that you can't stop thinking about cheating on your self-imposed diet.

Or that the sugars and carbs from the cake will affect your insulin levels.

Then there's the separation from a husband of twenty-eight years to consider. That was a blindside slam that still aches; not because he left, but because he had to rub in his affair with the younger secretary by marrying her.

Menopause, hot flashes, and weight gain are causing you to go agoraphobic. Your best friend a year younger than you was just given the news that she has stage 3 breast cancer. On top of that, you had to settle for a new job for half your previous pay and so entry-level you know you're going to lose IQ points and most of your self-respect the first week. How are you going to make ends meet?

Your life has met with crisis. You are faced with a big, daunting *now what?*

If any of the above hits close to home; if you are alone, frightened, and anxious; the first thing is to breathe deeply, count to fifty. I mean it. Set down the book right now and breathe. Come back when you're done.

I hope that helped, and I hope it's a tool you'll continue to use as you read this book, and after you've finished it. Your breath can be a simple and powerful noble friend to you. Use it.

Now, imagine your life as you will be living it in the best possible circumstances, because I assure you as the light of life and a cake of magnificent flavour, you will prosper, heal, and experience this next half of your life as miracle upon miracle.

Of course, miracles don't happen in isolation. As a smart woman who's been alive for half a century, you know you can benefit from direction and support. In the annals of magazines, self-help books, and countless websites you'll find information, advice, and guidance. Fortunately, and unfortunately, more than any other time in recorded history, we are inundated with contradictory and puzzling reports, recommendations, and stories about how to heal and how to succeed. Making sense of who to trust and what to follow is work.

My first recommendation? Trust yourself. This might be a new habit to develop, but I assure you it's worth it. Trusting yourself doesn't mean listening to all the chatter in your head; that chatter can whip you right into a frenzy. Trusting yourself may mean you need to suspend a belief system causing you to be overly stressed about your current situation. Trusting yourself is about quieting the mental chaos so you can hear a deeper truth. Once you trust yourself, it becomes easier to know who and what else is worth your confidence. Taking time out everyday to connect with yourself through meditation, prayer, or even a long walk can create wonderful results. Disconnect from the world; get away from the draining devices. Spend time in complete silence, go for that long walk without earplugs in, and just be with yourself. This is where the magic happens; where your inner voice, or whatever you want to call it, will show up. This is your trusted voice.

I call it my muse. On my own long walks, once I unload all the crap of the day, I make room for something else. The door in my heart creaks open and tada! Some amazing new idea shows up. The key is to capture those ideas, because I guarantee they will leave just as quickly as they showed up.

Once you trust yourself, reach out.

As a reminder from the introduction, you're not alone. You don't have to be isolated. My organization has spent years creating an environment for women where they can enjoy themselves, evolve, and be honestly appreciated as women. No one comes so well-prepared to points of crises requiring change and transformation that they have no need for support. I have been blessed with wonderful friends, mentors, and my beautiful family to see me through some of my darkest experiences.

Melodie, a long-time friend, showed up for me at a bleak time after my marriage had ended, and I was moving my family out of our home. Fresh from back surgery, I wore a turtle shell back-brace, which made it impossible for me to bend over or do much of anything. Yet I had to move. I had not seen Melodie for some time, yet there she was, like an angel, ready to give her time and love to help us. Accepting my own vulnerability and letting someone else into the current mess in my life was tough, but I couldn't have moved forward without Melodie.

In the Fabulous@50 community, I have a team of remarkable, supportive, magical women prepared to spread out, find solutions, and hear what you are experiencing and ready to re-experience. Know that they are ready and willing to welcome you.

Also, please remember that as much as Boomer women intimately know disadvantage (all I listed at the beginning of the chapter and more), we also know unprecedented advantage. We women have more opportunities and mobility than our mothers did. At our fingertips we have platforms to air our grievances and announce our triumphs. A simple Internet connection enables communication across the planet in real time. Personally, I love being alive right now.

In this book, you'll not only read stories of women facing enormous challenge, but also stories of those same women with a flaming light in them that will not be extinguished. My intention is that every element of womanhood is represented in these pages: the hardships and successes, the diversity, the courage, the sheer determination to rise above adversity and transform, and the willingness to heal by sharing stories.

We'll use stories from women belonging to the Fabulous@50 community to help us take a deeper look at the particular challenges and possibilities we Boomer women face, so you can draw strength and courage from their words. Their answer to now what? becomes a commitment to re-experience their lives. These stories make me so proud to be a part of this community of women and to be a woman period.

The stories in this book show that it's possible for you too to survive; land with both feet intact and grounded; and refresh your mind, body, and spirit.

In each chapter I'll focus on a few of those particular challenges and possibilities we face, taking a look at the state of things, at the *what is*. Then I'll wrap up the chapter with a section called *Ingredients to Gather*. Many of these will be the kind of ingredients that are already in you. They just might also be the ones you have to stand up on a chair to look for, because they've been sitting on the tippy top shelf, in the back, collecting dust. As you gather ingredients through the book, you're gathering all you need for your own fabulous re-experience recipe.

Through observing the lives of women that have had it all ways of favourable and unfavourable, I can say that we are both the bakers and the final outcome: the cake.

You might be asking yourself: *Why don't I feel as sure about that as you, Dianna?*

I say, for now copy my recipe. Until you gather all the tools, ingredients, and motivation to innovate, follow the ones who have come before you. There's no shame in using someone else's tried and tested recipe, and then, when you're feeling confident and comfortable, in changing it up and making it your own.

In my experience, a good recipe requires not just good ingredients but also knowing what you're hungry for in the first place. That is, knowing your needs.

In this chapter, we'll consider what needs you have and what issues you face in relationships, particularly marriage, as well as in health and healing. We'll look at some issues that may be destructive to your well-being in order to get you the support you need, as well as to clear the way for those miracles.

Separation, Divorce, and Loss

The breakup of a marriage can feel sudden, but a breakdown in a marriage may have been years or decades in the making. The end of a marriage with a sudden death or after a long illness carries its own unique pain. I have been both divorced and widowed and grieved both losses. If you're experiencing such a loss, your feelings will be many and varied, from sadness to anger and beyond. This is normal, and paying attention to your feelings will serve you well in healing and moving forward.

In the case of divorce, whether sudden or drawn out, the day comes when decisions have to be made to cut the strings, decide who gets the house, and if there's going to be alimony or child support. (Some of us Boomer women have children under eighteen.) How to explain it to the kids is damn hard, even if they are adults.

If there's been physical abuse, alcoholism, drug addiction, or any other form of neglect and disrespect, leaving may remove the immediate danger, but it doesn't make separation, divorce, and resettlement any easier. Years can span between resolution and closure. Often times in abusive relationships, women find themselves in severe financial stress. The husband or partner withholds money from them trying to control and keep them vulnerable.

For better or worse, finances are intricately linked with relationships. Just as broken or ended relationships come with emotional gains and losses, they also come with financial losses or gains.

On the other side of vulnerability, North American Boomer women as a whole have unprecedented purchasing power and influence and will benefit from a double transference of wealth in this century for the first time in our known history. Parents and husbands are estimated to leave anywhere from twelve to forty trillion dollars as inherited wealth.[2] No matter what money we inherit or don't, Boomer women can't avoid experiencing an influx of stress and strain from failed relationships.

21

Sheri W., born 1963

I knew he was cheating on me. We hadn't slept together for years. My life was full enough with three kids now grown up and on their own, charities, my own friends, and our families. I'll never forget the day, the morning, he announced that he was leaving me for his 23-year-old secretary. I was like a vaguely familiar stakeholder at one of his business meetings. He threw some papers at me that later I would read, discovering he'd left me everything. I had a bagel in my hand that I was spreading with cream cheese. When I looked up at his face, it was red and bulging at his temples. "Why are you so angry at me?" I asked. He left without another word. Ever. I cried. It was my birthday. I was 54.

⁓

In Canada, separated and divorced senior women are more likely to live in poverty than their married counterparts.[3] Still, these senior women are part of an economic class of purchasers. They communicate using cell phones and the Internet and are important social networkers within their communities. What they contribute to women's collective voices is as significant and important as women of wealth and status.

Divisions of wealth in the larger picture of our lives as citizens could be considered a political agenda, but I am here to help women wake up to their potential, know the tools and resources available to them, and be inspired and comforted. Just as we women can't be divided into nice, neat little boxes, the issues we face can't be compartmentalized. The political, as much as the relational, emotional, or physical, impacts our progress, so it's part of the conversation.

Margaret S., 1959

The baby was crying and he was yelling. My stomach turned from the foul smell of the liquor on his breath. His fist was curled up at his side. I braced for the punch. He was accusing me of having sex with one of his lunatic friends. I couldn't get away easily. He had me pinned up against the wall by his other hand on my throat. I had planned my escape. There was just the matter of getting cash from his wallet after he passed out. There should be enough to get me and the two kids a cab to the Greyhound station and buy the tickets to Winnipeg. Maybe some left for snacks. It was my birthday in a month. I'd be 20 years old.

⁓

Although politics will come up in this book, I'm a businesswoman focused on the most challenging issues Boomer women face, regardless of their financial circumstances. It may be difficult to feel empathy toward a high net worth CEO who's being dragged through a messy divorce when another woman has to negotiate for employment insurance and social assistance while living in a shelter.

Women experiencing poverty or facing that likelihood don't have to empathize with their wealthier cohorts.

Still, I suggest we temper our judgments and evaluations with a greater emphasis on the emotional and spiritual warfare against all women. A dozen and more reasons exist for any woman's current situation. The goal should be focusing on what that individual needs to find equilibrium as well as to stay upright and find her position relative to gravity, a force which elicits feelings of disgust for so many Boomer women.

Due to shared arrivals to this planet between 1946 and 1964, we are Baby Boomers as a generational category.[4] Those that have married financially successful partners, or thrived in a professional capacity and climbed to high corporate status of their own, share this cultural segmentation with women who have no high school diploma and have worked at low-paying service jobs all their lives. Highlighting the word share brings me to point out that the most beautiful things we can share are our stories, and the wisdom we've gained from them.

Maria C., born 1960

My body ached to have this baby. He insisted that I go to the clinic for a third time. It still pains me to think about what kind of mother I would have been. We were comfortable. His career as an artist was taking off. I kept at my administrative secretarial job even though I wanted to pursue theater. As long I was covering my expenses I could live the best lifestyle I could imagine. The drinking and the parties were always better when he wasn't around. He threw a big birthday surprise bash for me with all our friends invited. I don't remember what happened. Six months later he left me with everything, which I lost in a year to drugs and alcohol. I live in a one bedroom apartment on disability pension. I was 27 when he left. That was 28 years ago.

Wherever you find yourself on the crisis continuum, specifically in relationships, whatever pushes you into a new phase of your life at fifty or better (notice I didn't say older; feel this through to your core), you've got work to do. Now what? stands as an about-face from any expectations you had for the future you thought you were going to have.

Each story in this chapter highlights the different complexities of the emotionally charged dissolution of union, whether a divorce or separation. I remind you that we don't know what came before for these women or others.

Their husbands, lifestyles, and decisions come from their perceived inner value, something we as outsiders can't know. It's not really our business why a woman made the choices she made. What matters for her and for you—for all of us—is what we are ready to do now to grow and transform our lives.

It's the transformations in these stories that make them examples for us as Boomer women and our daughters and granddaughters.

These stories resonate in the present for some women as much as they could be about another person's past. Everyday, thousands face the pivotal moment of a decision that will leave them in varying degrees of uncertainty. As mothers and grandmothers, we know women our ages and younger facing similar issues alone, having to make decisions, and in need of support.

This need for support is what I choose to focus on; that is, offering inspiration and comfort to victims of emotional and spiritual warfare rather than judging their pasts or the circumstances they find themselves in. I don't know about you, but I didn't come with a set of instructions or a crystal ball to show me what my future held and how to handle it.

I'm glad to say that many movements and organizations—including Fabulous@50—that do not discriminate by age, race, or religion, are committed to providing assistance to women in crisis. Regardless of who you are, in the back of this book, you'll find a directory of exceptional agencies, coaches, free resources and help targeted for fifty-plus women.

Fabulous@50 has open doors where we celebrate all the diverse forms we gals come in. We are so many varieties of cakes and sweetness and magic. If one of my 50-plus ladies were to reveal a past as a man, I have come to a place in my life where the shock I might have felt as a younger woman doesn't matter. I would simply say, welcome to womanhood and the challenges we all face.

Despite our differences, we all still have those relationship hurdles that are not going away. Separation and divorce and the financial implications can result in less than ideal living conditions for Boomer women mentally, emotionally, and spiritually. We recognize that some Boomer women have a healthier financial outlook when a relationship terminates, but the emotional and mental stress remains the same. Regardless of the health of the relationship, the grief after loss is still present. How well we cope depends on many factors. In some cases, when the final paper decree reaches the woman's hands, she feels like a million bucks even though there's nothing left in the bank. I know a few ladies who couldn't wait to celebrate their divorces; they threw themselves huge parties

However, what about the case when a woman finds herself widowed and feels there's nothing to celebrate? Death of a spouse comes with a type of pain that requires coping skills different from those needed for divorce. However, both situations require the same considerations for a newly single person who was once part of a couple. I know, because I've been through both.

The grief I felt from my first husband's death was not quite the same as my divorce, but it had the same stages. And still, people's reactions are different.

What they say is more measured and sympathetic when you are widowed than when you are newly single from a divorce. It's awkward for someone to engage with a widowed woman; and trust me, it's awkward for the widow too. I can't describe the feelings I had when someone would apologize and offer their condolences.

I was only twenty. Could I handle it differently now if my first husband and I would have had thirty years together?

Sure I would. That's the beautiful magic of maturing. The mixture of experiences and new perceptions, which become part of the spiritual drawer at your disposal, heals and soothes in ways that did not exist in youth. Some of us once had no guides and mentors to deliver us from our old hurts and anger. At twenty, I was alone, I felt alone, and I managed by myself. At fifty-seven I assure you, whatever relationship loss you may be experiencing, you won't be alone.

That may mean you need to step out of your comfort zone and reach out. Our romantic relationships are important, but I urge you to prioritize building relationships with family and friends as well. The payoff is healthy connections when your great relationships become the candles on your cake.

Health and Healing

Physical, emotional, mental, and spiritual wellness are essential to long, happy lives. Strong minds and bodies shield the psychic blows that come with life catastrophes and crises. I'll introduce this important topic here and will expand on it in subsequent chapters. Tending to our health is essential and will serve us well.

Health issues for Boomer women can mean facing a life-threatening diagnosis. *Now what?* can be answered with life or imminent death. Or health issues can be serious enough to require a complete lifestyle turnaround. An illness like diabetes demands a new menu to reduce sugar and carbohydrates. Or if you had been leading a sedentary life, there's now an exercise regiment to implement. But rest assured, making these kinds of changes doesn't have to be complex or difficult. I've found that walking has improved my health significantly; it's a simple and easy strategy that costs some of my time but is well worth the investment.

Forget all the fear mongering out there for now. For Boomer women, physiological changes now nudge us towards adapting to new conditions like menopause and even shorter short-term memory. Adaptation is part of life, and we can accept it or fight it. It's a choice. We can feel deprived or allow ourselves to be invigorated. Sometimes less means more of the right things needed for longevity with strength and vigour. As a Canadian woman, it's important to acknowledge that I have the privilege of access to healthcare and wellness support that many women around the globe do not. I can reject that or gratefully accept and take advantage of it. We get to choose the attitude we'll live our lives with and what we'll dedicate our efforts to.

We must remember that our lives will affect the women who come after us, just as our lives, our health, and well-being are affected by the women who came before us.

Erma Bombeck, the American journalist and writer, lived her life in part as an activist for women's rights. In 1978 she joined the committee that fought for an amendment to the U.S. Constitution to ensure equal rights for women.[5] Our American sisters and their battles have mirrored ours on this side of the 49th parallel as far as rights to equal pay, benefits, and how we choose to treat our bodies.

In Canadian history, Emily Murphy stands as the woman who, in her own midlife after her children left home, decided to take charge of the movement leading to women being recognized as "persons." Women young and old benefit from Murphy's hard work against great odds to gain freedoms like the right to vote.

Emily Murphy stands as a reminder of the complexity of women and the struggle for our rights: she also happened to advocate for forced sterilization.[6] And her writings were laced with racism, anti-abortion, and anti-immigration sentiments. According to Mrs. Murphy, if you weren't born here, you didn't belong here.

I share this because Canadian, American, and global history shows paradoxes in practically all of the leaders, visionaries, and great thinkers. If it weren't for Emily Murphy and her activism that began in 1917, women might not have been considered persons within the Constitution. Yet her efforts also brought about thousands of forced sterilizations to Albertans in the 1970s.

If Erma Bombeck hadn't advocated for women's rights in the United States in the 1970s, feminine hygiene products may have never been advertised in the media. Now we can shop for advertised brands without shame, for tampons in the same aisle as ribbed condoms with extra lubrication, and yet the history of tampons includes significant health dangers.

History is complex and so are the people who populate it. The point here is that the complex women who came before us fought hard for many of the freedoms we enjoy, and still there are battles to fight.

It's obvious that women with insurance and health care in place for themselves have less to worry about then those that live in poverty, without access to healthcare. How do we get everyone access? Cancer, heart disease, and Alzheimer's are prevalent among Boomer women, and research and education are more important than ever. How do we get at the root of these things?

Personally, I depend more on alternative methods of managing my health than I do on conventional Western medicine. However, I don't discredit or ignore my doctor's advice and diagnoses from tests and lab results. How can we blend and value the best of both worlds?

Depression ranks as another serious health issue, and we'll return to that and further effects of aging in the next chapter. For now, please remember that your health and safety are the first order of your concern. When you find yourself in crisis, get these to the top of your to-attend-to list.

If you have just been diagnosed with a disease, this is the critical moment to rethink your diet and lifestyle. When the doctor told me I had cyst on my spine, I felt like I'd fallen into a pit of jagged rocks. Although I'd been experiencing chronic pain for at least two years and doing my best to push through and pretend it wasn't as bad as it was, I never expected the problem would be anything serious. Like I did, you might be thinking that whatever's going on with your body can be cured with a few simple fixes. All that fatigue and heaviness will go away once you take some extra iron supplements added and a short vacation. After all, you have plans, right?

Having plans is all the more reason to consider your physical well-being, and it's important to remember that plans can change. This isn't always a bad thing.

Madeleine L., born 1958

University was tricky. School wasn't my cup of tea—ever. Not graduating from high school to get married was nothing that kept me awake at night. Becoming a twenty-something divorcée with a new boyfriend and better prospects for my life—going for a degree in social work— put me in a happier frame of mind. I was going to be able to make a contribution to the world and that felt good. That made me proud. I dug into coursework without worrying about how much of a struggle it was. I knew I was smart, determined, and that was all I needed to get through this. The day I sat in the doctor's office waiting for the results from the biopsy, I was sweating so much there were huge wet stains under my arms. The pronouncement that I had uterine cancer left me speechless. She patted my hand and asked me if I needed some water. "No thanks." My mouth was dry, but so was my mind in that moment. I was scared. But not to death. That was 33 years ago. I am going to visit my son and his wife who live in Costa Rica. On my 57th birthday.

❧

From Issues to Ingredients

Here's where I jump back in with reassurance about letting go of the plans we once had and making way for new and even better maps for our lives, health, and relationships. My story includes the tragic death of my first husband. I had my entire life planned with this wonderful man I adored more than anyone. Then as life does, it took a right turn, and my twenty-one-year-old husband died in an explosion. Just like that, *kaboom*, it was over. My second marriage was supposed to be my white-picket fence experience, and although I was blessed with two beautiful children, that relationship ended in divorce and serious surgery.

Your story may be more or less tragic than mine, but I'm more interested in what connects us than what separates us. As I see it, what draws us together is our identity as Boomer women who are experiencing and re-experiencing our lives. Nearly all of us will experience menses, childbirth, menopause, sterility, physical aging, and maturity.

Our cohort of Boomer women in their late forties to early sixties have experienced one-half of the twentieth century and are living out the rest of their lives and talents into the twenty-first century. We enter it grossly misunderstood and with most of our needs ignored or deliberately downplayed by marketing executives, male politicians, and a society that has grown up hyper-focused on youth, beauty, and self-absorption. I don't hate it though; I see it all as an opportunity.

Ladies, we have to keep working on our recipes for fabulous lives. Emily Murphy and Erma Bombeck brought awareness to women's issues in critical decades of the twentieth century. They both wrote books in their own voices that represented the women of their time.

You and I are living in 2015. How will we use our voices and our lives?

I happen to know what I want my life to be about until it's over. I plan to advocate for those I have the most in common with—that means you! I am humbled by and in awe of the lives of courageous and determined Boomer women like you.

I want this book to provide inspiration and tools and to send a message to the world about what we need, want, and are willing to accept. It's not what the marketers, men, politicians, or our mothers and daughters think. We have spent decades being on our best behaviour, dedicated to fulfilling others' expectations. We've neglected and been denied those *just for me!* moments.

Now that we find ourselves in crisis, those same people we have been responsible for and answered to don't have satisfying answers for our *now whats?* Our tastes and sensibilities are more complex, dynamic, and creative than people give us credit for. What we find on the shelves or in the world market is not in tune with our potential. We need products and services that make sense for our future, the one that we hadn't planned for. Boomer women are not only smarter than we are taken for, we are wise. Oh, yeah. We are wise and tough and still womanly, sensuous, and alive.

The women I've known who have overcome huge obstacles come through with a complexity of character not easily described. Boomer women have had the children, paid the bills, been the concubines, been abused and cajoled, educated themselves, and apologized if they asserted themselves too much because that turned them into "bitches." We've done it all and been it all for everyone else, and now we're ready to do it all and be it all for ourselves. When we give ourselves those *just for me!* moments, our efforts become *just for us!*' We pave the way for other Boomer women in our cohort. We inspire each other and also pave the way for the women who will come after us. Our efforts to take care of ourselves and rewrite the recipes of our lives ripple out and resonate.

In support of you, every chapter offers ingredients for you to add to your recipe, ingredients I trust will feed your need to refresh your mind, body, and spirit to live into an answer of the *now what?* I learned the art of baking from the heavenly concoctions of my grandmother, and I learned the art of re-experiencing because of her. I know it's not too late for me or for you to be fabulous at fifty or whatever age you happen to be. So let's get cooking. We have some cakes to bake.

Ingredients to Gather

Relaxing

In a perfect life I would have a personal chef. I love to eat, but don't like how much time the process of cooking takes away from my work. When I had a body cast that limited my movements, cooking was nearly impossible. The kids and I worked out a system, and most of the meals we had at that time were simple.

Crisis situations call for creative ways to manage daily tasks like preparing meals, and they call for simplicity. Which brings me to a first simple, but powerful ingredient in support of your well-being: relaxation.

Remember when I asked you to put down the book at the beginning of this chapter to breathe while you counted to fifty? That's part of it.

Breathing techniques are taught everywhere: on the Internet, in yoga classes, and at gyms. If you haven't tried breathing consciously, you have my word that learning the best way to use your diaphragm and take in deep breaths works to settle you down. Breathing is one of the simplest ways to relax your crisis-weary body. It's not the only one.

Some women pray, some adopt a positive affirmation, and some do meditation to ground themselves in gentle quietness. Whatever we do to relax, giving our minds a rest heals our hearts.

Prioritizing Physical Well-Being & Safety

Panic can be the strongest feeling you have. If your situation has reached a level that requires drastic actions, you literally may not be in the mood to find a way to relax. Believe me, I get it. For now, you might just need to take action. You will need a place to stay if you have to leave your home. You will need a source of income if you are losing a job. If you've been horribly depressed, you will need professional support.

Take care of your physical health first. A strong body absorbs shock that much better. Look to the resources provided in the directory at the back of the book for ways to support your well-being. If there is urgency in your medical situation, start with manageable changes first like cutting out sugars, adding a salad to your meal plans, or going for walks.

This is the time to trust yourself, to listen to that voice within. You don't have to go into a deep relaxation, but do take a deep breath or two and ask yourself what needs to be prioritized right now so you are healthy and safe.

What do I need to do right now to be healthy and safe?

1._____

2._____

3._____

Noble Friends

Finding someone to keep you accountable and on task helps. Crisis thrives in isolation, so this is not the time to do it alone. Surround yourself with a support team. Use the space below to write the names of people you know who are positive, honestly helpful, and who will be there for you.

If you can't think of a single person to list, list characters you find noble from movies or books, or feel free to write a description below of the noble friend you'd like to find.

_____

_____

_____

_____

_____

Look for Clues

If you haven't started one, a journal helps. If you have been keeping one, this may be the perfect time to re-examine some of your entries and look for hints at old patterns, concerns, or dreams that you are not committed to.

What My Subconscious Has Been Hinting At

_____

_____

_____

_____

_____

_____

_____

Having trouble with this one? If you haven't been cultivating self-awareness, getting to these clues can be tricky. Try this: if you've had a dream, especially one that's been hard to forget, jot it down in the space. Or write down a moment that stood out to you today or this past week. It's not essential to get to the core of your hidden issues just yet. For now just pay attention.

Identifying Your Now What?

Something I've learned as a business woman is the thirty-second pitch—basically summing up what I'm about into a short delivery. I'd like you to do the same, particular in summing up your current crisis.

You might bristle at this. How can you be expected to sum up your situation into one or two sentences? Well, earlier I warned you that there would be work, and here it is. If you're having a big reaction to this and want to understand it, feel free to turn to Chapter 8, *Reactor Factors*. Your process doesn't have to follow a linear path. Follow your awareness and use this book in a way that works best for you.

If you're still here with me, now's the time to try it. Get focused, and sum up your crisis in a sentence or two.

_____

_____

_____

_____

_____

Good, now consider what you need. If you need money, how much do you need?

_____

_____

If you need a specialist, what kind (lawyer, acupuncturist, consultant, life coach…), and who can direct you to one?

_____

_____

_____

_____

_____

Gratitude

Try to end this chapter with a new list of things to be grateful for. Enjoy yourself and play. I recommend breathing and counting to fifty and then writing down as many as fifty things you are grateful for today. I know one woman who did this and wrote out the same thing fifty times. That's fine.

Gratitude heals, no matter the size and scope of your list.

If you don't already have a gratitude journal, check out the Fabulous@50 website. (www.fabulousat50.com) This gratefulness habit may be the best one to acquire over your lifetime.

What I'm Grateful For

_____

_____

_____

_____

_____

_____

_____

Now, turn to Chapter 2 for a great little exercise to incorporate into your designated relaxation time. There you'll also learn more about the stress you may be facing and about something called *post-traumatic growth*.

Reflections of a Boomer Woman

DRIVING TO 50

I popped the CD into the car player when I stopped for gas in some tiny Saskatchewan town. The slow, sad songs surrounded me; after 15 minutes I had to pull over to stop the music and my tears. My daughter had made the medley, and her choices reflected her feelings for me and her hopes for my new life. It was the first time I had cried over the past three weeks when my world had turned upside down.

I was 48 and had always lived comfortably in Winnipeg with a wide network of family, friends and colleagues at hand and some career successes under my belt. However, creating a strong relationship had eluded me; I had married twice and was recently separated from my second husband. The economy was stagnant, and my consulting business and health were suffering. When an unexpected job offer came from Edmonton, I snapped at the opportunity to wipe the slate clean and start again.

So I headed west with my small Ford hatchback stuffed to the gills. I had decided to delay finding a home until I arrived, worried about choosing the wrong location or price until I got to know the city. But how to decide what to bring for 3-4 months of vagabond life? I narrowed it down by using the letter C: clothes, computer, CD player, golf clubs… you get the drift. It all seemed like a lark until those damn songs came on; I already missed my children and though they were in their early 20s and out on their own, I still wanted to be their mom in all sense of the word.

The next few months went by in a whirlwind. I lived in three places – a hotel, a furnished student sublet and finally a rental townhouse, where I could finally have my own furniture moved west. I had three visits with my ex to see if we could still patch things up before finally leave my wedding ring on the floor of his car. But on the plus side, I loved my new job and working with a free rein and some great staff to transform and brand the organization. And I loved the energy of Edmonton and the freedom I had to explore it – playing tourist in my free time by going to festivals and attractions, hiking the river valley, listening to live music. For the first time in my life, I was independent – I could eat, sleep, play and work whenever I wanted.

Nine months after my arrival, my world crashed down again. My employer removed the position I had and me along with it. What to do? Go back to Winnipeg, to Calgary where some family lived, or stay put. Edmonton won out, and I set about finding a new job, a network and friends. Yes, that was the one thing I hadn't worked on – friendships. Working 12 hour days and some weekends, being single and not knowing anyone when I arrived had not helped. I'd also refused to date to give me time to get my emotional equilibrium back and to focus on work. It was time to get more balance in my life.

An online search showed that Edmonton had lots of singles clubs, so I bravely ventured out – alone - to two clubs: one that offered social sports like bowling and golf, the other a Wine and Dinner club. Though I'm straight as an arrow, my first objective was to meet other women!

How else could I find someone to attend these functions and do other fun things like shopping, lunch and theatre. It worked like a charm and I soon found myself surrounded by friends and plenty to do.

A year after my dismissal, those same friends threw a fabulous 50th birthday party for me at a beautiful log cabin at Pigeon Lake. By then, I had a new job, had purchased a house, and yes, had a new man by my side. In the midst of the party noise and laughter, tears sprang to my eyes again, but this time they were tears of gratitude for all the blessings I'd received.

Andrea Collins

Chapter 2
Post-Traumatic Growth

Our stresses, anxieties, pains, and problems arise

because we do not see the world, others, or

even ourselves as worthy of love.

Prem Prakash, *The Yoga of Spiritual Devotion:*

A Modern Translation of the *Narada Bhakti Sutras*

~❧~

We must have a pie. Stress cannot exist in the presence of a pie.

David Mamet, *Boston Marriage*

~❧~

If you're still breathing, whatever crisis you're facing right now will make you stronger. Maybe not in body, but your mind and spirit will be supplied with a new-found strength and purpose. Despite the struggle, your breath will fan that flame inside of you.

As you stand in the middle of the tension and uncertainty, you may not believe what I am saying or be able to take it in. You may even reach for a piece of pie, hoping that stress cannot exist in the presence of it. That's okay. You know what you need, what works for you to relieve stress. Feel whatever emotions rise up, and then let them go—this is a process that heals and transforms.

Although we'll start here by focusing on struggle and stress, please remember that the title of this chapter is *Post-Traumatic Growth*. The post means we're talking about the time when the struggle will be behind you, and the growth suggests what can come after it. So ladies, despite your current suffering, trust that honestly facing it will strengthen you for what's ahead. Trust that we're moving in the direction of hope, possibility, and transformation.

Stress as You Know It

The stress in your life might cloud your view for healing and transformation possibilities, or even identifying first priorities. The drama from those around you can confuse and further complicate your situation.

Your parents might be acting like your divorce is an attack against them and their values. *Why didn't you just stay in the marriage? Wasn't it more important for the children? What does love have to do with staying together?* They lay on the guilt like they never have before. Your kids may be barely talking to you.

The best friend since high school hasn't returned your calls since you told her about your husband's confession that he had an affair with her years ago. She was never one for confrontation, but you want closure and her side of what happened.

Or perhaps no one you usually confide in seems open to or comfortable with how to deal with your husband's recent disclosure that he's gay.

Oh, my...

Along with our own crises, sometimes this added trauma and drama of friends and family creates the high stress level that floods our bodies with the chemicals cortisol and adrenalin. Too much cortisol can leave us physically weakened, vulnerable to hair loss, fatigued, or lead to more serious conditions like heart disease or diabetes.[7]

In addition to daily roles and responsibilities, Boomer women also often find themselves in caretaking roles, tending to the pain and suffering of people they love like elderly parents facing Alzheimer's or cancer or loved ones suffering from addictions. Because denial often accompanies addiction, it can be hard to find appropriate or timely treatment.

Addictions may simmer quietly for years until they boil over into crisis. As in, you won't let your daughter come visit anymore because every time she does, something goes missing from your house, including money from your wallet to support her meth habit. You don't remember being mean or hitting her. Both you and your husband worked hard to make sure she had the best education and after-school activities that included ballet and piano. You ask yourself: *how do these things happen?*

I don't have those kinds of answers. But I do know that gambling, shopping, sex, alcohol, and high-risk sports or activities can all become problematic when they overtake our normal routines and responsibilities, when they hurt our loved ones and us, as I experienced with my second husband's gambling addiction. Some Boomer women facing their own addictions are now ready to change, as are the women who have faced family members with addictions. So, now what?

Treatment?

Medicine?

I say we need some different definitions for disease, what constitutes treatment, and maybe we have to stop trying to cure things with drugs in the first place. Some of the researchers whose work I've referenced in this book have strong opinions about the pharmaceutical industry influencing psychiatry for the sake of business rather than the sake of wellness. If we've lived through a whole half-century of advertisements focused on fixing problems with medications that only mask the symptoms and can create even more problematic symptoms, what has our entire healing platform been founded on?

No one gets better after the medications stop, according to Martin Seligman. As a past director of the American Psychological Association, Seligman and several of his colleagues have turned away from the spoon that fed them for decades.

But there can be many who benefit from taking prescribed medications too.

I was prescribed anti-depressants as a younger woman, and although I was very resistance at first, I don't think I could have gotten through what I did without them. I needed to restock my shelves (serotonin) so I could make better decisions. I only took them for a year, but I believe they saved my life.

Denise M., 1961

My little brother had a crack addiction from the time he was 18. He was in and out of rehab, in and out of girlfriends, then a wife who couldn't control him was in and out of their apartment if he got violent. Every time he was out of money, or needed a place to stay, I made room. But every time he left he made sure he took something with him. Addicts sell it to the drug man so you will never see it again. When I finally decided to have kids, my husband and I knew that having him around was not good. But he was my brother. I loved him. I had spent so many years saving him from the street, and jail, and bad relationships that maybe it was too long realizing I had to save myself. Mom died a year ago. We are getting ready to move to a new city. I will miss everyone. I hate moving. We used to have to move every other year when I was growing up. I had to get used to a new school, make new friends, and start over too many times.

This year I turn 54. My brother isn't here. I'm not sure how I feel.

❧

Some critical and dangerous situations to our well-being result from mental health problems and addictions. Serious addictions are stressful matters, whether you suffer from them yourself or they belong to someone close to you. They need attention, direction, and healing. If your sensitivities are such that you feel other people's pain as deeply as if it were your own, the stress can come from so many directions that you have no idea how to start the healing process. In subsequent chapters, I'll offer ways to deal with your emotions that will empower you and your loved ones.

For now, I dedicate the focus of this chapter to one of the most severe and complex issues of Boomer women's lives—high stress—as well as how to heal from it and experience new and positive emotional growth and well-being. We don't have to succumb to stress or be swallowed by it, and later in this chapter I'll share more about something called post-traumatic growth. But before growth comes the trauma or the crisis.

Right at this moment, Boomer women ready to move on from the *now what?* need clarification about the trauma they have faced or are experiencing. Researchers, therapists, and psychologists consider trauma a one-time event that leaves an individual terrorized and overly vigilant. Crisis, according to psychotherapist and clinical psychologist Barbara Rubin Wainrib, is a "predictable experience" such as birth, illness, divorce, and so on.[8]

Predictability doesn't make the issue less tolerable or easier to navigate. Both trauma and crisis take their tolls.

Trauma or crisis can leave an isolated and lonely Boomer woman tired, disappointed, self-critical, and even clinically depressed. No wonder.

Your husband may be driving you crazy with his demand for intimacy when it hasn't felt right for ages, and you aren't sure if the problem is him or you.

Financial problems may multiply with the recent diagnosis of an elderly parent with arthritis and limited mobility. The sister-in-law is pushing for homecare that no one can afford.

A new daughter-in-law has been bed-ridden since her baby was stillborn, and your son is beside himself with his own brand of grief. Nothing you say can comfort him or her, and someone has to make the funeral arrangements.

In moments like this, when we are helpless to ease the pain of another human, we Boomer women, who are supposed to be the caretakers, can question our purpose.

Corliss B., 1959

My brother was six years old. He was riding his bike in the street with his friends when a car hit him. He was in a coma for two months. When he recovered my mother couldn't afford to care for him and had him placed in a care facility. After my mom passed away I became his legal guardian, responsible for his care. My husband and I left our province to take teaching jobs. I left my brother in the care of our youngest sister. I knew she had problems. When she was diagnosed as bipolar, it didn't seem too far out. She was depressed as a child and for years before Mom died she was a handful. She got into bad situations with guys, drugs, and the law. Eventually she found her way to university to earn a degree in physical education. She lost every job she had. I judged her. My husband judged her. No one could talk to her or reason with her. She would get angry and derogatory at me, claiming I was better than her. She wanted to have a normal relationship, kids, and a stable life, but we all knew it wasn't likely to happen unless something drastic changed. My little sister has been in and out of institutions and hospitals. I am a grandma now with two beautiful granddaughters I adore. I'll spend my birthday with my family at the lake and think about my brother and sister. So as usual, the day won't be without some sadness.

This birthday I turn 56 years old.

❦

Negative thoughts affect our physical well-being, so if we focus on our woes, our stress levels rise as does the likelihood of depression, even in its mildest form. High stress is like an IV drip plugged directly into your main artery.

The problem is that there's usually no caring, professional nurse standing by to adjust the drip levels to what you need for optimum functioning or to reposition he needle when it's not comfortable.

So you may have to learn how to take care of yourself in a new way, which might involve reaching out to others for help. Whatever it involves, self-care in the face of stress is essential and can be life-changing to the recipe that is you. If you need some self-care immediately, jump to the ingredients at the end of this chapter. Otherwise, let's see if we can come to a deeper understanding of how stress, crisis, and trauma function in our lives.

Shedding Light on Stress, Crisis,
and Post-Traumatic Stress Disorder

Stress can be grouped into two categories: distress and eustress, or good stress, which boosts our energy to stay out of danger, finish tasks, and reach goals. We can experience this when we graduate from school, get married, have babies, and compete for top positions in sports or business. Pioneer researcher Hans Selye (1907-1982), who coined the term eustress,[9] spent his life studying and theorizing the series of physiological responses to perceived threats. He concluded that both distress and eustress were adaptive measures all humans experienced on a day-to-day basis. The perceptions of the stressors as bad rather than good influenced the development of physical and psychological disorders in an individual.

Scientists and researchers have come to a reasonable understanding—I hesitate to say conclusion—of the physiological mechanisms responsible for our flight, fight, or freeze responses. Hundreds of thousands of books, articles, websites, and theories offer ways to deal with too much stress. You'll find some that I recommend, particularly for Boomer women, at the end of the book in the resources directory.

Right now, let's get the idea of what stress, crisis, and trauma do to us. During stressful situations, a flush of chemicals—cortisol, norepinephrine, or adrenalin—affects all our tissues, organs, and skeleton.[10] When this flush is excessive and prolonged, the results damage our immune system, which in turn increases our susceptibility to chronic disease. Too much cortisol can eventually lead to adrenal fatigue and create a whole host of other health issues that can easily be misdiagnosed if a practitioner isn't considering the whole life of a patient. Since we Boomer women often face misdiagnosis and less-than-stellar medical care, we need to take a serious look at both the quality of care and the kinds of care we want to address our health issues.

Darcie S., 1964

My parents used to fight every day they were together. I and my four brothers would be huddled together on the sofa crying. It was ugly. We grew up thinking that our parents' inability to communicate without fighting was normal. I used to hate coming home when I got older. I was glad when I got a job as a janitor after school. When I graduated from high school and got married, my marriage wasn't like my parents'. He would put me down, but it wasn't in a vicious way. We never fought. But every day I cried when I was alone. I was listless and unsure of myself. By the time my first son was born, I was crying even more. I developed thyroid problems and Crohn's disease that was treated, but I still had this crying thing I did. The doctor said to me that I would be fine if I dropped fifty pounds. I lost thirty but I was still depressed. I eventually divorced my husband. It wasn't until four years ago I found out about what our body goes through when we experience constant stress and crisis. I had thought that my parents' fighting was not a big deal. But the fact that there was no peace in that house—ever—likely contributed to my health issues that were mental and emotional that eventually affected my body. No one had answers that helped me very much fifteen years ago. I meditate, have a new career, and stay away from my parents.

I'm 51 this year.

⊰≈⊱

Before we join arms to rally for our benefits, let's go deeper in understanding what goes on when we are stressed—or worse, traumatized. After a traumatic event, simple challenges become larger than life and not so simple to tame. After prolonged stress, we don't feel like ourselves. We can become indecisive, jumpy, out-of-it, brain foggy, and chronically moody.[11] Because we are trained as young girls and women that others' needs come first, we often ignore these symptoms of stress or slap labels like PMS onto them.

In his book, *Controlling Stress and Tension,* Daniel Girdano reveals that post-traumatic stress disorder (PTSD) did not enter psychiatric terminology and diagnostics until 1980. It took a while for the medical community to accept that "persistent, increased stress arousal" was not just a result of wartime, but rather a crippling disorder requiring extensive recovery and therapy.[12] According to Girdano, an incident or event that is "overwhelming beyond normal coping mechanisms" pushes high stress into extreme trauma.

If a Boomer woman as a child or teenager lived in a home where sexual, physical, or mental abuse occurred daily, does this not qualify as persistent traumatic stress? Of course it does. But I know that I'm not the only Boomer woman who wasn't diagnosed until adulthood with chronic stress resulting from years of mental abuse in my childhood. When we are younger our bodies can bounce back more easily from stress, mild or severe; and even as adults, we might not notice the slow drain that stress, especially in high levels, has on our bodies.

Or we may know how to reduce the effects of stressors because we have educated ourselves. Some of us have incorporated daily exercise or cognitive therapy into our life recipes. For example, when we feel angry we are able to course correct rather than blaming or reacting. (For managing intense emotions, you can jump ahead to *Reactor Factors*, Chapter 8.)

If we can afford it, we might request days off from work to get a break from annoying co-workers. Some of us meditate, spend time with friends, or binge on a dozen cookies—my favourite is chocolate chip—as ways to adapt and cope.

We balance joyful sugar treats with the right choices of fruits and veggies.

If this isn't your experience, don't worry. If you're not sure how to manage stress, or are desperately trying to break out of a mold that's no longer comfortable, I'm here to guide and support you.

For the Boomer women whose lives have been clouded by depression, addiction, or some inner belief that they are not worthy of empowerment or financial security, I'm here to tell you that the time to transform your fortune is now. No matter how bad it is or was, this transformation is possible.

41

Yelgy P., 1949

My first marriage had ended in divorce. The job I had as a curator relocated me to Cairo, Egypt, where I learned to speak Arabic. My second marriage to a wealthy African businessman was like a dream. He was handsome, charming, and worldly. We lived in Paris. The birth of our son changed things. He became controlling and abusive. Every day was living on eggshells. He would get angry because the food wasn't the right temperature. If the baby was crying, he would yell at me to stop him or he would do something about it. I was terrified. I lived everyday with fear. I was starting to lose my hair, a band of fat started growing around my mid-section. I was tired, brain-foggy, and jumpy. One night he wanted to have sex, and I didn't. It was starting to become painful. Usually I just gave in. But this night I decided that I was asserting myself. He yelled, "You will never talk to me like that again, missy." He forced his fist into my mouth, knocking out three of my front teeth and tried to pull my tongue out with his hand. It needed 32 stitches. My jaw had also been broken. From the hospital I fled Paris and returned to the US, to a different state so he wouldn't find our son or me. I still have nightmares. I go on dates every once in a while. This year I am returning to college without a major.

On my birthday, I will be 66. My son is taking me to dinner.

❧

I heard the story of a Boomer woman who lived with a highly abusive parent in her childhood. Around the age of four, her mother would threaten to kill her, walking around the house with a butcher knife when they were alone together, ensuring her daughter's terror and absolute obedience. That this Boomer woman was diagnosed in her forties with PTSD from the early childhood trauma wasn't a surprise to me, but it was to her. She thought she was crazy. For years she had blamed herself and used illegal drugs along with two bottles of wine a day to self-medicate. She lived most of her life as an addict and alcoholic and drifted into reclusive and avoidant behaviour. But that wasn't the end of her story.

What she did for herself—to push past negativity and debilitating life issues, to heal and to grow—is at the heart of this chapter. Tired of being alone and in a haze of wine and drugs, this woman checked herself into rehab, found funding, and went to college. It took everything she had to get herself to do it, but she is proud to say that she currently attends university to study linguistics.

It doesn't take wartime or a devastating killer cyclone to reduce a person's life to anxiety-ridden, negative, and persistent distortion. Often devastation happens in supposedly safe institutions or in the privacy of homes, as it did for this woman.

Knowing her story and those of other women striving and thriving past trauma put me in a different mindset on a day when I rode my bike to a meeting. I love riding my bike rather than taking my car because I can stop and talk to people. It was a perfect, Alberta summer day, and I wore a light tank top and shorts, credit card and phone tucked in my back pocket.

When I paused at an intersection, I saw a white-haired woman sitting on a wheel-chair by the curb. Her whole self looked like it had been worn from abuse, years of rejection, and fatigue. From her sullen face etched with deep wrinkles, I would have guessed her to be in her mid-seventies or older.

She looked up at me and asked, "Do you got a cigarette?"

A little stunned, I thought to myself: *That would be the last question you would ask someone riding a bike looking like a health nut.* I responded, "I don't smoke."

She said, "I used to be into fitness when I was your age."

That tweaked my curiosity, and despite myself I blurted out, "How old are you?"

"I'm 60."

We were just three years apart in age. In that moment I saw a living example of how a body can store stress. The damaging, long-term health effects from PTSD on the body, mind, and soul can result in drug addictions (that includes nicotine), violence, suicide, and vulnerability to chronic diseases. Early childhood trauma can leave permanent marks leading to homelessness; 36 percent of Canada's homeless population are survivors of severe traumas including conflict and abuse.[13] I don't know what circumstances led to that lady sitting on a downtown street hoping to score a cigarette from a generous smoker. But I was reminded of how hard life can be on Boomer women and what can happen to us when we can't or won't take care of ourselves.

Often it can feel like we don't have self-care as a choice. We're working and have families, after all. There are appointments to attend on time, laundry to do, and important relationships to nurture. We may be staying in violent, destructive relationships and marriages because that's all we know. These relationships don't have to be obviously physically threatening to wear away at us. They can be emotionally abusive. Our savings, cars, and homes may be tied up with partners who refuse to cooperate with us if we leave. If our children are still at home, we have their welfare to consider. We have so many things and other people to consider, all the time. I understand this.

Vicki F., 1964

I was pregnant with my first child out of wedlock. The dad moved to Alberta, and after the baby was born I followed him from my home and family back East. It was there that I met and eventually married a co-worker of his. Things were pretty good until my husband started gambling. He was on a roll. Most of his family had no idea what was wrong. Neither did I. We went back and forth so many times until I finally had to move. After a few months away I found out I was pregnant. I moved back to the West and we had a different life for a while. Then the stuff started again but not gambling. He was suicidal. I had my own issues to deal with. My mom's abandonment of my brother and me when I was four still bothered me. I went through a period of losing my hair, sleep problems, developing skin rashes, and having yelling matches with my crazy mother-in-law. I drink too much but I don't plan on stopping. I have no excuses. I do what I do. Four years ago my husband revealed that he had been sexually assaulted when he was

11 years old by an older man. That's taken a lot for us to work through. We don't have a sex life. He works six days a week. He turned 51 this June. He got a bonus from his boss: a seven-day trip to Hawaii. I've never been to Hawaii. It will be fun, if I don't get a sunburn.

I turn 51 in August.

⁓

In my second marriage, I was ready for him to leave after a decade and a half of his excessive drinking and gambling that had left me with what felt like 200 percent of the responsibility for our family. But it wasn't easy for my two children. Even if our marriage had been less than stellar and loving, they would still suffer the loss of their dad in a divorce. By then, I faced surgery for the tumour on my spine, and I was going to lose my home. Was I under enough stress to consider it falling in the category of persistent, increased stress arousal?[14]

Well, I hadn't witnessed a murder or violent death as a soldier might in war nor been a victim of rape. My single event trauma was the sudden death of my first husband. But at that point I was reeling from a lifetime of critical events and turning points, and I finally chose to make decisions based on what made sense to my heart and soul.

The first one of those was getting a divorce.

Some crisis situations (divorce, bankruptcy) can be handled with planning over time; trauma may require an immediate choice that uproots you from everything you've ever known. Whatever is true for you, as I said in Chapter 1, physical health should be the first priority in your transformation.

You might start with the stress and PTSD screening questionnaires at the end of this chapter. If you've been ignoring excessive stressors or a particular trauma and are noticing that your physical health is suffering, it might be time to contact a therapist or doctor.

Get the blood work done to know your iron, thyroid, and blood sugar levels. Find out ways to relight that inner flame, one step at a time, to help you regain strength, flexibility, and wellness. Healing is possible, and one name for it is post-traumatic growth.

Post-Traumatic Growth

The stories throughout this book reveal of Boomer women who overcame significant challenges and healed from serious trauma and distress. Some have returned to school, have new opportunities, or are finally getting much needed rest.

The point is growth can come after trauma, stress, and suffering.

My own journey has been full of tears, laughter, joy, and pain. I still dream about a personal chef, and although I'm not there yet, I have been able to sometimes enlist some cleaning help. My business requires so much of my time that I don't always have the energy to think about cleaning bathrooms, vacuuming, and dusting. Occasionally having someone in to clean has been a big step for me.

Before reaching some success in my active business as an event planner, speaker, consultant, and graphic designer, I had to do it all: chores, kids, parent meetings, birthday parties, driving back and forth for appointments, and more. The challenges of being a Boomer woman who has been a widow, divorcee, wife, and mother have all been mine to deal with. I'm sure you can relate to feeling spent from expertly juggling responsibilities and challenges—and perhaps to tucking secret wishes, like hiring a personal chef, away in your subconscious.

Whatever your yet-to-be-manifested dream is, let's work together to see if we can build our lives in a way that filling those dreams and wishes becomes possible. Rather than focusing on the stresses and struggles from our crises and traumas, how about we put energy into healing our bodies, minds, and spirits to become more positive and resilient?

A major piece of the stress, crisis, and PTSD puzzle is recovery. Researchers have seen people not only transcend expected results for improvement, but also become stronger, more resilient, and wiser. At the same time that clinicians and researchers were deciding what to call the symptoms of severe trauma, they observed an interesting phenomenon. Despite horrendous and devastating events leading men, women, and children to suffer physically, mentally, and emotionally, a portion of the sufferers turned their focus to renewing inner strength and experienced what Peter Levine calls "authentic transformation."

In his book *Waking the Tiger*, Levine determined that the human mind had capacity for "profound metamorphosis" and spiritual awakening; resilient people could not only survive trauma, but emerge with a renewed sense of identity.[15]

In the 1990s, the work of scholars Richard Tedeschi and Lawrence Calhoun on post-traumatic growth led the theory of *positive psychology* to take hold. Researchers began to question how some of us are just that much tougher, more resilient, and self-controlled than others.[16]

Levine defines *tenacity* for survivors as the ability to hold on while the weight of struggle pulls on you, and *hope* as the capacity to sustain heartfelt enthusiasm. Despite stress and trauma, Levine and others observed in some survivors a light that refused to go out, a movement toward life well-lived.[17] The Boomer woman I mentioned earlier who was terrorized by her mother but went on to heal and study linguistics is a prime example of this.

Martin Seligman, the force behind the positive psychology movement to understand happiness and well-being, calls life well-lived *flourishing*—also the title of his 2012 book.[18] For me, flourishing and thriving are close relatives; by definition both are actions that lead to success (a highly personal definition) and prosperity. With that in mind, I also see striving to achieve our goals and live above the rage of depressing, negative, and dangerous acts in the world as thriving. We flourish and thrive when we align our definitions of success and prosperity with our values and goals. (There is more on values in Chapter 4.)

Some people are more resilient in stressful situations than others. Age, fitness level, and strength can affect how we handle trauma.

In *Walking the Tiger* Levine suggests that the ability to discharge energy and take action rather than freezing or collapsing can also be a reason why some people are able to move through trauma easier than others.

I'm not a scientist or researcher, but I can look to my own experience and the experience of other Boomer women I've encountered for guidance and insight.

In my own recovery from painful shocks, surgeries, struggles and turning points I found a place inside of myself that was ready to move forward because I was ready to trust the future. I was optimistic that my future held a safe place for my family and me. I was hopeful that my experiences had made me wiser. I trusted that my choices from that point on would be the right ones. I relied on spiritual grounding—an unshakeable source of inner strength for me—then and now. And I'm not alone.

I've met many women who have been through so much, yet come out stronger without any bitterness or resentment. My friend, Jo Dibblee, author of the internationally best-selling book *Frock Off: Living Undisguised*, has lived an unbelievably challenging life yet is one of the most positive, confident woman I know. Jo has survived neglect and trauma yet thrives in her personal and business life.

Spirituality doesn't often factor into research, but it does matter. To me, spirituality is about one's search for meaning and purpose, something that goes beyond religion. Mostly, it's about what's inside of you—intuition, inner voice, or muse—and learning to trust it. What's inside of you doesn't need to change.

Whatever you believe, know these things: you are resilient, you are magical, and your recipe for resilience and optimism needs to be part of your daily routine.

As you make your own journey toward thriving, you will likely find that the routines and habits you've grown comfortable with will require the greatest change. You might be in the habit of ignoring your stress at the expense of your health

However, managing stress can be a simple matter of recognizing what is stressing you out, the feelings it creates, and acknowledging them; this is a new habit worth cultivating.

We can't eliminate stress, but we can manage it in healthy ways and find balance in our lives. It's work, but I know that we Boomer women aren't afraid of *that*. We've been working hard, one way or another, all our lives. We've earned our stripes, and it's time to use our efforts for our own well-being.

So gather your journal and pen, and get ready for some updates to your ingredient lists.

Ingredients to Gather

Grounding Revisited

To revisit and build on some ingredients from Chapter 1: Mindfulness has been around for centuries. The practice that has roots in Buddhism has become mainstream in the West.

Personally, I've incorporated it into daily routines that also include intense work-outs bike riding in the summer months, and cross-country skiing in the winter all while being present by noticing my surroundings. I think about gratitude, about the people in my life, and the quality of my life, and just allow the experience of being happen. I ask myself if I need to slow down. These daily efforts of mindfulness reduce stress and allow me to rebalance. When I feel rundown, which happens when I get close to an event that has me running for fourteen-hour days, I relish the moments that I take to meditate, slow my mind, and check in with my body.

In Chapter 1 I offered a grounding exercise. This one is a variation with a bit more intention and requires greater focus on your breathing.

Find a comfortable position. You are safe from distractions and no one can demand your attention. Imagine holding a flower in your palm. If you have access to a plant, or a real flower, take it in your hand.
Breathe deeply through your nose for a count of five, and with your mouth closed, hold for a count of five.
Release the breath through your nose for a count of five.
It can be noisy. Note the sensations you experience.

Oxygen is one of the most underrated cures for what ails us when we're tired or out of sorts. Plants are this planet's air filters, so let's not underestimate them. A small bit of gratitude to our plants and flowers does our minds a bit of good too. If you are not a plant person, plan a visit to a flower shop or a conservatory. Of course there are outdoor parks, which are the best way to experience nature, but it's also fine to recognize the more controlled spaces where growth takes place. Greenhouses and conservatories have a different kind of energy than the wild, open spaces of parks and forests.

You'll see what I mean by the differences if you've never noticed before. So take some time if you have it. Otherwise, move on to what you do have time for. A few minutes of mindfulness a day can work wonders for our wellness.

Most of us don't breathe deeply enough or slowly enough to employ our dia-phragms in the process or smell the world around us. Some of us have poor pos-ture and scrunch the abdomen and lungs. Some of us learned good posture from our teachers, like the third-grade teacher a friend of mine remembers fondly. This wonderful woman spent some class time each day reminding everyone to "sit up straight!" She would go around with a ruler and gently push her students' backs to stop them from hunching over. Whether we learned this or not, we can take a mindfulness cue from this teacher to pay attention to our breath, posture, and sur-roundings for a concentrated amount of time every day.

As you experiment with mindfulness, I want you to know that at least one other person cares about your progress. So feel free to write to me about your experience.

Balance

I have a fairly regimented routine. I know where I have to go and what I have scheduled a few weeks ahead. This helps me to manage stress and create balance, to make sure I have allowed for enough stress-relief to accompany what may be stress-inducing.

If your life right now tends more towards chaos, the reflection questions below can start you on the road to understanding stress, its role in your life, and when it is too much. As you reflect, remember that stress isn't only linked with trauma or crisis. We can be just as stressed getting ready for weddings as we are for divorces. Boomer women have daughters and some granddaughters getting married and having babies. You may even be preparing to walk the aisle for the first, second, or third time yourself. When I planned my third wedding in 2013, I based my decisions on how to have the event with as little stress as possible. Life with stress is normal, and how we deal with it can prevent illness of body, mind, and spirit.

Feel free to use the space below or your own journal for your reflections. And here's an extra challenge for the first question: can you answer it with one sentence rather than with one word? If not, that's okay, but give it a try. Clarity about your life is the goal. So ask yourself:

How have I been handling my stress?

_____

_____

_____

See if you can write into greater clarity. If you've been eating too much, drinking, isolating yourself, or crying, see if the sentence can be expanded this way, "I have been handling my stress by crying because…"

Be willing to acknowledge that whatever you've been doing to handle your stress might not be working. You may have been going to the gym or hanging out with friends, but unable to get any genuine comfort. As you move onto the next question, imagine what might bring balance into your life.

Is this what I need to have balance right now?

_____

_____

_____

Here are a few additional questions to help you consider your levels of stress and get you started on a new recipe for balance.

How are my relationships? Healthy   Unhealthy   Non Existent

Do I have enough noble friends? Yes   No

How much stress is in my life I feel is overwhelming?

On a scale of 1 to 10: _____

How much of the stress in my life is normal living?

On a scale of 1to 10: _____

How is my physical health? Bad   Fair   Good   Excellent

How is my dental health? Bad   Fair   Good   Excellent

Sleep is an often underrated ingredient for overall well-being and health. Lack of quality rest can add to the difficulties of making better decisions and finding balance, so consider:

How much sleep do I get? _____ hours/night

What is the quality of sleep? Bad   Fair   Good   Excellent

Do I have trouble falling asleep? Yes   No

Write a lullaby here for yourself.

_____

_____

_____

_____

_____

_____

Do you remember your dreams when you wake? Yes   No

Write your latest dream recollection here:

_____

_____

_____

_____

_____

Dreams contain subconscious information that can give us great insight about our current situations. I'm not an expert on symbols or meanings, but I have found understanding in my dreams by writing them down first thing in the morning and then re-reading them later in the day. What may not seem obvious at first can become a clear meaning to something later. Keeping a dream diary or journal to make notes can be a good way to recognize patterns and issues that escape our consciousness. If you don't remember any of your dreams, it might be just as beneficial to take your waking moments to jot down images, symbols, or thoughts that are with you right now—things that might seem mysterious like dreams but can also contain helpful information.

Boomer women have work, family, friends, and themselves to attend to. For some, life can be so hectic that finding time for mindfulness and creating balance sounds absurd. I experience times like that. When I do, I have to take time by force—even just ten minutes—for my sanity, whether it feels like enough of not. On that note, I would suggest that we release guilt, an intrusive emotion we women can fall into and become lost. For now, let guilt go. (There is more on that in Chapter 4.)

Most of all, as you work on finding balance and getting the stress in your life in check, I recommend you follow your intuition. Go with solutions and techniques that feel right to and for you, and feel free to explore the resources at the back of this book for more exercises, quizzes, and recommendations.

If you were able to come up with numbers for some of the questions above on stress and sleep, here's where you can do a little analysis:

_Subtract the negative number (overwhelming stress) from the positive number (normal stress) and total it here: (i)_____ stress level._

Average recommended hours of sleep are 6-8 hours.

_(ii)_____ average sleep hours._

_Write (i) and (ii) here: (____, _____). This is your total stress-to-sleep ratio._

When you add together the two numbers in your stress-to-sleep ratio, see if the resulting number is close to your sleep hours. For example, if your total stress levels are -8, + 5, beside your average sleep of six hours a night, you would arrive at (-3, 6) for your total stress-to-sleep ratio, which equals three. An example of an ideal stress to sleep ratio might be (0, 7.5). When your positive and negative stress levels added together are 0, your total stress-to-sleep ratio would total your sleep hours. This number reflects your circadian rhythm and natural resting disposition.[19]

Some women seem to require fewer sleeping hours for healthy functioning, and everyone's rhythms are unique. Ultimately, this measure may be helpful for Boomer women who haven't given much thought to their own basic needs.

PTSD Quiz

Take this yes or no quiz to honestly consider trauma in your life. You can find similar quizzes online. More yes responses could mean it's time to reach out for professional help. Remember that these types of short quizzes are not here to diagnose any physical or mental health conditions but rather to support you in gaining clarity for your next steps.

If you've had trauma but adults around you minimized the symptoms and your experience, you may never have been able to gauge those experiences and their relevance to your health. Look over the list of symptoms. Consider if you had them as a child. Use your journal to write down your thoughts and feelings about the past and who influenced how you saw yourself and the world (We'll revisit this in Chapter 4.)

Screening for Posttraumatic Stress Disorder (PTSD)

If you suspect that you might suffer from PTSD, answer the questions below, print out the results and share them with your health care professional.

Are you troubled by the following?

Yes No   You have experienced or witnessed a life-threatening event that caused intense fear, helplessness, or horror.

Do you re-experience the event in at least one of the following ways?

Yes No   Repeated, distressing memories, or dreams

Yes No   Acting or feeling as if the event were happening again (flash backs or a sense of reliving it)

Yes No   Intense physical and/or emotional distress when you are exposed to things that remind you of the event

Do reminders of the event affect you in at least three of the following ways?

Yes No   Avoiding thoughts, feelings, or conversations about it

Yes No   Avoiding activities and places or people who remind you of it

Yes	No	Blanking on important parts of it
Yes	No	Losing interest in significant activities of your life
Yes	No	Feeling detached from other people
Yes	No	Feeling your range of emotions is restricted
Yes	No	Sensing that your future has shrunk (for example, you don't expect to have a career, marriage, children, or normal life span)

Are you troubled by at least two of the following?

Yes	No	Problems sleeping
Yes	No	Irritability or outbursts of anger
Yes	No	Problems concentrating
Yes	No	Feeling "on guard"
Yes	No	An exaggerated startle response

Having more than one illness at the same time can make it difficult to diagnose and treat the different conditions. Depression and substance abuse are among the conditions that occasionally complicate PTSD and other anxiety disorders.

Yes	No	Have you experienced changes in sleeping or eating habits?

More days than not, do you feel...

Yes	No	sad or depressed?
Yes	No	disinterested in life?
Yes	No	worthless or guilty?

During the last year, has the use of alcohol or drugs...

Yes	No	resulted in your failure to fulfill responsibilities with work, school, or family?
Yes	No	placed you in a dangerous situation, such as driving a car under the influence?
Yes	No	gotten you arrested?
Yes	No	continued despite causing problems for you or your loved ones?

Reference:
Diagnostic and Statistical Manual of Mental Disorders, Fourth Edition. Washington, DC, American Psychiatric Association, 1994. Taken from the Anxiety and Depression Association of America (ADAA) www.adaa.org

Reflections of a Boomer Woman

THE NIGHT THE MASK CRACKED

On *August 9, 2002*, at 1700 hours, my husband Les and I were on our way in to Edmonton from our home, west of Stony Plain. We were driving on the Yellowhead, a divided four-lane highway. It was a rare occasion that Les and I were both working the same shift, so it was nice to be able to drive in to work together. But our plans were about to change.

A GMC Jimmy – gunning it to get across two lanes of traffic – did not see us. The next thing I knew, we were in the ditch having been hit just short of the passenger-side door. He had hit us so hard that the impact had moved the motor off its mount.

An ambulance ride, an emergency room visit and finally a doctor to check us out. No broken bones, just some bruising; but as anyone who has been in a motor vehicle accident can attest to, there are some things that do not show up right away. I had torn all my abdominal muscles and had a serious shoulder injury from the seat belt. I went to work the next day, tried to work a couple of dayshifts, but then my shoulder seized and I could not even turn my head. I had to stay home and rest.

I had been home for a couple of months when one dark night at about 0300 hours, I found myself sitting in our living room. Everyone in the house was asleep; there were no lights on and I sat in my chair silently crying, wishing I had died in that car accident. It was as if a mask that I had been wearing for so long, one that helped me do my job as a police dispatcher without falling apart while taking the calls, cracked and all of those suppressed emotions were coming up at once. I had had a glimpse of those emotions a couple of weeks before, when one of my coworkers had come over and mentioned a file where a child had called the police when her father had been injured in a farming accident. The father had died before help could get to them; I had started to cry.

Thankfully, I was able to recognize that I needed help and sought it. The first psychologist was not a good fit so I went looking for another one. Fortunately, I found a good match the second time. During my visits with her I developed tools to help me recover. While I still could not do much, I did a lot of reading. Books can be very healing. One of the books I read changed my life: a book by David Schwartz called the Magic of Thinking Big.

There was a line in the book where two men were conversing.

One man was a clerk and wanted to be a manager but was giving all the reasons why he could not go back to school or start working toward becoming a manager. The other man looked at him and told the clerk that now that he had heard all the reasons why the clerk could not become a manager, he wanted the clerk to go home and come back in two week and explain to the other man how he could do it. Just that one thing shifted my thinking.

The motor vehicle accident was the fourth car accident I had been involved within 10 years. I like to believe that after the first three I still was not heading in the right direction, so God made sure I was immobilized long enough this time to listen. My knowledge came from the books I read because I was unable to do anything else. It took a long time and a multitude of treatments but I was fully mobile and, except for my shoulder bothering me occasionally, I was able to go back to work full time and carry two or three university courses a semester while working those hours.

I count the accident as a blessing now. Because of the accident the doctors found some medical issues that had not yet made themselves known and I was able to have those dealt with. In fact, the accident probably saved my life.

Sometimes it takes being hit hard to wake us up. I learned that I was much stronger and smarter than I thought I was; I learned to live in the present and enjoy the moment because it only takes a moment to lose everything. Life is for living, the past is behind me and the present is a gift.

As I finish writing this, I glance up at the clock. It is 0338 hours and I am sitting in my living room and everyone in the house is asleep. This time though, there are no thoughts of tears and the lights are on.

© Janet Wiszowaty 2011

jwiszowaty@shaw.ca

Chapter 3
Reality, Myths and Tests

'Cake is for the weak,' Mom always says.

Funny, I thought it was for birthdays.

Danielle Joseph, *Shrinking Violet*

Do you remember walking on the sidewalk as a kid, skipping carefully over the cracks? If you stepped on them there was the possibility that you could break your mother's back. Or was it the devil's back?

Old wives' tales, superstitions, and misconceptions have proliferated in every culture throughout history.[20] To Dark Age peasants in Europe, the earth was flat. To wander off and reach the edge meant sure death. Some people in the world still wear talismans or carry them in purses or wallets to protect them from evil spirits or bad luck. Don't get me started on professional sports players and their rituals and superstitions. Or watch people laying down that five-dollar bill for the Lotto Max lottery ticket. Why is it folded in half, face-up, rubbed five times in the top right corner while the ticket buyer refers to this as their lucky day? The Dark Ages was when again?

Most women reaching that 50-plus mark have a lot more to worry about than how to fold their lottery tickets. Still, we all regularly act on so many small superstitions and assumptions that we might not even be aware of them, and this chapter is about becoming aware of what we do and why. It's about learning to trust what we know and discover more than what "truths" are handed to us. It's about deciding which assumptions or misconceptions or superstitions might hurt us and which are harmless—like blowing out all of the candles on our birthday cakes to ensure a wish comes true.

Now, I maintain a healthy scepticism, but I still make or buy birthday cakes for family and friends, watch the birthday boy or girl blow out candles, and take great joy in being a part of the celebration. I also remind myself that no matter what I wish for on my own birthday, I don't have the power to, say, wish away the suffering of loved ones. I do have the power to support their well-being and to show them how much I love them. This chapter is about that, too: facing reality and making healthy choices.

According to numerology my name, Dianna Lee Bowes, is an 5, a soul urge number.[21] People with this number allegedly want to follow a life of freedom, excitement and unexpected happening. Travel and the freedom to roam is very attractive to a 5, which makes us adventurers. I'm not an expert in numerology. Rather, I do what a lot of people, not to mention corporations, I know do: use what information suits me and discard the rest. If you believe in and practice numerology or astrology, divination, or feng shui, I don't have any arguments against it. If that's how you make your living or choose to live your life by…well, thank goodness we live in a world where we can have so many different careers. I'm not interested in criticisms of spiritual practices for failing to be rigorous, evidence-based, or scientifically robust. I've gone to tea readings and visited energy healers. I include medicines that are herbal and considered alternative as part of my healing regimen. I know people who might judge some of the things I've mentioned as witchcraft or the devil's work. Not here to debate any of it.

Like I said, we Boomer women have more pressing matters to attend to, such as learning to discern myth from reality in terms of what works for us, finding out for ourselves what we think rather than assuming everyone else knows best, and living with integrity in alignment with our values.

For years I wasn't feisty or disagreeable. Like many Boomer women, I was trained to be kind to a fault. We can be so full of self-doubt that we never assert our opinions for fear of being rejected or thought of as stupid. I put my faith in God because that feels right to me. I let my actions follow my core values, and that includes taking part in things that intuitively do not feel harmful or dangerous to me. That also includes helping people regardless of their beliefs. So what if someone believes in numerology? If my name happens to jive with a numerological tenet that describes a character trait that I embrace...again, so what? There may be some other forces at work that science and researchers don't have answers to yet.

Also, we can't assume that researchers—market researchers in particular—always have our best interests at heart. Timothy Caulfield, professor and researcher from the University of Alberta and author of *The Cure for Everything*, maintains that our current understanding of "the language of science" is unduly influenced by corporate marketers.[22] They manipulate our loyalties to products and services, more often than not with statistics and research that may be highly speculative. Corporate marketers may not be in the practice of witchcraft when they use neuromarketing, but Big Business and the media do seem to want a certain blind loyalty along with our money. It's enough of a problem that I suspect we need protection from their efforts. Talisman in the purse, anyone?

Eve R., 1963

It was getting harder to deal with our situation. My husband had finally graduated with his education degree but he wasn't finding a permanent teaching job anywhere. He substituted but the work was few and far between. Our three kids were sick most of the time with colds, flus, allergies, and our son was having trouble in school even though we spent a lot of time with him. I liked my job as a nursing attendant but on my income, we didn't have enough to keep up with our bills. Live was definitely stressful. Nothing was life-threatening or desperate but it was nagging and defeating. Our relationship was growing distant. It wasn't me that was getting tired. He was losing interest in lots of things as he started to look for other work. One day, one of my co-workers and I were talking. She had read a book on feng shui. I had never heard about it before.

She offered some of the suggestions in the book that included putting a mirror between our fridge and stove to reflect prosperity back into the room. There was also adding purple cushions to our living room and adding some plants in the kitchen. Two weeks later my husband found a permanent teaching job. We wouldn't have to move. Our whole family was better. It's 16 years later. We are still doing extremely well. I never added any more feng shui cures to my home.
This year I turned 52.

⌒∾⌒

Kidding aside, I am a businesswoman who understands what it means to market to the consumer. I know my demographic, because I am my demographic. I know what they want, and because I genuinely care about my customer, I do my best to offer it to them. I am also a consumer with needs for products and services for my business, lifestyle, health, and motivation. When diagnosed with a tumor on my spine, I was a single parent with two teenage children. I needed accurate, reliable information on how to deal with surgery and recovery and what I needed to stay strong. Keeping track of new discoveries and facts felt like keeping daily vigil to information.

With the Internet, we have more access to information than ever before. According to Shawn Achor, a Harvard lecturer, the average North American takes in 11.8 hours a day of information.[23] This number reflects a 60 percent growth in the last six years. While I valued being able to access information and do my own research when I was ill, I also found myself overwhelmed by it. *What do I pay attention to? What matters? How does it connect to what I believe, feel, need and value?*

I believe that this extra overload can add levels of stress in a dramatic way that keeps even those of us without crisis off balance, slightly angry, and fuzzy-headed. Have you heard of a condition called *brain fog?* It's no joke.

The Internet has become our addiction and information our drug of choice. But out of all that information, science, and marketing, how do we know which is fact or fiction, myth or reality?

I say we can find the answer within ourselves.

Reality

According to Caulfield, not only is science itself flawed sometimes but so are the scientists and researchers who draw conclusions from the data the government spends trillions of tax-raised dollars to support, which means we pay for the flawed research. Governments and politicians rely heavily on our participation in accepting conclusions, new-found truths, and invented remedies that can negate century-old treatments, discoveries of the last ten years, or if you're an Internet hound like me, the last ten days. Our understanding of our minds, bodies, and spirits change rapidly with the latest scientific discoveries, statistical analyses, and medical agendas from Big Pharma.

Diane G., 1958

My profession is as an instructor in a technical college that teaches medical programs, along with some alternative treatments like massage therapy and reiki. I have a nursing background and consider myself grounded in science, with practical methods for healing as my main field of practice. I follow most of the professional guidelines for nutrition, But I love food and have since I was a teenager my weight has yo-yoed like every serial dieter I know, and every new diet one of my girlfriends tries I jump in with them. I have probably lost two thousand pounds over my lifetime and gained back three thousand. Seriously, think about it: I have lost in some years one hundred. I have gained it back plus some. Lately though, as I have passed my 57th birthday headed for my 58th birthday, being slimmer isn't that important. I have my three dogs, a great career, and travel all over the world. My life has been pretty good. It's when I think about my best friends that have husbands, kids, and grandkids—it was all I wanted when I was in high school and in my twenties. By my 45th birthday I started to lose hope. Losing that last 28 pounds; I don't think it's going to happen. This summer I made a second trip to Paris with one of my friends I've known for 15 years.

This year I turned 57 and paid off my mortgage.

What Caulfield, in true Albertan fashion, gives me is healthy scepticism towards so-called experts who distort the "facts" they deliver to consumers, often offering information without the actual research to back it up.[24]

What I'm here to give you is support—sometimes also in true Albertan fashion—in navigating your journey, which at the moment may be in physical, spiritual, or psychological crisis. As you take in information here and elsewhere, as you sort faction from fiction and myth from reality, I say the best thing you can do is learn to trust yourself and your intuition.

During the last fifteen years, I've learned to trust my intuition, my body's internal signals, timings, and synchronicities, all of which have led me to an array of supportive books, healing modalities, and new understandings.

I've learned to pick up dropped hints from acquaintances like, "Did you read the latest book on post-traumatic growth?"

Or I'll be sitting at a coffee shop in a meeting and notice someone next to me reading a book with a title that includes the subject of post-traumatic growth.

My younger fearful and traumatized self didn't know how to trust or access her intuition. Now I recognize these moments. I think of them as spiritual nudges or wake up calls, directing me towards a new piece of knowledge that I will grow from. This isn't to say that we should act on every repetitive dropped hint. If we acted on all of the repetitive hints we get from advertisers on TV, we'd have homes packed with pharmaceuticals, cleaning products, makeup, furniture, and contraptions all guaranteed to save us as soon as we buy them.

Honest and heartfelt spiritual guidance from yourself feels different than someone, or some corporation, pushing their agenda. Others with such agendas may only be trying to control you and avoid their own healing. You can learn to know the difference by listening to yourself. Your body will tell you.

I always check in with my body first, and it never fails me. When I'm looking for answers, I go for a long walk and just listen. I recently had to make a very big business decision, but my body was screaming that it was a mistake. I got what I like to call extreme butterflies, something that makes me lose my appetite and more. Even though I found it extremely uncomfortable to go back to a meeting with a changed agenda, it was definitely the best decision for all of us. If I had not listened, I'm sure it would have ended in anger and disappointment, possibly even in court.

So why would you believe me? I'm not a scientist. I am a lifelong learner, perpetually curious, and pretty smart. I seek the best for those that matter to me: my family, friends, my Boomer women, and myself. As I have grown and matured, looking on this last birthday and the age that I celebrate, something inside of me wants to assert itself. Since I started the e-magazine earlier this year, I have been on a rampage about the way media shows women over forty-five. If you flip through a magazine, the majority of the photos you see us in are pharmaceutical ads. Studies show that Baby Boomers are the ones with the buying power, yet they don't market to us. Oh dear, don't get me started.

The bottom line is that I want to make a difference for as many people as I can. Is it because I have two Ns in my name instead of one? Does my soul urge number, 11, propel me forward into work that comes from my spiritual values? Did the last birthday wish when I blew out the candles of my cake start to manifest? Maybe.

Most of all, I want to make this kind of difference because it feels right to me.

I have learned and grown considerably from life-altering situations, but not so much that I am finished with learning about myself or that I may not still change how I live or think. I'm an open, discerning listener who continually checks what she hears and sees with her body's intuitive, steady self-healing process. Being open to new learning is a quality I respect and trust in others and in myself. I don't call myself an expert but I'm getting there, because I really want to understand how to help people, and I commit to cultivating that understanding daily. For instance, if I say the first order of business should be to get your health in order, I draw that conclusion from my experience and that of many other women that I've encountered. This leads me to the first of two examples of myth-busting we'll explore in this chapter: one in service to your health as first priority in a turning point, the other in service to your happiness. We could devote a whole book to myth-busting, but when you're in the midst of a now what? the two myths we'll bust in this chapter are essential to your well-being and to creating a solid foundation for growth and transformation.

As we bust both of these myths, I'll also offer some tests, basically questions that will allow you to get honest with yourself on your path to fabulousness.

Myth #1: Moderation is Good Enough.

According to Caulfield and his research, the best fitness and body benefits come from resistance training and high intensity interval workouts that leave you sweating and breathless. Although I trust that most trainers don't want anyone to be torn, bleeding, or crawling out of a gym after a workout, some debate exists about whether or not you should hurt badly after a workout.

Regardless, Caulfield was surprised to find that moderate exercise does not have the same health benefits that vigorous and intense workouts do. A particular study by physical activity researcher Gary O'Donovan and sport and exercise physiology professor Rob Shave concluded: "The public erroneously believes that moderate activity offers greater health benefits than vigorous activity."[25]

The reality, according to Caulfield, is that for optimum physical health, reduction in disease, and long-term wellness, vigorous workouts trump moderate activities.[26] Doing just anything to get off the couch and out of the house is not enough. Walking the dog, going for a leisurely swim, or playing catch with our kids or grandkids may be excellent activities for our emotional stretches and mental cool downs, but apparently we shouldn't be thinking that it's good enough for our physical body.

So what constitutes a vigorous workout?

Test: *Can you speak more than two or three words after your vigorous workout?*

That's it. If you can tell a whole story about your crazy neighbour immediately after your workout, it's not vigorous enough. If the most you can say is *Wow* and *Whew* after your workout, you're on the right track. So if you're doing something you believe is intense, this is your test for doing it correctly or vigorously. Give it the proper cool down afterward and you're good to go. Caulfield writes that we should do this three or four times a week, twenty minutes per workout.

The research suggests that rethinking our exercise routines to make them more intense, increases our resistance to age-related illnesses and the symptoms of severe stress. Recently, I joined a group resistance-training program, and the last few sessions have left me sore for a day or two after. Even though I had been working out in the basement for years, plus walking, the intense workout with my trainer has returned me to the physical condition I was in ten years ago. I am 57 years old, and I am as strong, if not stronger, than my 30-year-old daughter. Even though the workouts are hard, and I am sore, I feel so much more energized and sleep better than I have in years. If I miss one or two sessions I am okay, but once I miss more than that, I can feel my body start to soften.

My desire for good health and longevity overrides my want to avoid the training, and having a group to support me and keep me accountable works well. Speaking of which, I'll say it again here and repeat it throughout the book: it means everything to your overall health and recovery from high stress, illnesses, crises, traumas, and injuries to get a positive and nurturing group of noble friends in your life.

But first, try this.

Test: *Can you find positive words to describe yourself while in your crisis situation?*

Noble compatriots have no problem affirming you, whether you're in crisis or not. Noble friends are compassionate and helpful, provide support and guidance, and are in it for the long-term until you succeed in meeting your goals. The words and efforts of compassionate people build us up. Earlier, I mentioned that noble friends might not always be gentle. A gym trainer certainly isn't. What most of us need is not a slew of meaningless compliments, but rather input that feeds our drive and forward momentum.

A question: are you doing that for yourself?

Here's why I included the above test: to truly, deeply heal you must be your first noble friend. If you cannot find positive words to describe yourself, then it's time to ask if you want to be a friend to yourself. You might even try asking: *If I was a noble friend to myself, how would I describe me right now?* See if the answer changes. Sometimes the friends we make outside of ourselves, even the noble ones, may have to leave us. That's why you start with you and take good care of that first noble friendship. If you're looking for immediate comfort, and I mean right this minute because you need a jumpstart to your transformation, look in the mirror. Literally.

If you can't look your own lost self in the eye, take a long, deep breath. This is not the easiest thing to do. Try again. Be compassionate to that reflection.

When you become a noble friend to yourself and embrace your own potential, other noble people will come into your life to guide and support you. In this moment, I'm reminded that we are here to teach that which we are to learn. I have had to learn to be kind to myself. I know what the lesson involves.

Are you saying supportive, encouraging words to yourself or are you saying negative words about your body or personality? Whatever the nature of your crisis, how your turning point is taking shape, start with addressing the part of yourself that may be less than compassionate and helpful. So, time to get back to the mirror to practice a compassion workout. Don't worry—in this case it can be moderate and not vigorous.

Test: *I look in this mirror and I see my first, most important noble friend.*

Can you say this comfortably? If not, then you have some work to do to unravel the myth that you can't be your own noble friend. And if you have this work to do, you don't have to feel alone. This is a tough exercise for a lot of people, especially women who have been separated for years from their true feelings and intuition, mostly listening to their inner critics. You may want to look at Chapter 6, Reduce the Inner Critic, to read up on the inner critic.

Give some time to your reflection. Once you can establish some level of ease with looking in the mirror and learning how to be compassionate with yourself, you are entering a new reality. When you get to Chapters 4–6, there will be more work to get to the core of your self, to realign with your true values in service to your transformation.

For now, let your first noble friend convince you to go for that workout, and don't worry about mirrors.

Reality

In Chapter 2 I talked about PTSD and post-traumatic growth. Ideally, I explained my understanding of it well enough for you to see that tenacity, hopefulness, and optimism are three character traits that researchers have found specific to those considered resilient. I would say that resilience is what I had in me to be able to recover from the crises in my life and to move forward.

I touched on the work of Martin Seligman, who wanted to further the study of this resiliency in the 1990s and created a branch for psychological studies called positive psychology. From there, extensive, rigorous scientific methods and measures were applied to studies to understand happiness.

Some scholars have pressed for deep and unprecedented study on how to help people reach their full potential and be engaged in healthy relationships and meaning. Seligman contends that our connection to people and our quality of relationships gives us a sense of meaningful living, which in turn determines our level of well-being. I'd add that the quality of your inner relationship, with your spirit, must be tended along with your other relationships.

Since Seligman began his work in the 90s he has revised his theories. The movement has been from authentic happiness to flourishing. His theory of well-being suggests that it's less about an idealized notion of happiness and more about taking direct steps to living a flourishing life. According to the theory, to flourish an individual must have several core features, including positive emotions and a sense of meaning and purpose in life. Individuals must also have three of six additional features: self-esteem, optimism, resiliency, vitality, self-determination, and positive relationships.

Seligman and his colleagues have pioneered this movement in order to steer away from the disease model of mental health, in which there was something to cure, to the wellness model of mental health, in which there is something to attain. Much hard evidence exists for amazing recoveries from devastating circumstances when self-control and perseverance are applied along with the hope (the will) of faith (understanding) to overcome these adversities.[27] All of this is to say that as much as any other treatment or medication, your hopeful perseverance will go a long way toward your healing and growth from whatever ails you.

A brief reminder: wherever you are right now in your process, let that be fine. Release the anxiety that you have to do anything more than what you can comfortably allow into your mind or routine at this moment.

You have plenty of time to get to where you want to be. It all starts with a choice, and that can happen in a second. I understand that transformation can be difficult, especially when you may have to realize that what's been in your mind as truth is actually a myth. When we have pressing issues to address, crises or otherwise, it can be tricky to stay calm and unrushed.

So please take advantage of the ingredients I've offered for mindfulness, breathing, and journaling.

It's important to turn your focus away from stress and take a breather. Exercise if you want to, vigorously or moderately. Either one may be hard to do at this point, but get into some form of action.

The reality is that all these actions trick the mind into degrees of serenity, likely from mood-stabilizing serotonin.[28] Changing things like using your non-dominant hand to drink your water, taking a different, safe street to go visit your friend, or trying something new (like a cake recipe), creates new neural pathways in our brains. You don't even have to eat the cake. Bring it to a nursing home and share it with folks that would appreciate your kindness. Most of all, we want to increase our openness to new experiences, reminding ourselves that as we come through our turning points, we will be better prepared to re-experience our lives with vigour and wisdom. In other words, to be happy.

Myth #2: When We Are Successful, We Will Be happy.

In his books, *The Happiness Advantage and Before Happiness*, researcher Shawn Achor extends the work of Seligman and others in exploring the themes of happiness and success. From his research, Achor draws the conclusion that there is a progressive order for reaching our potential, and it doesn't start with being successful and then finding happiness or bliss. The array of data from neuroscience and brain studies show the successes we imagine—finding the perfect job or partner, or having a lottery win—are not actually what will make us happy.

Another excellent book that explores this finding, to the detriment of our romantic notions, is Sonia Lyubomirsky's *The Myths of Happiness*. Like Achor and Seligman, Lyubomirsky, a University of California, Riverside psychology professor, has worked primarily in the science of happiness. Amidst all the jargon, data, and statistical calculations, Lyubomirsky, Achor, and Seligman come to the same conclusion: we have been misguided in our perceptions of how achievement and memory serves us.

Lyubomirsky suggests that we won't be happier when [fill in the blank with your ideas of what you would like to achieve] but rather in experiencing the memorable moments that lead to those achievements.[29] Seligman sees positive emotion as a learnable commodity that helps people flourish. Through his exploration and research, Achor has concluded we must first believe that change is possible and worthwhile before we head out of our comfort zones and into active change. All of which is to say that grounding and creating serenity come first and that includes learning to be our own first noble friends.

From there we can find clarity. As Boomer women, we have lived for decades with someone else's voice running through our heads about who we should be and what we should do. We are input overloaded, sometimes with information that has mislead or harmed us, and sometimes with information that has uplifted and healed us. To deal with this conflicting mix of messages, information, and advice, our inner searches require deep dives below all the noise.

We have to reach into our hearts and minds for our own answers to what will work to make us happy.

I don't expect the overload of paradoxes to decrease, so it's time to develop our own filtration systems so we Boomer women can get our hands on quality information that doesn't silence us into submission or return us to numbness, and so we can bust the myths, the extraneous fluff and garbage, that will not contribute to our well-being. In service to myth-busting, I subjected myself to Achor's four tests, basically questions to ask yourself that rate the signal (quality) to noise (quantity) ratio of incoming information your brain processes.[30] I found this test enlightening as I am like many of you who get distracted and off my path with the clutter and confusion of all the information, products, and distractions.

Test No 1: *What are you paying attention to that you will not act on?*

If you spend time on the Internet or listening to the radio about the latest trouble in a third-world country or hanging out on Facebook with the miserable boyfriend problems of your cousin two provinces away, and you are not going to do anything about it, it's just noise.[31] Basically all situations, news items, or gossip that don't require you to act or be directly involved, don't serve you or your well being. Unless you truly feel compelled to send money to help earthquake victims, fly over to a third-world country to work with women and their children, or hook your cousin up with an awesome new boyfriend, let it go. Move on to the issues or matters that will allow growth, that can be resolved, or give you something back. If you panicked at the words just for me in the intro, this might be hard to hear. Don't worry; I'll return to the important idea of giving yourself something back in Chapter 13.

Test No. 2: *What are you paying attention to that you will not use immediately?*

How many times have you bought something to try, like the new facial lifter from Europe on display in the spa parlor, that you are never going to use? You buy it because you're concerned about those sagging jawlines and crow's feet but don't have the money to get cosmetic surgery to fix it. (I know this is a loaded topic). You buy the gadget, or the magic serum, or the latest book because you see it on TV or Facebook. Or you click on the sidebar while surfing the pitfalls of body fat measurements, another obsession. You watch the model on the you tube video transform into a firmer, sleeker version of herself thinking that could be you one day in the future.

The bottom line?

If "it's not going to change you or the way you do things imminently," ignore it.[36]

The only reason the ad was on the sidebar in the first place is that you have been using Google. This Internet giant uses computer programs to make e-notes of your clicks and visits to tempt you with advertisements you're likely to investigate.

Achor recommends that whatever information falls into the category of irrelevant or untimely be tossed into the noise pile. The kind of information you want to keep is the stuff that adds to your resiliency and optimism. Being fixated on your lines and wrinkles before you can do something about them is key here.

Some Boomer women embrace those wrinkles, sags, and extra pounds, some don't and are willing to take measures to change them. Let's put that one on our no judgment shelf for now.

What we want to achieve with this exercise is to cut away the excess stuff we are not going to use, now or ever. In the practice of feng shui, a major cure for blocked energy is to do away with clutter, and I can feel the truth of that in my bones. For me, clutter includes what we read, watch, and think about.

Test No. 3: *What are you paying attention to that is a prediction?*

Clicking through our Internet world we can end up on some pretty interesting pages. As I was searching for information on pitfalls, I came across the site www. weightology.net.[32]

The site creator, James Kriege, holds two masters degrees: one in nutrition, the other in fitness science. In a June 2010 report, he asserted that body fat measuring is predictive of future weight-loss with a 3–5 percent margin of error. When does that matter? It matters if you have the money to spend on hydrodensitometry, skin callipers, BIA, and DEXA scans to find out if you can be healthier and skinnier than you already are.[33]

Then comes the onslaught of "new" fitness testing and monitoring that will gladly suck up all your hard earned money as you focus on future predictions and results more than present wellness. Living in that kind of doubt and fear increases stress levels and diminishes your quality of life. For Boomer women who want to be living with balance, start with giving your attention to information that does not qualify as predictions or forecasts.[34] As part of his methods for reaching and sustaining success, Achor recommends we shelve predictions and forecasts as noise, and I agree.

Test No. 4: *What are you paying attention to that is a distraction from you actual goals?*

Your life is in crisis or you are recovering from trauma. You have people who need you and your attention. Some of us find ourselves alone but still have responsibilities that need our attention. We honestly don't have time for distractions, specifically the ones Achor describes as leading you away from your goals for overall well-being. Social media that is entirely for leisure and casual contact, YouTube videos with grumpy cats, your insensitive partner's snide comments, drugs, family drama, sex, or your favourite novel can be pure noise and major distractions from goals. Taking on turning points and transformation requires a lot of energy and requires us to minimalize distractions.

I don't believe that it's easy, but I wholeheartedly believe it's worthwhile. You are worthwhile. It takes most of our mental, emotional, and spiritual vitality to limit distractions and wisely use our resources. More distractions than necessary and we wind off our paths. Frustrated, annoyed, and self-doubting, we can slip into fatigue and complacency and fill our futures with the myth that once we get our perfect partner, the perfect job, or have more money then we'll be happy. It's not going to work that way. If you pay attention to all those distractions, you'll lose sight of your goals.[35]

So to bust that myth once and for all…no, we don't need to be successful to be happy. But when we are happy and alive, we are certainly more likely to be successful.

Soon, we'll move on to Chapter 4 where we will get to the real you who's been hidden away for reasons including, but not limited to, a lack of nurturing, oppression, and other people's expectations. My intention is to infuse the real you with optimism, determination, and noble intent for positive living. For now, how about a few more ingredients for your recipe?

Ingredients to Gather

Thanks to positive psychology and the research that led to it, we can now see a major movement away from focusing on fixing our broken minds, bodies, and spirits, and toward focusing on creating well-being. Instead of the drugs or talk therapy that can sometimes keep people immersed in crisis or trauma, research indicates that learning to cultivate positive emotions and actions can lead to a more fulfilling life.

This isn't to say that learning how to be more positive, to find meaning and purpose, and to create opportunities to be kind and thoughtful to others and oneself is all happy faces and bright colors. It can be hard work. Making ourselves happier often requires us to change. According to Rubin Wainrib, with change there is not only loss but also reward.[36] We sometimes forget that we can be recipients of fortunate situations that result in change. It doesn't always have to be bad things that happen to us. Imagining good things coming our way is reasonable and a great start to building positive mind muscles.

So, have your journal handy? Your pen? Learning takes practice, so let's get to work.

Clear out some quiet time, and imagine
that you're flying to meet with Oprah.
She will be giving out endowments:
one for you, one for a charity,
cause, or a worthy individual of your choice.

How are you going to use your cheque, and to whom is she going to write the other cheque?

_____

_____

_____

_____

_____

If you have more than one charity, would you be willing to have Oprah write the other cheque out to that charity rather than you keeping if for yourself? One thing I've discovered in the midst of my own suffering is that shifting my focus outside of myself and extending kindness to others can be tremendously fulfilling and healing. Numerous answers are possible, so be creative as you explore. Write. Draw. Color.

_____

_____

_____

_____

Practice positive muscle building. Find the most positive ways to answer this question:

What will you lose when you change?

_____

_____

_____

_____

When we let something go, there's an empty space left, and that can feel scary. As your own noble friend, this is an opportunity to take care of yourself. What can you feel right now—no matter how critical your situation or crisis is—that has warmth, softness, ease, and comfort?

Breathe gently into the palm of your hand.

That's right. Your breath. You have all those things—warmth, softness, ease and comfort—within you. You are here. You are magic. You are cake. You are worthwhile. You are your first and best noble friend. Tend to your health and happiness. Educate yourself via the resources in the back of this book and otherwise. Build a strong information filter. Strengthen your intuition.

Get ready to re-experience your life and soon enough, just a few chapters ahead, to set some goals. But first turn the page to Chapter 4, where we'll meet the real you.

Reflections of a Boomer Woman

〜✍〜

My Magnificent Life

As I drive away from Starbucks, her words keep reverberating through my head.

"You're life's about to change." That's what Debra Kasowski announced during our coffee as her pretty green eyes sparkled. I just smiled and looked down at the floor saying nothing.

"How could it?" I thought to myself. "It's just a book about fitness." It took a while, but I realized that she was right; my life was about to change, but not the way I imagined it would.I met with Debra that day because she wrote and published a book and I was about to embark on that very same quest. I'd been thinking about a writing book for a while now. I'd started to write down ideas, outlines and even a few chapters. But, I really didn't know what I was doing. I had never written anything before, thus the coffee meeting with Debra.

She gave me some great advice and also asked if I would share my story with her women's group. I quickly agreed, but the next second my stomach started to churn with nervousness. "What did I have to say that anyone would be interested in?" the voice in side my head was telling me. That was the same voice I was battling whenever I had second thoughts about writing a book.

Months followed and I shared my story with Debra's women's group and after that, many others because I started to meet so many amazing women at every event. My circle of friends grew and grew, I've lived in Edmonton all my life and how did I not know these amazing people before?

When I spoke in front of a group, it was about how I lost weight, finally drawing a line in the sand and taking charge of my health. But, as I continued to speak about my journey, the part about how I got there started to creep in. I soon understood my story started long before I got fit and healthy and lost the weight.

All along, I was writing what I thought was my book about health and fitness. But, the real story was about resiliency in life, being accountable and believing in one self. Sure, there was the health and fitness part but that was just the turning point. I wrote and published my memoir called Saving Her. Saving Me. On My Way to Something Magnificent., November 2014.

Writing taught me so much about myself, the woman and mother I was and who I am today. It was difficult to be that open and honest with my life, but it was a very liberating and freeing experience, cathartic in a way.

I wrote many versions of the book, many of them for just me. Writing allowed me to finally be able to let go of the past and move forward to the future, thus the subtitle On My Way to Something Magnificent. That's how I felt when I finished writing my memoir. I was finally on a path to something magnificent. My magnificent life.

While on this journey of writing, I learned so many new things, opened my mind to new ideas, met so many amazing people and continue to grow and learn. I surprised even myself with the dedication I had for writing and re-writing my memoir.

That voice inside my head is still there, but just like before when I was getting healthy and fit, I'm getting better at squashing it and replacing it with what I call a warrior voice. It's still a daily practice for me to keep the right voice front and center. The voice that reminds me be accountable, believe in myself and be resilient, just like I write in my memoir. I've come such a long way, and every day I wake up with gratitude and excited to continue living this magnificent life ahead of me.

Debra was right! My life was about to change, but not because of the book I wrote, my life changed because I did and I continue to do so.

With Gratitude,
Bonita Lehmann
Dream Big Accountability Partner & Life Coach
Best Selling Author and Speaker
www.dreambig-liveamazing.com
bonita@dreambig-liveamazing.com

Chapter 4
Re-Establishing You

when you come to me come to me with cake

in your pocket come to me nicely

with that soft kinda cake that's mostly icing

come to me ready and rude

bring me angel food

angel food

Ani DiFranco

You may have spent the last 50-plus years with an identity that no longer feels right for you or the circumstances you find yourself in now. Turning points have revealed an inwardly powerful woman ready for transformation. You're already working on a new cake recipe, one much more to your liking. It's far more delicious, lighter, and tempting, with a dash more of confidence, knowing, and expertise than the recipe you had been using.

For those not quite at the 50-year mark, you still feel the effects of the Boomer women's struggle between who we were supposed to be and who we are. As you work on your own recipes, you are also invited to be part of our magical transformations.

Where We've Been

Boomer women grew up in the middle of the twentieth century, a time when many women were expected to hold down two forts: home and career. The first fort consisted of Industrial Age traditions that taught conformity and obedience.[37] Urban Alberta high schools were supposed safe havens where girls learned how to cook and sew in home economics, went to sock hops, and necked with boyfriends in their cars. Any woman who wanted to further her education could be planning for university, especially if she was smart enough, but she was supposed to keep that a secret. It wasn't polite to acknowledge your intelligence if it shifted you into an elite bubble of giftedness.

Boomer women squashed into humble disregard for their abilities spent their teen years resigned to ignore their true selves and do everything to fit into the norm. Some Boomer women who had emotional support for their gifts experienced a different freedom, but most sunk into a spiritual sadness, one unrecognized and unspoken. Better for you to just accept your place in your home and community than to whine or undermine the status quo.

Better for you to just make one of the few acceptable choices as a homemaker, teacher, nurse, or secretary. And why wouldn't you want to?

There was nothing wrong with these occupations, and there still isn't.

However, if you've never been truly comfortable because these acceptable choices didn't take your strengths into account, minimized your core values, and silenced your true inner magic, you've suffered, and you probably didn't bother to, or were unable to, protest.

Where I grew up, Central Alberta in the great Canadian North, the 1960s and '70s were pretty quiet in the public protest department. We watched news on television consoles that needed two strong people to move, played our favourite music on vinyl records, or listened to the radio. The most we knew about protest was via media. Civic and sexual revolutions of the '60s and '70s, when most of us Canadian Boomer women were girls and young teens in junior high and high school, pushed out a new agenda of socially acceptable behaviours that shocked communities all over North America. Although in some places women found opportunities for sexual freedom, access to birth control, and being part of feminists' protests for equal rights and pro-choice, what we Canadian Boomer women knew of our southern cousins' radical anti-war movements on college and university campuses protesting the Vietnam War was only from the six o'clock evening news.

Our reach into world affairs as global citizens grew at a crawl. The technology that satellites brought us would soon deliver the Internet, along with personal computers to access more information than we could ingest.

In July 1969 we Boomer women watched the televised moon walk by US astronaut, Neil Armstrong.[38] As young girls we were mesmerized by his, "One small step for a man, one giant leap for mankind."

The 1972 Canada-Russia hockey summit shut down our regularly scheduled class, and we were allowed to roam the halls while the game announcer gave us the play-by-play over the intercom, all the way through to Canada's victory.[39] I still do love our sports teams, especially the Edmonton Oilers.

Our female celebrities were political wife Margaret Trudeau; Anne Murray, the soulful singer from back East; and actress Margo Kidder, who co-starred in Superman as Lois Lane.[40] In this part of the country, we listened to rock & roll or country-western music. The occasional polka or fiddle music at rural community weddings or anniversaries meant that young girls still had to know step one-two-three if they wanted to avoid stumbling all over a guy who asked for a dance that involved being held closely.

Fashion reflected our community's cultural sensibilities. Most of us didn't go too far off the top. In my school we had no shameless exhibitionist who showed off her cleavage, wore too much makeup, or had some rude saying splashed across a too-tight T-shirt. She would have been sent home. You may laugh, but I kid you not. In the 1970s when I was in high school, our city schools enforced dress codes. Take a look through some of our yearbooks, and I'll bet you'll find similarities with mine. In my yearbooks you won't find nose piercings, tattoos, shaved heads, purple and pink hairstyles, or exposed collar bones. It would have been pretty tough to be a biker chick if you were in a country-western worshipping farming community, right next to a Hutterite Colony.[41]

God forbid you were struggling with gender or your sexuality. As sad as it is to admit, the homophobic nature of our towns and cities was extreme to the point of homosexual men being at risk of physical violence. A childhood friend of mine remembers a young man in the late 1970s who would dress as a girl; other men chased him down and beat him up regularly. Gay women, I have to confess, were not even on my radar growing up, although now we welcome all women, gay or straight, to Fabulous@50 functions without a second thought.

All of that is what I and some of the Boomer women in my community remember about our early lives in Canada. I grew up in Edmonton, Alberta, a progressive city surrounded by farms, wheat fields, and livestock pastures. Collectively, our urban Albertan experience from the '40s to the '90s had no shortage of connections to the land and agriculture. Take a drive along any main Alberta highways in the summer and you'll still notice farmed and ranched fields as far as your eye can see.

By the 1970s, the forestry and oil industries were firmly situated in our affluent economy, dominated by men, trucking, and environmental destruction.[42] Most individuals or families who worked at it had opportunities to own their homes and land with reasonable mortgages, send their children to college or university, enjoy accumulating nice furniture, cars, or big trucks (this is Northern Canada), and look forward to a comfortable retirement. That was life for our parents. When it came to our turn, we hit a bump.

The oldest of the Boomer women reached their mid-30s in 1980. Unlike their parents and generations before, Boomer women were able to delay starting their families or getting married, or not, to take up a space in the growing workforce that was also feeling the effects of an economic downturn. Inflation created economic times with less to spend and more to pay with each new decade. Despite this swing in the economy, in North America women and girls could take on the same jobs and responsibilities as their male counterparts, just for lower wages. Most of my friends and their older and younger sisters close to our age, lived with an incredible amount of independence.

We came and went as we pleased because we had our own apartments, cars, jobs, and ambitions, with very few restrictions or censorship. I can't speak for different cultures or the girls my age who lived in abusive, oppressive homes that did not allow them the kind of freedom I had. Yes, I lived with emotional abuse, but I was quick and able to escape a life of total repression. None of my aunts or uncles really cared enough to pay attention to me because they were wrapped up in alcohol, drugs, and being angry towards every one. The drama in my childhood home was sometimes so over the top that it resembled a Hollywood fight scene. Some of you know exactly what I mean from your own experience.

Still, despite my aggressive and violent household, I grew up pretty tame. Really, I was. The chaos and resultant turmoil in my grandparents' house made me avoid confrontation and work to stay invisible. Although I became a passive, insecure child, I still wouldn't describe myself as shy.

I loved being around older people, my friends, and of course my boyfriend.

I actually felt the most authentic around my high school boyfriend. I married him.

Evelyn H., 1956
On of the hardest things to be called when you are growing up is ugly. It started when I was in junior high. My four younger brothers, their friends, even my mom when I asked her if I was pretty said, "You have a nice mouth." That day I went into my room and cried. It was awful. From then on I was ashamed. I would spend the rest of my school years feeling like no one would ever like me. It was the 1970s and a rural community. Most of the guys were pretty simple, you know…farmers or cowboys. I wanted to leave home as soon as I graduated. I went to the city with one of my girlfriends. She had discovered makeup and hairdos. She wanted to be a nurse. Whenever we would go out, the guys would come to her first, ask her to dance. I would sit there alone 'til it was time to go. I stopped going to bars. It wasn't hard to stop. I didn't like drinking. So I spent the next seven years thinking that no one was ever going to look at me. I went home for a long weekend. One of the guys I had gone to school with was there fixing a truck. He was a mechanic. He was shy. We talked. We started dating. Three years later we got married. Two years ago, he died in a car accident. He used to call me his queen. I turn 59 in December.

⤫

As a young girl, I don't remember meeting anyone so confident, daring, and un-conventional that she stood out. No one in my immediate group of high school friends had ambitions beyond getting a job, or perhaps getting a degree—but only for teaching or nursing—then settling down into lives as wives and mothers. Even if she had a dream of becoming a movie star, a famous singer, or having a model-ing career, no girl spoke such a thing aloud. After all, this was Northern Canada. What that stood for in my teen years and even as a young adult was not the same for someone my age growing up in Los Angeles or across the ocean in Paris or Hong Kong.

I never heard someone speak of traveling the globe as a world famous musician or marrying a millionaire. None of my graduating class ended up on television or the radio or in record stores on album covers. Guys swooped up the pretty girls early. One of my Boomer women remembers her school's most popular, pretty, and smart girl going out with one of the least handsome guys in their school. When someone asked her what she saw in him, her brown eyes sparkled.

"He writes me the sweetest poetry," she said.

We welcomed being wooed by poetry or songs, but we certainly didn't demand or request it. We didn't ask for what we wanted or voice our dreams and desires. We teen girls were going to grow into God-fearing, hard-working women born of traditional stock, born of women who did the same.

None of us were groomed or prepared for a life of creativity, celebrity, or leader-ship.

If a man asked one of us to marry him, no one worried that it would throw a wrench in her career or ambitions because we were supposed to want marriage. If we got lucky and had a sensitive, loving man who wrote us poetry…well, if it didn't pay the bills, it wasn't important.

To be clear: creativity, celebrity, or leadership are not the end all, be all of fulfillment. That's not what I mean by bringing it up. If we as Boomer women have lived our lives with faith, dedication, and love for our families and community, we have done most of the work required for spiritual fulfillment. What I do mean is that if we've been indoctrinated to believe our talents, gifts, and desires are irrelevant to our personal and professional growth, or if our true voices were silenced so we didn't stand out too much, or if we flounder in confusion and quiet bitterness because we feel like we've been missing something, then we need to re-establish our authentic selves, which is ultimately what this chapter is about.

Re-establishing you and rediscovering the magic that's always been in you, sparkling within your true desires and unique gifts, is a key part of the now what?

Where We're Going:

Re-establishment, Authenticity, and Core Magic

Boomer women who have been hiding their dreams from their own lives have been withholding the best part of themselves from the world. We need you now more than ever, as I feel we have a responsibility to ourselves and the young ones to show our authentic selves. The loss of dreams is a tragic thing.

That girl who was called ugly and never tried out for local theatrical productions would never know that she could bring scripts to life, create believable characters, and deliver joy to audiences.

Bullied at school and abused at home, a young girl with dancer's legs and dreams would run away and end up with a brutal man who beat her so badly she was left paralyzed and in a wheelchair for the rest of her life. She used to imagine putting on ballet shoes and twirling across a stage.

Or what about the bookish, precocious girl whose narcissistic mother hated her talent and called her stupid on a daily basis? That girl grew up working menial jobs, battling depression, and slowly forgetting her hope to be a writer. The world will never know her prose and discover something of themselves in her characters that could heal a long-held emotional wound.

Or the wife who wants to travel and see the world, to capture it on film, but the husband she loves wants to stay at home. She sank quietly into a depression and spent the rest of her days with crippling arthritis, her knack for photography never be pursued.

The daughter turning 55 who cared for her aging, sickly parents for the last 15 years. Although she never stopped dreaming of her own business, she couldn't afford to lose the benefits from her job.

She retired never marrying or fulfilling her dream.

Millions of Boomer women have lost pieces of their authentic selves to responsibilities, illness, upbringing, abuse, trauma, and expectations. Millions more have come to find themselves in life crisis, facing change, and not knowing who they are. They sink under expectations to act their age, do the right things, try hard not to be rude, mind their manners, be home on time, get a real job, get their head out of the clouds, and for God's sake lose some weight. How can a person get out of mud like that?

In the previous chapters I've addressed stress, crisis, and myths. There may be no myths worse than the ones that would dismiss our inner power and womanhood. No crisis greater than realizing we're about to lose the last of our authentic selves. No stress more painful than suppressing our dreams.

Serene J., 1948

I would be the first woman in my family to go to university. The generations before were wives that stayed at home tending the gardens, livestock, and children. Even though I excelled at math, physics, and sports. I chose to be a nurse. It didn't take long to see that I knew more than some of the interns and training doctors. It was all I could do to keep quiet when one of them would flounder with a diagnosis that I had figured out from observing. Honestly, I didn't disrespect any of them. Not as they did to me and my fellow nurses. My knack for figuring out the patients' problems made me think that maybe I should go for it and study medicine. I thought to talk it over with my mom. She said, "Don't be stupid. You're a nurse." I didn't disrespect her either, but I grew distant from her. I married a lovely man who was an accountant. We had one daughter who was smart, assertive, and talked about being a doctor when she was four. Maybe it was me mentally forming her into what I had wanted. I don't have any regrets about staying with nursing. My daughter graduated from med school and is an obstetrician and gynecologist. This year I turned 63. I am taking photography.

⌒⟳⟲

Parents, guardians, and teachers taught us to be obedient in word and deed, all in the name of what was for our own good. We grew up saying the proper things because we wanted people to like us, and we still do. Even now, by not following the rules of our family, community, and society, we risk being isolated and rejected. But by following those rules, we might be taking even greater risks.

Boomer women who have distanced themselves from their authentic selves learn to live with less than they deserve and learn to criticize and diminish themselves for not being satisfied with what they have, even though what they have may be far from physical, mental, emotional, and spiritual well-being.

These are dangerous lessons. I think we would do better to educate ourselves in other ways, like learning to take care of and listen to ourselves, so that we can re-establish what has been lost.

What is the truth about re-establishing you? Does it mean going backwards?

A big no to that. You are not trying to be like your mother or to relive your 20s. I personally love being 57. The maturity, wisdom, and confidence I have now was not there when I was 20 or 30. By the time I reached 40, I had some profound insights that gave me the inner strength to make decisions that felt right even if they seemed risky. Re-establishing me was about aligning my insights and values with my decisions and actions.

Finding the part of yourself that Wayne Dyer (one of my most beloved teachers) calls the "dimension of real magic" means aligning how you move through life and what you do with the invisible self that is your spirit, your values, and your talents.[43] When you achieve that alignment, the right dreams and goals (for you) manifest, and you begin to live as if nothing is impossible.

Up until now your crisis situation may have held you hostage. You are loosening those bonds by prioritizing your physical and mental health, using the tools in this book and other tools you choose with your own intuitive brilliance.

Now it's time for the emotional transformation that comes with the work of re-connecting with your inner self. Begin to re-establish you by finding your authentic magic.

That can mean sorting ourselves out and distinguishing ourselves from where we grew up, from our families, the politics, the social and cultural beliefs that shaped our minds and behaviours. That can mean maintaining some old values and taking on new ones. That can mean stepping more fully into roles we weren't trained for and learning to adapt to things like advancing technology. All of that takes some bravery. In the twenty-first century, if Fabulous@50 didn't have a blog or Twitter and Pinterest accounts, the organization may not have made the same gains as an Internet presence. I'm proud of the work that's been done to get it to the top and of the efforts of so many talented, positive, and fearless warriors who have helped me along my way.

As a businessperson, I benefit from the Internet for communication, social interactions, and business acumen. My livelihood relies on metrics, page hits, and demographics. Of course, we don't have to adapt to everything, especially if it doesn't serve us. I know Boomer women who have no interest in the Internet, no desire to post on Facebook, or to tweet. It doesn't align with their core values. It makes no difference to their quality of living or communication.

What's important to point out is that some adaptation is necessary, especially what is in service to our fulfillment, professionally and personally. We don't thrive in isolation, so we have to make our way out into the world. From my own core magic, I started Fabulous@50 in service to Boomer women, to do what I can to help them connect with one another, to share my knowledge, and to bring self-esteem and love back to their lives if those things been gone for a little or a long time. I have heard Boomer women say that they are tired of being ignored, of having their needs and values downplayed, and I've found the Internet an effective tool to address these issues.

I also haven't taken my eyes away from the need for safety, heartfelt expression, and friendship.

We should have all of these in order to thrive as Boomer women. When you are at a turning point and preparing for transformation and re-establishing yourself, you need assurance and support from outside and in. When you operate from your core values and magic, you operate with so much more power and efficiency.

You may be dealing with a divorce, a job loss, or an unexpected tragedy. Maybe it's all three at once. As you deal with confrontations, negotiations, and arrangements, you'll find that coming from the confidence of knowing your authentic self will not only give you courage but also make you all the more effective. Acting with noble intent from our core selves allows us to move magic back into our lives and transform crisis into opportunity.

If this kind of transformation scares you, if you fear you might lose something as you step into a new version of yourself, remember what I shared in the ingredients section of Chapter 3: what we gain after the loss that comes from change can be magical.

In *Excuses Begone* Dyer writes, "Old habits die readily when you get your ego out of the way and live by the four cardinal virtues."[44] In his books, Dyer often refers to these four cardinal virtues from Lao Tzu: respect or reverence for life, natural sincerity, kindness or gentleness, and supportiveness. I recommend you read more about these virtues, which can be so helpful in your transformation. In the meantime, just notice as a few of them come up in the Ingredients section below.

Now that we've considered where you've come from and where you are, you have the opportunity to investigate how your values connect with your emotions and your strengths. My sincere hope is that you'll leave this chapter with more powerful ingredients to move out of crisis and into flourishing, with love.

So get your journal handy and your pen ready; there's good work to do.

Ingredients to Gather

Values, Emotions, Strengths

Unless some of you have proof that fairies or wolves brought you up, you had a parent or a set of them, guardians, or teachers who gave you an introduction to values and morals. I call these acquired values.

If you're a Boomer woman who didn't receive enlightened mentoring in your early years, you might be more than ready to let go of those acquired values. For instance, the value of fitting at the expense of genuine self-expression, or the value of politeness or niceness at the expense of honest emotion.

The values many of us acquired were overshadowed by traditions that suppressed and ignored our emotions and disconnected us from our authentic selves, keeping us from becoming fully embodied women whose talents, gifts, and natural tendencies are respected and valued.

Now is the time for you to discern what matters to you and what you value. I call these chosen values, not the ones that were given to you, but the ones you claim for yourself. Of course you might find some overlap; you might find that you want to choose some of the values that were passed on to you.

The following questions are here to help you explore both your emotions and your core values and identify and re-establish the true you, the one you want to share with the world.

What emotion comes to mind right now?
How do your values line up with this emotion?

_____

_____

_____

Choose from the sample list below

Values

		Emotions	
accomplishment	faith	anticipation	bored
abundance	family	courageous	depressed
adventure	friendship	afraid	centered
autonomy	freedom	longing	free
balance	fun	dreamy	invincible
beauty	gratitude	happyin	consolable
community	harmony	passion	cheerful
concern for others	inner peace	thankful	motivated
creativity	learning	hateful	joyful
cooperation	nature	kindness	eager
	pleasure	confused	indifferent

If you were asked to share your greatest strength with
the world what would it be? Why?

_____

_____

_____

_____

_____

**If you need a prompt to get started, here are some examples
of you how might show strength. You may be:**

enthusiastic	idealistic	dedicated
spontaneous	persuasive	empathic
tolerant	determined	intelligent
optimistic	independent	strong
curious	brave	analytical
practical	tactful	friendly
inspiring	honest	patient
humorous	versatile	tireless
disciplined	loving	hardworking

Remember, you no longer need to come from positions or notions of meekness or fear that you will be shunned, insulted, or ignored if you are outspoken and self-respecting. No more moving over, apologizing, or bowing to bullying, disregard, or snobbery. Take delight in your powerful, true self.

When you do, when you are rooted in your core values and magic, you act with sincerity from your true nature.

What do you do that is an act of natural sincerity?

_____

_____

_____

We see the difference when someone responds to our genuine acts of friendship, cooperation, and concern vs. when they respond to our forced behaviours and actions. Yes, there are times when we might need to *fake it till we make it*. We may have to smile (more on that in Chapter 10) when we don't feel like it or be in gratitude when the situation is less than ideal.

If you have a tough time with the exercise—and it's okay if you do—try to relax, breathe, meditate, and wait for your mind to clear.

You may be way too hard on yourself right now. You may be offering more judgment than compassion. Remember, you are your first noble friend. Also, know that a sincere act doesn't have to be magnanimous like helping the homeless or giving a thousand dollars to your favourite charity. It's fine to start with making yourself a beautiful cup of tea or admiring something lovely. For example, smiling at a garden you find beautiful is a sincere act. Or just enjoying it without smiling. Yes, it's true. Genuine, natural sincerity doesn't have to be expressed in big external action. For example, if internal enjoyment gives you a sense of deeply felt warmth and calm, you are still connecting with your core self.

Have fun spending time with yourself, as your first noble friend, imagining and visualizing sincere acts of compassion and generosity. There's nothing to hide or feel ashamed about. There are no right or wrong answers here.

Sensitivity and Service

When was the last time you were insensitive?

_____

_____

_____

_____

Manifesting kindness shouldn't be that hard and usually isn't for us when it comes to our loved ones. Most of us are considerate—some to a fault—sensitive, and peaceful. Dyer suggests that gentleness or sensitivity is the embodiment of a woman. I think that's part of womanhood, and I'm more interested in this question: if we have been insensitive, or unkind, and lacked consideration, where was it coming from?

**What made me act with insensitivity, unkindness,
or without consideration?**

_____

_____

_____

Did you act from your core values? If you were unkind to someone that treated you unfairly, were you justified?

Here's where you might fall into the trap of guilt, anguish, and beating yourself up. I challenge you to avoid the trap. Write down what you believe made you react the way you did, and move on. Take a few moments or more if you need to, and release the negativity attached to the situation.

You are getting stronger by the minute. Trust that as you get into the habit of releasing more of the negatives and memories of hurts and traumas, the more you are going to be able to access your core values and think about re-establishing your life uncoerced, with a renewed sense of positivity, and full of potential.

When was the last time you experienced comforting, giving, or serving someone?

_____

_____

_____

_____

_____

_____

I want to emphasize that giving, serving, or supporting doesn't have to mean grand, sweeping gestures of altruism. In Chapter 3, I used an example of Oprah writing cheques to you and others. She also happens to be a Boomer woman who suffered hard times, abuse, and struggles in her early years. Oprah has the resources to write big cheques, but you may not. Know that whatever you offer in sincere service— whether it's a cheque, a piece of cake, or a kind word—has great value.

We've done a lot in this chapter. It's work to re-establish yourself when you've been living nearly half a century separated from your core values, strengths, and emotions, when your real magic has been minimized or dismissed so you could blend in, fit in, or please someone else.

You may be recovering from an abusive relationship, recuperating in bed after surgery, or lying awake late at night after putting your dying mother to rest. You may be thinking that you'll never get married again. That you're too old to start your own business. That there's no way your toxic parents will ever change. This is where I reiterate: it's not too late for anything to happen, and you're not alone. I'm here with you and have faith in you and the work you're doing.

Up until now, you may not have considered what you were missing or what made you act and think the way you did. You may just be learning that you're allowed to be both selfish and selfless.

Know that as you progress you can and will develop greater strength that leads to more balance than you ever imagined was possible.

As heavy and hard as this work has been, I also trust that at the same time it is easing and empowering your spirit and preparing you for magic, sweetness, and delightful re-experiences.

By doing the work on yourself, challenging your belief systems, and getting clarity on paradoxes, values, and emotions, you open yourself to resiliency, what I discussed in Chapter 2. Go back over it if you need to. If you're ready, try this affirmation:

I flourish. I am unshakable. I have what I need.
My surroundings are sacred, full of grace, and
each thought that fills my mind contains
the seeds of love and peace, which sink deeply into
my heart, revive my spirit, and connect me to
the source of life, unconditional love, and infinite
healing.

You are doing important and valuable work, so give yourself time every day to journal, meditate, pray, rest, and breathe Spend time with flowers and plants too. We need them and they need us. So take in some oxygen, and turn the page. I'll see you in Chapter 5.

Reflections of a Boomer Woman

~≈~

To Re-Experience

Several years ago I found myself poised on the precipice of new life paths. At that time I was: recently divorced, a very busy mother of three, a devoted daughter to an ailing mother, and consumed with caring for everyone else, at the expense of my own dreams for the future. Since that time I have learned how to dream and manifest, allowing me to be able to re-experience many aspects of life.

I was asked, "What do you want to create in your life next?" What did I want to experience? Well, first on my list was to re-experience myself as a single woman, with a zest for life, and a longing for travel and adventure.

I embarked on a lifetime dream of doing humanitarian work overseas. I was heavily involved (and still am) with Medical Mercy Canada. I, and two friends joined the volunteer team going to Nepal in 2011 to host a free health camp in an under serviced part of the country. After our work in Nepal we then extended our travels to northern India for amazing, memorable adventures. I knew it was an incredible blessing to have the freedom to travel the world. I have done a considerable amount of travel in my lifetime but this was the first trip I had gone on as a single women, in over 2 decades. I was reclaiming me, and what makes my heart sing.

Six months after my trip, I found myself interested in finding a relationship. Or at least a few dates. I had been flying solo for the past four years and I felt it was time to brave the dating world.

My life did not often bring me in the path of single, eligible men, my age. Dating online, I have to say was a brand-new experience. It was definitely uncharted territory. It did, however, lead me to the re-experience of falling in love.

I did not set out with a list of what I wanted to find in a man, as many people do. I set out with an affirmation of what I valued within a relationship and I held no expectations as to when it might happen. I wanted to find a relationship based on mutual love, respect and support while filled with laughter and adventure. I trusted in a higher power as to how this relationship would manifest.

I think that re-experiencing love at this age is magical. The pressures that a younger woman faces don't exist. I was not trying to find a man to marry and make babies with; I wanted to find a man I could share my life with. I have been incredibly fortunate in finding a man who wanted the same. We started our relationship without expectations other than to enjoy some time together. Our relationship is now over three years strong. Each and every day I feel we share mutual love, appreciation, and support. We are very different people and our differences bring us great amusement and delight.

Being in this relationship helped me love the parts of me, I wasn't sure I even liked.

Now that I had love in my life and had filled my adventurous spirit, I was ready to turn my focus on a career path. I needed to decide what I wanted to do when I grew up.

Formally, I had been an oncology nurse, so returning to that career meant returning to university for two years to complete the RN Refresher

Programme. Taking that leap back into school after twenty five years, was rather daunting for my middle aged, peri-menopausal brain to grasp at first. With time I found a system that work for me and I was blessed with many rewards: increased confidence; a renewed love of learning; and I was blessed with the support of my family and friends cheering me on.

The life path I am on now is beyond the wildest dreams I had four years ago. But it started with the smaller dream and an openness to risk a step. Bit by bit, my life has opened up in new and wonderful ways. It's not always easy but it's always fabulous.

Joanne Neweduk
Calgary Fabulous@50 Director
www.fabulousat50.com
joanne@fabulousat50.com

Chapter 5
Reinventions Made Easy

Someone once said that there are always flowers

for those who want to find flowers. I think that's true.

But I also think that there are always cakes for those

who want to find cakes.

C. Joy Bell

~~~

You have re-established you, or at least you've gotten started. So how you are going to enjoy this next phase?

You've discarded myths that no longer serve you; cultivated positive emotions and taken care of yourself in the midst of stress; shed decades-worth of beliefs that weren't yours and weighed you down with depression and bewilderment. The crisis you've been dealing with begins to resolve. It's left you exhausted but optimistic, which may be out of character for you. The old failures, crises, and traumas have actually become excellent ingredients to add to the recipe of who you are. Rather than labelling them as bad luck or yourself as a victim, you realize they've made you resilient. Now when someone reaches out to you, whether in a positive or negative way, you stay grounded and springy. The toothpick in your cake comes out clean.

Your next challenge: how will you reinvent yourself and your life? Reinvention can mean anything from making simple improvements on what's already good to making major changes. For some of you, reinvention could be a shift in your perspective or beliefs about the world or yourself. For others it might be deciding you will no longer be part of an abusive relationship.

In his book *Flourish* Martin Seligman reminds us that the absence of sadness, anxiety, and anger does not automatically make us happy.[45] For most people, the experience of *Now what?* starts with a kind of emptiness. Along with the emptiness, you also have a new level of conviction that you deserve a refreshed body, mind, and spirit. It's at this moment in the turning point that you can manifest other possibilities and build into the empty spaces. As Wayne Dyer writes in *Real Magic,* we realize that we've "restricted ourselves to a very few emotional choices," when actually, we have many.[46] Makeovers, careers, and lifestyle changes are exactly what are on the menu, but you're still deciding what to order.

As you do, be aware that your reinventions might shock the people you love. They might not be ready to welcome a new you—at least not yet. Our loved ones may be the least prepared for a personal chef in the kitchen cooking up healthy meals because their old mom or old wife has now been called to be a leader for a higher cause. It can happen. I say, be ready for anything.

Your whole life has groomed you for this moment. For some Boomer women that will mean roles as leaders, visionaries, and advocates for change. For others it will simply mean to live with well-being, love, and safety, maybe for the first time in their lives.

Our reinventions are as unique and varied as cupcake flavours, and we choose them based on what we think we're ready for, which is based on how we see ourselves.

First, you should recognize the major ingredient you may have been missing for a long time. That is, the essence of you, what's at the core of your being. For a long time I had buried the essence of me so deep I couldn't find it, and not loving myself made up a lot of the dirt on top of it. Maybe you've also done this.

Essence and Self-Love

So, you have some new ingredients to bake up something delicious: a new you. Hard to think of yourself as delicious? That's okay. Get used to it! Boomer women are still sexy, sensuous, alive, and magical. We need respect, honour, and to be celebrated.

The time for blind obedience and compliance is over. The time for being invisible, as I did to survive in my chaotic and violent childhood home, is over. You could accept invisibility as your authenticity, because most of us Boomer women saw our mothers and grandmothers do just that. I know I saw it in my grandmother. But why would you? You are meant to be seen. You are meant to be vibrant, breathing, and creative. This is your true essence as a living being.

Take a second to breathe. Here at my home, it's just finished raining. The air is fresh. While I write, I can hear the birds chirping. On my coffee table, I have a terrarium that a friend gave me a month ago for my birthday. The plants in it have grown since then. Flowers, plants, and cake are wonderful things to receive on our birthdays because they signify growth, beauty, life, and celebration—all of which make up the essence of humanness. This essence is the very thing we as women bring into this world through our children. I know of women who can't have children, and I respect those who have chosen not to have them even if they are able. The point is, women are creative beings; it's built into our bodies.

As for me, my two children have allowed me to grow and celebrate life in so many ways. It hasn't always been wonderful or easy for us. Experiencing challenges is also part of life and growth and humanity. Difficulties give us spiritual workouts to build our positive mind muscles and perseverance. There was a time when I fought regularly with my daughter Amber, and yet we both came out of those battles with that much more love, respect, and better communication than we had before. I have watched her grow and blossom into her own person. Every day I marvel at her beautiful spirit, her dedication to live fully engaged, and her plans for a life full of possibilities.

Our daughters and other young women we know have come into the world given a different set of values and beliefs than we received. They have tools to invent themselves we didn't have when we were teens and young adults. They do have freedoms and struggles similar to those we experienced, but the choices they have about their careers, lifestyle, and futures is only limited by their own creativity and how badly they desire it. We've experienced different limitations.

Dini P., 1958

I was 39 when I had my first and only child. My daughter's father was in her life but not in mine. He was still married when our baby girl was born and divorced afterwards. Personally, I never missed the marriage part with the worry that he was out with some other girl. I had been told by my doctor that I could not get pregnant. No excuse though for not taking precautions. But it was a pleasant surprise, and I love her so much.

I have given her everything she wants. Now that she's ready for college she's been wandering around not sure what she's going to major in. I started a jewelry business for her that she can take with her wherever she goes. She's an excellent designer and builds the most stunning earrings and necklaces. We have gone to fairs and markets locally and the money is pretty good. Lately though, she has been showing no interest in jewelry and has been talking about going to Quebec with a friend of hers. She's been with me her whole life. I suppose the last fight we had was because I couldn't say how much I was going to miss her if she went so far away. I'm frustrated. I want her to be happy. I'm actually thinking of travelling myself. I think that was what made her so upset. I wasn't trying to talk her out of moving away. Now I'll be able to do things I hadn't done before for myself. It's a weird feeling. This year on my birthday I turn 57.

⤜⤛

We are not like our daughters, even though I would say that as Boomer women we have more in common with them than with our mothers. Our Boomer rock n' roll icons are still rockin' out of the intercoms in malls while we shop, but '70s retro fashion looks different on our daughters than it did on us when we were growing up. Most of us aren't interested in going backwards to relive awkward survival in a man's world. Some of us lived with a romantic naiveté that men would complete us. We yearned, pined, and agonized over having boyfriends, getting married, and being secure in the way our mothers imagined our lives for us. If this is still an issue for you, I implore you to love yourself first. Become you first noble friend. Embrace your re-established you with all your heart and soul. Watch everyone else follow your lead, as you claim your essential womanhood.

As a 50-plus Boomer woman, or those a few years younger or older, you are loosing your inhibitions, false hopes, and stigmas about being a woman. We talk more openly about what was taboo back in our mothers' world because it's so important to our well-being. Some Boomer women are still shy and uncomfortable discussing topics like vaginas, sex, and orgasms. On the Fabulous@50 blog, you'll find an article titled "Shrivelling Vaginas" by Joanne Neweduk, the Calgary division director of our association, who also happens to be a registered nurse and life coach.[47] Joanne spent time researching the issues of menopause and interviewing women's health experts Vivien Brown and Rupinder Toor Mangat to get more details on a condition called vaginal atrophy. I highly recommend you check out the blog on the Fabulous@50 website and read the article. It may just save your marriage or relationship.

The point is, to take good care of ourselves, we Boomer women need to get comfortable with and honest about our bodies. Businesses and marketers do too. Much shifts in our bodies to accommodate fluctuating hormones, mood swings, and bladder issues, along with life issues like relationships, careers, and everything else. Yet marketers seem to hyper-focus on protective undergarments that have no panty lines or passing on ineffective diet trends for Boomer women. They miss the mark entirely by not offering us products and services designed to honour our individuality, common sense, and dynamism. Rather than playing to the mass market that we are not, tailoring intelligent and creative messages to our reinvented selves wins more of our loyalty. When we do get valuable and usable information that heals what ails us and leaves us healthier in bodies, minds, and spirits, then we're ready for adventure, fun, and sex that matches our essences and identities.

As an example, thanks to Joanne's article more women know to approach their physicians and gynaecologists about vaginal atrophy and to have it treated. There is no rocking chair waiting for this Boomer woman or any of my ladies involved with Fabulous@50, unless it's to rock one of our beautiful grandbabies to sleep.

This brings me to another component of our true female essence. Not so much about motherhood but love, along with sharing and receiving it. How much sweeter can it get? Without love we cannot thrive, flourish, or be comfortable with who we are. For those of us who have lived without love for our bodies, who have hated ourselves for failures, or who have been blind to our strengths and talents, love has seemed like it's elsewhere. I assure you, it's not.

Janice V., 1947

Bulimia was not on the radar so most of my family didn't pay attention to me spending time in the bathroom. I'd say I wasn't feeling good, and it was put down to my sensitive stomach. Binging and purging became worse during my college days. One night on my way back to my dorm, my overcoat filled with all kinds of baked goods and chocolate bars, two dogs came from out of nowhere. They sniffed at my pockets that were stuffed with food. I was also holding to my chest more goodies, so my arms were literally full. If I let go to try to get the dogs off me, or toss out a morsel I would lose the grip of all my booty. I started to make a run for my dorm. Two other dogs joined the race. Some of the baked goods fell out of my grasp. The dogs helped themselves. As I got to my dorm room, sweaty, wheezing, and terrorized all the goodies fell to the floor. I looked down at the mass of crushed muffins, Danishes, donuts, cookies, and chocolate bars. That weekend I did serious soul-searching. I left my homework and cleaned up my room. When I went back to the cafeteria, I marched past the sweets and reached for an apple. It was literally the first time I made it my first choice.

I never told anyone about my eating disorder that I overcame, not even my husband who I consider my best friend. I have retold the story about the dogs chasing me because of food I had stuffed in my overcoat. Until now, I left out the part that I would have stuffed it into my face then spent the rest of the time puking it out, hating every minute of it, and myself. I do eat cake on my birthdays.

I turn 68 years old soon.

❧

You are, actually, love. Believing this—or not—defines your identity and how you perceive your contributions to the world. Without love, we languish in a spiritual depression, stress eats up our physical energy and our days, relationships seem meaningless. We strain against responsibilities, expectations, and the status quo. According to Dyer, this struggle comes from our "habit of allowing others to influence us, to push us around, or be a servant."[48] We Boomer women have some hard habits to break, but if we deeply inhale our courage, tenacity, and magic, what we breathe out is pure, essential, restorative love. It doesn't have to be unconditional love just yet. We have to be strong in ourselves in order to offer love to anyone else.

Beatrice N., 1959

I started first grade happy and cheerful. Then as the year wore on, I was getting anxious about going to school. This was first grade and my older siblings had no trouble. Both my parents worked shift work so after school there was no one that could help me. I passed those first two years but just barely. My third grade teacher was short-tempered, abusive, and yelled at everyone through most of that year. When I couldn't answer a question, or my homework was substandard to her liking, she would bring me with my desk to the front of the class. I was there for most of that year. One day I broke down. I couldn't stop the tears, hard as I tried. My classmates sat terrified for me as she started to yell at me to be quiet and stop sniffling or she would have to give me the strap. I ended up with five hard welts across my behind. She pushed me so hard back down into my desk, I nearly passed out. My siblings came to get me from class. We walked home. I told them what happened. I also remember telling them if I had to go back to that class I would run away from home. That night, I could hear my parents discussing what to do. They saw the marks on my backside. The teacher was gone when I got back to my class. By then, I was so far behind I never caught up. I moved along to high school, but there were no expectations for me to go on to a post-secondary education. After fourteen years as a waitress and cashier, I could see where it was going to take me. I ended up going back to a community college. I did so well I went further and eventually got a master's degree in education. As a principal of an elementary school, I know each one of my 270 students by first name, their parents and guardians, and at least one of their favorite things. This year for my 56th birthday, I received 270 hugs.

❧

Although learning new habits is hard work, it is also possible. Along with positive psychology's strides in understanding resilience, neuroscience research shows that we can learn, unlearn, and relearn as much as our fantastic brains can absorb to our last breaths.[49] We have access to the writings of wise and compassionate spiritual leaders and teachers around the world. Knowing that your essence is love and your identity founded on that, doesn't preclude the need for physical well-being or safety. Knowing that doesn't make it easier when you need to get a restraining order for an abusive spouse uttering death threats, when your adult son has been taking money from you to support his drug habit, when your new female boss keeps trying to humiliate you to get you to quit, or when your aging mother continues to push your buttons to near meltdown every time you see her. So as we move forward, I offer another reminder to take care of your health, safety, and well-being first. If need be, set the book down. I'll be here when you come back.

As I've shared throughout this book, we need time, space, and support while we transform. Some of us at 50-plus are just reaching an understanding that our identities are independent from external sources or opinions. We are taking first tentative steps to our core selves, realizing that our emotional intelligence, life experiences, and hidden talents have actually supported us through the struggles, challenges, traumas, and crises through our whole lives. We are also learning we are not weak when we are kind or modest. Maybe the marketing world avoids or pigeonholes us because our core essences and identities are so luminescent, breathtaking, and strong. God forbid if women who have been silent suddenly wake up to their inner lights, because by ruling their minds, bodies, and spirits, they can rule the world!

So get out your crowns and tiaras, ladies; it's time to gather up some new royal ingredients.

Ingredients to Gather

I think reinvention is the easiest part of the transformative process. I say that because reinvention can be playful and experimental rather than permanent.

A New Name and Love at the Center

When we were little, some of us got to play and pretend. Whether you did or not, I'm inviting you to play right now. If you want to participate in this little bit of make believe and reinvention, why not start with giving yourself a new name? Some of you have never been comfortable with your names or longed for Hollywood names to match some idealized perfect version of yourselves. This isn't about perfection; it's about playfulness. So rather than choosing a name to reflect who you should be, choose a name to reflect who you want to be or who you know you are. No way to do this wrong, so have fun!

Write a new name for yourself in the center of the first circle.

Note: If you have trouble with the exercise, it's okay to write your original name.

In the second circle write *love* **in the center.** Feel free to embellish however you like.

This is a good time to write down your thoughts and feelings. Pay attention to your body and make note of any itchy or painful spots, any tension or discomfort. How did it feel to write love in the center in the second halo? Did you smile to yourself when you wrote your new name in the center of the halo? You don't call it a halo? It's a golden circle? It's a donut? Good. This is a great time to give this circle some description. It could be a piece of gold jewellery, a sun that gives healing rays and warmth, or a button that when pressed makes your personal chef appear.

Take a minute to write here or in your journal.

_____

_____

_____

_____

_____

_____

_____

_____

_____

Now take some deep breaths, quiet your mind if it's full of any chatter, and let it go up into the air. Once you do, I ask you to visualize those two circles, one in each hand, coming together.

Describe how the circles come together or stay apart.

_____

_____

_____

_____

Regardless of what name you chose to put in the center of the first circle, or whether the circles want to be separate, honour the result of the visualization. Strength and growth comes from how quickly you recognize there's no need to stress about the results or whether you do the exercise or not.

This next little quiz is about taking a look at how you love yourself.

I give myself love easily.

Yes   No

I give myself unconditional love easily.

Yes   No

I believe that we aren't in a world were we can safely practice unconditional love towards every one of our fellow humans. Some situations require us to be vigilant and cautious. I also believe that one day in the near future we will have a very safe world. I am not sure how it will manifest, but I blame my confidence on the optimistic, resilient, and authentic person I have grown into. If many of us can get it straight about love, and letting it start with ourselves, that spreads to others; we become a collective of authentic, trusting, and passionate beings. We will always find flowers and cake, as C. Joy Bell writes. Let's make sure that we can find love too, where it resides in our hearts and souls, and make it the first ingredient for transformation. I suggest that reinventions will feel easier and easier as you see your two circles fit together.

Imagining Next Steps and New Possibilities

As you plan for your next steps, goals, or ideas, try a variation on the circle exercise above.

Instead of your name, write your goal or idea in the first circle.

For instance, you could write, _write a book_. Then, again, write love in the second circle.

Visualize holding the two circles in your hand, and see if they come together. Finally write about what you feel or notice.

If you're not good at visualizing, trace the circles here onto another sheet of paper and cut them out.

See how it feels to hold the circles apart or together in your hands. If you're exploring a reinvention that's a big step or maybe costly, take your time. Nothing has to be decided immediately. In upcoming chapters, you'll find tools and exercises with more detail on how to approach decision-making, handle your inner critic, dig deeper into wishes and dreams you may have forgotten, and be rebellious, which sometimes is healthy for everyone.

Now is a good time to think about some simple, less demanding reinventions. When it comes to metamorphosis, celebrities provide some inspiration. For instance, Madonna, a Boomer woman, is a model of fashion style transformation.[50] She may not be everyone's cup of tea, but the point is to try something you might fear but is relatively easy. One idea: go out for lunch or to work without makeup.

Or if you don't wear makeup, would you go out or to work with some? This is about trying little challenges that make you a wee bit uncomfortable. So if you don't wear makeup, I'm suggesting some blush, a touch of mascara, and maybe some lip-gloss.

Or what about a hair appointment for a new 'do or color choice? Small steps that tickle your knees are usually better than big ones that make you want to throw up.

If you were never a curious person before now, try asking more questions, explore old relationships with family or friends in new ways, or investigate new ways to be helpful. Remember, we are trying easy first.

If you haven't worn a dress for decades, put one on today. If you don't have one in your closet, you can visit a store that carries second-hand retro fashions. See if wearing that old prom-like dress dredges up some old memories, good or bad, that you might want to journal about. For that kind of work, you may want to turn to Chapter 7, *Realizing Forgotten Dreams*.

Okay. Check into your stress levels. Get comfortable again. Then imagine this:

Something magnificent has just happened. What is it?

_____

_____

_____

_____

_____

Is it magnificent because of something about you that you're-reinvented?

Imagining or visualizing is an important tool we can use for re-inventions. If we get good enough at it, we can use our minds to prepare all manner of things to manifest in our lives. In *Real Magic*, Dyer writes about how he learned to prepare himself for his drive to work every day.[51] By seeing himself calm, leaving and arriving peacefully, he managed to get to his office in a better frame of mind. What if you did the same, visualizing your own trip to work, to see your mother, to visit your son's messy apartment?

Researchers have been able to see into the brains of subjects who were given instructions to visualize, such as shooting a basketball into a net. As the subject visualizes this, the area of her brain that controls that part of the body also lights up, meaning more blood flows to the area. Building a picture in your mind may well be a scientifically proven way of achieving goals, and we'll dig deeper into that in Chapter 7.

For now, we're moving along to Chapter 6 where we discuss not only your past, but what to do with it. Thanks for staying with me. I am here with you too. Let's keep on.

Reflections of a Boomer Woman

⤳

Running Out of Time

Some would say I have lived my life running at full speed. Finished high school early, started University at 17, graduated by 21, full fledged career at 22, Mom by 24, participated in the start up of a now very large, respected non-profit while becoming a Mom, started and ended a marriage with a raging alcoholic, left the non-profit world for entrepreneurship, raised 3 amazing, successful, young men, created a business that at it's peak generated 1.7 million dollars in revenue. Now, at 51, working with Mexican, Chinese and Russian companies to create a standardized training and certification process to support companies doing the work that is my purpose. Rarely do I feel tired or overwhelmed, and to be honest when I turned 50 I felt afraid. Afraid I'm running out of time, I have so much more to do and experience! I know what over the hill actually means. On top of that a breast cancer scare has only made the fear more real.

So as a problem solver for others, I have met my first real challenge of solving the impossible, I don't have the power to stop the process of aging. I do have the power to choose my response and attitude towards it. So, everyday is a gift, I keep acting as if I will live forever, and trust that when my times comes, I will run towards that too, grateful for a life fully lived!

Rae-ann Wood-Schatz
Born July 9th, 1964

Chapter 6
Reduce the Inner Critic

It doesn't take a hurricane to blow out

a birthday candle. Let this be a lesson in love

—and cake etiquette.

Jarod Kintz, *Love Quotes for the Ages*

If you're a Boomer woman, you probably know what it's like to be barraged by unhelpful inner voices. Our inner critics rage around, blow hot air with hurricane force, and make such a racket that it can be impossible to hear the gentler voices within, the ones that can gently blow out the candles on the birthday cake and make wishes come true, without making a mess. Even if we've felt bullied in one way or another into our current existence, we don't need to bully ourselves to find our way into reinvention. Voices of love and compassion and intuition aren't always loud, but the good news is that it's possible for us to turn down the volume on the inner critic voices and tune in to more helpful and nurturing input.

Since we Boomer women were children, external voices reinforced the inner critic. While nothing slows down the myths, fabrications, and deceptions of big business, pharmaceuticals, and the media in offering cures, relief, and distractions from suffering, we, in all of our resilience, know something they don't. Boomer women are waking up. We may still hear the voice of inner critics, but we're also remembering to listen to intuition, to the voices of compassion and wisdom within. We are waking up to our inner warriors, who have been held captive by our youth and beauty culture, by obsession driven by fear of aging, dying, and loneliness.

The institutions that have dictated our options for everything from retail to healthcare and entertainment, have no love for us as human beings, let alone 50-plus women. The advertisements that have blazed across television screens, magazines, at the cinema, and sit passively on sidebars waiting to be clicked on, guide us to our obsessions. Marketers want us to be infatuated with their products and services. They want us to stay in fear of growing older and being alone, to feel unsafe in the world. The last thing marketers want is for us to learn how to love ourselves; it's much better for them if we believe we have to buy love instead.

The media and other negative voices from our childhood and beyond would have us believe that we need fixing because we are imperfect and flawed. That we should hate our bodies, including the wrinkling and sagging, and whatever else separates us from popular images of hard bodies and perfect skin. That we should live in fear of being abandoned, lonely, and rejected by our husbands and lovers because having a partner is the ultimate measure of personal happiness and success. That having a relationship is more important than the quality of love it offers.

Some women, Boomer and otherwise, have firmly rejected all of these beliefs, transcended idealized versions of beauty by embracing their actual physical, mental, emotional selves. They have relationships with partners who respect and love them.

These graceful, positive, and mature women exist everywhere and at every age. If you know of a woman like this, you might feel intimidated or confused by her confidence to accept herself as she is. I urge you to move past that. Seek her out, speak to her, and request her noble friendship. Women are natural communicators, yet many of us were never taught to ask for help or seek out mentors.[53]

Most of us also haven't said many things loudly enough for marketers—let alone our family, partners, or friends—to understand us and what we need. Fifty-plus women have learned to turn away from themselves, their inner voices and intuitions. They've learned to seek out external sources of pleasure, safety, or comfort through relationships that actually decrease their energies and reinforces their inner critics, unhelpful voices that have been with them since childhood. In the midst of the stress or crisis of crucial turning points, these voices seize the opportunity to surface and block women from transformation.

If we begin to sift through the myths and deceptions perpetrated on us for someone else's profit, find the right information to guide our evolution to be empowered and healthy women, and build walls of well-being and success around our community of women, the outer and inner critics don't stand a chance. But we have to build towards that strength, small steps at a time. If you become part of the Fabulous@50 community, you will meet women who have begun their journeys to find themselves, enjoy what they've worked hard for, and continue learning and growing. They have questions about their bodies that are changing, their relationships that need fresh perspectives, and they want to find supportive kinship with like-minded souls

Alice T., 1953

My first Disney movie was Snow White. I was six. That night I has a dream that I was being kissed by seven boys. And no, I didn't grow up to be a prostitute. I was an average student with average looks. The more popular girls that got all the attention made me and my friends jealous and whiny. We would get together at lunch time bitching about these girls, making them into our problems why we couldn't get any of the guys to look at us. I don't blame Disney movies for my pathetic teen years. It just seemed that no one talked about what was real about relationships and love. My girlfriends and I had no idea, but we talked lots about love when we didn't have a clue. Our parents didn't have the answers. My first date was with a guy everyone thought was great. He raped me. I never said anything until I was 37 when I finally got some therapy. I made it to adulthood to get married, divorced, and remarried. I let my kids watch Disney movies. My daughters talk about love a lot differently than I did. They get mad at me when I share my opinion about what I think it should be. I've never shared with them what happened to me. They say I am old-fashioned but then laugh that they love me anyway. Funny. This year I turn 62 years old.

We Boomer women value community, and we understand that we do not live in a vacuum. We are learning the importance of looking honestly at ourselves, looking inside our hearts and minds. We're willing to ask ourselves tough questions like how have we been treating our loved ones? We worry that it hasn't been good enough. Has it been obsessive and suffocating, rather than a gentle, nurturing, loving, and positive relationship? Does the way we treat our loved ones reflect how we were treated as young girls? We worry about these kinds of things. Did you ever promise yourself that you would never grow up to be like your parents? You're not alone. In Chapter 9, we'll get back to the idea of legacies.

For now, it's time to look within our hearts and minds with a particular goal. I direct your focus to the inner noise, the worry and self-deprecation that may have been growing in you since you were a child, because it's time to reduce the inner critic and increase your inner strength, power, and resolve.

Reducing the Inner Critic

Anyone who takes up a pen to start writing faces a common creative struggle. You begin with a blank paper or page on the computer screen, and your eyes glaze over as the mind works to come up with the opening line. At this point many writers, Boomer women or whoever, find their confidence go up in flames with the hot blowtorch of a voice set on stopping their progress. Most of you know exactly what I'm talking about because most of us have a voice just like this. The inner critic that got its start when we were kids.

The adults around us, older siblings, and our peers in schools or extra curricular activities often contributed to the senseless destruction of our self-confidence, trust, and unconditional love. It started the minute we were delivered from our mother's womb. Count ten fingers, ten toes, two eyes, flailing arms and legs, squawking, terrified—good. We were bundled up and whisked away so quickly and efficiently from our drugged up moms as soon as we were delivered there was no time for mother-daughter bonding. While strangers fed and cared for us our parents recovered from the stress of our births, made plans for our names and bought pink booties and everything else in pink because we were girls. *Don't think about choosing another color. Don't cry.* We were adorned with frilly lace and ribbons, knitted bonnets, and treated more delicately than our male counterparts. Remember, you're a lady. Don't be too loud. Mind your manners. Be nice, for goodness sake.

You want to do what? Girls don't do that. You'll never get a husband that way. Put that book down. It's giving you too many wild ideas. If it's good enough for me, it's good enough for you.

Most of us Boomer women were exposed to at least some of the above, the same kinds of conditioning of worthlessness, shame, and disconnection from our core selves.

Beulah G., 1954

My parents were farmers and both of Eastern European heritage. My dad was abusive. I had seven other brothers and sisters that lived in fear of him. He always had his rifle with him. Although there may only be the occasional coyote, it didn't seem like there was enough dangerous animals to make it necessary for firearms. One night when he was drinking, my mom was busy washing up the twin boys, I think they were not quite two. I was seven. He was calling for her to bring him some more liquor. We could hear him bellow as we all did the last bit of chores so we could be ready for school the next day. I went running for the house to help my mom. I heard a whole lot of crying and screaming from the house. Dad had butted mom in her face with the rifle, broke her two front teeth while the two babies had slipped out of the basin and fallen on the floor. There was blood, soapy water, and panic all over the kitchen. My dad left, jumped in the truck, and didn't come home for two days. My mom got herself dentures. We all got out of being farmers by becoming teachers. My oldest brother and I worked to pay for our siblings to go to university. We were the last two to get our degrees. We stuck together, and none of us cried at our dad's funeral. Mom did. We never talked about anything. Having two parents that never talked to you was like growing up as orphans. We never worried about love, whatever that meant. Not until I had my own kids, did I get what it meant to love and be loved. My mom died five years after my dad. I couldn't get out of bed for two days.

This year I turn 61 and retire from teaching.

～∼

These voices from outside ourselves fed the voices inside, particularly the one that crops up to keep us you in your place, or at least the place that someone else assigned to you long ago. It's time to tune in to other, more helpful voices.

For instance, I've developed an inner defender to overcome the inner critic, and that has helped me burst through to the opposite of worthlessness and to feel the warmth of a bright, new sun that shines proudly on me. Of course, sometimes I still struggle and hear the whispers of my destroyer and guilt tripper, but I understand the inner critics better as I research healing.[54] Understanding goes a long way, and that's what this chapter is about. You don't have to smash your inner critic to bits right now, but as you begin to understand it and where it comes from, you can also begin to reduce the power it has in your life and make way for transformation.

Talking about the inner critic with other women can help. The Fabulous@50 chapters organize women to support each other, so consider this a reminder that you are more than welcome to join us. Open discussion about something that's hidden in the darkest parts of ourselves can be liberating and enlightening.

As we bring the inner critic out of the shadows of shame and into compassionate light, we might also discover things we didn't expect.

In my own research to understand the inner critic, I found Jay Earley and Bonnie Weiss's book, *Freedom from Your Inner Critic* (2013). Through their work, I learned our inner critics are not always there to hurt us but to protect us. In explaining the critic as a possible protector rather than a deliberate destroyer, Earley and Weiss assure us that as we make friends with the inner critic, we can connect with our inner child and reprogram our lives. The intention of our inner critic is to protect us from pain.

Even though it may feel challenging to do, the best way to deal with your inner critic is to show appreciation for its efforts and make a positive connection with it. For instance, when my inner critic pops up and asks: *Who do you think you are?* like it did when I gave a talk in Victoria, I made it a part of my presentation and acknowledged it. Not only did that create more cooperation between me and the inner critic, it also created opportunity for connection with other conference attendees who knew exactly what I was talking about. Also, sometimes, when my inner critic shows up, I know it's time to reach out for some support from a coach or a trusted noble friend.

All of which is to say, you can use your inner critic as a resource and build a trusting relationship with it. We can un-blend or detach from the bad feelings about ourselves that play the harshest roles in our lives, recoup the beautiful and loving child within and re-experience, and savour our lives.[55]

How many of you had trouble with the mirror exercise? How did you do with telling yourself you were worthy of love and wanted to be your own noble friend first? If your inner critic piped up and derailed your attempts by filling your head with words like *stupid or crazy*, if you wanted to cry, or stopped trying in utter disgust, then what Earley and Weiss provide might begin to heal you and your inner child.

Earley and Weiss do reinforce the fact that each of us has a unique combination of inner critics, and we may give them names to help us define and identify them. Whatever we call them, in order to heal we need to befriend these inner critics and reintroduce them to our core values. When we accept and work with them, instead of fighting them, we can decrease the animosity within ourselves, allowing us to use our energy to do the healing we need to do.

Sarah L., 1964

Attacking was a game in our family. They all did it so I had to get better at it than they were. What gave me the power to not be hurt by them was by being harder on me than anyone else could. I wanted those people to love me, but there was no way it could happen. I grew up competing with all of them: my parents, my two sisters and brother. Christmas holidays were like world wars, family get-togethers were trash talks, and nothing anyone did was good enough to gain anyone's respect or admiration. I would crush my attempts to do well in school and in the sports we were all a part of by over-extending myself till something would fail. I had some sort of cast or sling for most of my early life because a bone or tendon would snap. College was a little bit better because I picked the furthest away I could be. I missed them even though they were like vampires that sucked out every ounce of my goodness when I was around them. I made sure I did only what I had to and graduated with mediocre standing. It was in college that I had my first gay affair. That was horrible trying to imagine what those monsters were going to say about that. I joined the military and my father, for the first time in my life, congratulated me when I was given the rank of staff sergeant. I retired then entered the police force. I don't talk to my siblings, and I never go home for Christmases. I live alone but three years ago I started to go to therapy for serious depression.

This year I celebrate my 51st birthday.

~∽~

Inner critics come from parts of our wounded inner child that may have been disciplined, forced into submissiveness to someone else's idea of acceptable, frightened somehow into obedience, or verbally or physically attacked. Regardless of the reason for verbal or physical disciplining, these actions left us with varying degrees of perfectionism, guilt, impulse control issues, undermined self worth, or destructive and conforming temperaments. As Earley and Weiss write, "It's time for your suffering to end."[56] They are proponents of a therapy modality called *internal systems family therapy* (IFS) that was developed by Richard Schwartz in 2000.[57] If you want to investigate the healing tools they've developed, you can visit www.selftherapyjourney.com for an array of quizzes and information designed to help you understand self-defeating behaviours and the inner critic.[58] Or check the back of the book for other resources on similar therapies.

I am not a therapist, nor can I whole-heartedly endorse Earley and Weiss's work. However, I see great value in their approach, that is, "creating a cooperative relationship" with all the parts of our mind, dispatching our curious natures about how the inner critic has been protecting us, and eventually separating and befriending it.[59] In my work with Fabulous@50, I've noticed how Baby Boomer women in particular have allowed their inner critics to hold them back from following their dreams, by undermining their self-confidence and self-esteem. If you want to re-experience your life, that needs to change.

Get your journal and a pen to try out a few questions and exercises to help you reduce that inner critic and care for your inner child.

Ingredients to Gather

More mindfulness

Please ensure that you are practicing mindfulness. Making it a part of your daily routine, along with journaling lends strong and powerful reinforcement to transformation. If you've been practicing, by this time you are likely experiencing the sensations of more peace, inner calm, and love for yourself. If you felt none of these before and feel like even a small amount exists now, then something wonderful and magical is happening.

Try this exercise to add to your mindfulness ingredients:

Breathe slowly. Begin with a warm breath on the palm of your hand. Close your eyes for 50 seconds. Yes, count from 1 to 50.

Were you able to count without stopping? Record your thoughts and feelings here or in your journal. Did the inner critic surface? What did it say? If there was nothing out of the ordinary, you could go to a place in your mind that pokes the critic to awaken it a like a dragon in a den. Breathe and observe. Note what was going on in your body. What was your breathing like? Did you have thoughts vying for your attention? Was this an easy exercise, or was it a little bit tough? Take whatever amount of time you need to record as many details of what went on in the near minute of quiet.

_____

_____

_____

_____

_____

_____

Getting to know your inner critic.
Inspired by the work of Earley and Weiss, a question for you to consider as you explore your inner critic:

What are some of the internalized rules I must obey to be loved?

_____

_____

_____

_____

_____

_____

The need for external validation can come from the need to conform and obey the rules, whatever we perceive them to be. We have learned to be reliant on voices from our culture, the media, our partners, or our friends to tell us that we're good enough, pretty enough, or perfectly fine the way we are even if we don't feel that way. For 50-plus women who have spent most of their lives working hard to fit into their family, community, and work, it can be a challenge to take validation back into their control and regain balance.

I say you are capable of regaining this balance. Learning to deal with your troublesome inner voices and follow what your heart tells you will be an ongoing challenge, but I know from experience that it's possible to meet this challenge, especially once you focus on your own happiness and desires for a fulfilled life.

As you get to know the inner critical voices, it can help to identify the voice you hear the most often throughout your day. This is the inner critic that Earley and Weiss describe as the one you have the strongest relationship with, the one you would most closely identify as your *self*.[60]

As you work on identifying your most vocal inner critic, you might consider the seven types of inner critics Earley and Weiss identify: perfectionism, guilt, impulse control issues that relate to addictions, rigidly obsessing towards negative traits like laziness or incompetence, undermining self-worth, shaming, and conforming to others expectations.

What voice do I wake up with in the morning and hear most often throughout the day?

_____

_____

_____

_____

Perhaps there's more than one, and it's hard to pick. However, many show up, Earley and Weiss recommend that you try not to silence or ignore them.[61] Solutions and healing come from taming them, cooperating, and permitting them to unveil their parts in your life.

Kindness to the Inner Child

We understand that the inner child is wounded and needs healing. As you work through the process of dealing with and befriending your inner critic, you can use some of these small exercises here. The more thorough work in Earley and Weiss's book and on their website, provide insightful ways to reparent your inner child.[62]

These techniques, used in the internal family systems therapy seem like a good place to begin to heal the wounds of the inner child, so feel free to investigate them.

Another way to tend to your inner child is to cultivate curiosity.

Can you relate to feeling curious?

Think of something that would bring out this wonderful temperament. When we were babies, beautiful creatures full of wonder, we delighted in discovery. Some of us lost this delight long ago.

My heart breaks when I think of every child who has experienced harm in any form. For those of you who experienced great tragedy, torture, or pain as children and are here now with me, breathe the loving breath into your hand. My heart is with all of you who are recovering from past trauma or are in crisis now. Be gentle and kind to yourself.

Let your fingers touch your cheeks, gently, caressing your face and tell yourself this quiet truth:

I am magic. I am beauty. I am love

Are you able to feel compassion in your heart for yourself? Remember to check in with your breathing. If it's fast, try to gently slow it down. If it's shallow, and coming from your upper chest, try to take in deeper breaths from your lower abdomen. Straighten your shoulders if you are scrunched and collapsed. Say the following:

I am connected to all parts of my being. I am healthy. I am flourishing.

Children are so open to learning and love being inspired by a good hero. Same goes for our inner children. Wayne Dyer is one of my heroes. Another is Albertan author, businesswoman, and politician Lois Hole, a lifelong learner who never lost her curiosity or love of people. Who is your teacher or hero? How did they come to your life? Remind yourself by filling in the space here or in your journal.

My teacher or hero is:

_____

_____

_____

With our heroes and teachers behind us, let's keep up our inner work. I am rooting for your inner champion.

Now on to Chapter 7. It's time to delight your inner child and your adult self by strengthening your creative muscles and realizing your dreams. Stick with me; we're on the way to something fabulous.

Chapter 7
Realizing Dreams

The event happened on my birthday. I don't

remember the date, I only know it

was my birthday because there was

no cake or presents.

Jarod Kintz, This Book Has No Title

When it comes to your dreams—the ones you've had since you were a little girl, the new ones that just popped up out of your teacup this morning, or anywhere in between—here's an important reminder of something I shared earlier: it's not too late.

It's not too late, and there are no rules or requirements.

Some of us dream of dense chocolate cakey sweetness, and others of the kind of delicate sweetness of a handful of berries with a touch of natural honey in plain yogurt. Some of us dream of being on stage at a loud and lively event. Some of us dream of finally finding a quiet studio to make art. When it comes to dreams, there is no right or wrong. This chapter covers creativity and manifesting as two unique, intuitive, and perfectly normal human activities that we Boomer women can engage in to fulfill our dreams.

An important note about creativity and manifesting: they're about building up, not tearing down. For 50-plus women in the midst of crisis and difficulty, life may be even harder for them because they are hard on themselves, in the habit of letting the inner critic have the microphone and tearing themselves down. If you're in this habit, I urge you to give yourself a break. In the last chapter we covered inner critics who crop up to punish and berate when we try to extend ourselves beyond the rules and norms surrounding us.

If you've been able to identify the inner critic that keeps you from achievement and well-being, you are on a new, clear path to a transformation that you can't even believe. You may also have been cultivating mindfulness, finding some quiet time to relax and de-stress, and visualizing to arrive at a space in your mind where you can see, feel, and hear your life opening to possibilities. If all of that is true, great; if not, don't worry. Work at your own pace. You'll get there, and when you do, I'll be here to celebrate with you as you manifest your dreams.

Mona M., 1958

Growing up my interests were horses and science. My college degree was in waste water management. Things that were airy-fairy had no place in my life. My husband was equally logical and science-minded. Our three sons were brought up the same, but it was the youngest one that threw a wrench in the family that shook us all up. He was artistic, I guess effeminate, and unlike his two older brothers, never had a girlfriend in high school. He was bullied, beaten up a few times, and cried more than I was used to.

I wasn't insensitive to him. I just wasn't sure what to do about it. One day when we were at the stables, he finally broke down about his sexual orientation. Together him and I told the others. What changed was our closeness and love for each other became that much stronger. He attended art school then encouraged me to take up painting and sculpting. I was never so amazed in what could be formed from clay. My work sells in galleries. As I get closer to 60, and am settled into what my body is comfortable with after nearly nine years of menopausal symptoms and a diagnosis of osteoporosis, my art is changing and so are my interests in spirituality. I grew up as a Presbyterian. I took up meditation, yoga, and read books on topics my parents criticize. My husband balks at some of it, sharing his views on the science that hasn't proven some spiritual things yet. I am not fazed by any of it. I was so sure about so many things that I found out later needed more flexibility in thinking. I thank my son for that.

On my 57th birthday I will be at the Esalen Center.

∼

Speaking of manifesting, it's time to let the statement "what we mind becomes matter" become your reality. This idea comes from physics, neuroscience, quantum mechanics, and a slew of modern great thinkers and philosophers. You may argue that this doesn't apply to you, but maybe you should be arguing with the Dalai Lama, Stephen Hawking, or the scientists and researchers who have published findings on neuroplasticity, the brain's remarkable ability to heal and adapt[78] or the work from positive psychologists that prove well-being and an ability to flourish as teachable skill sets. This research gives me hope for a better world, in particular, better lives for Boomer women.

As the results show, we humans are a creative bunch, perfectly capable of living to the full extent of our potential. Because of what we're learning, accepting, and ready to be responsible for, we get closer and closer to this fulfillment. We Boomer women are strong and dynamic, and with the right tools to find our core magic, we can discover profound and creative ways to solve not only our own problems but also to be magical solutions in the world. In Chapter 3, we had a look at only a few of the myths that have permeated our culture. I find it remarkable that most of everything we believe depends on our perceptions and that we have the capacity and the freedom to change those perceptions and beliefs. Our intuitive selves may have been lying dormant because we've been pushed to behave and conform to rules dictated by our families, communities, society, and the media. How many of us try something because our friends have, even if that inner small voice says that what they're trying isn't for us?

You know what you're ready for, even if you only know it deep down for now. So if you know you need to do some more work on your inner critic, the voice that interferes with your intuition, and are just beginning to look into options for therapy or treatment, it's perfectly fine to stop where you need to stop, slow down, or back up a bit.

Also, know that incorporating creativity and manifesting into your routines can only enhance any efforts you're making to resolve some of your crises and come up with goals and plans that truly suit your re-established self. As you move through this chapter, I encourage you to outline some goals, knowing you can fill in the details as you go through the rest of the book as all that you've been learning, questioning, evaluating, and imagining feels more fully integrated.

Manifesting

Manifesting requires certain skills and practice. To expand your learning about manifesting, I suggest Wayne Dyer's method, elaborated in his books, *Wishes Fulfilled* and *Real Magic*. Dyer writes that the way to begin manifesting is to feel the feeling of reaching something desired.[79] That can be tricky.

You might ask yourself: *How do I feel something I've never felt before?* If you've never had a lot of money and struggled with borderline poverty or barely paying the bills every month for most of your adult life, the feeling that comes from security through abundance may be hard to trust. I know I'm inviting you into some hard work to move out of crisis mode and into learning mode. Along with other Boomer women in my community, I understand what degree of mental work manifesting can take and how tough it can be to acquire new habits and skills. Being comfortable with the ambiguous and unformed future you want also takes some getting used to. Know that you can get there.

In the meantime, you're not alone. Reading books by thought leaders for motivation and inspiration can help put you in the right frame of mind to relax and believe your success is achievable. Also, don't forget to look to noble friends and other supportive people for guidance and motivation. Years ago, I had to be convinced through coaching that I should follow my intuition and passion to start a woman's show, which eventually became the Fabulous@50 organization. This turning point required hard work from me.

The first woman's show that I produced—full on with guest speakers, entertainers, and vendors— was exhilarating and terrifying all at the same time. I had no idea if the trade show was going to succeed or fail. It existed in the quantum space where nothing was formed yet. Weeks before the event, I struggled with the feeling that I had more to do but I didn't know what. Stress filled my mind and body.

A little voice said to me: *You've done everything else, Dianna, so all you can do now is stand naked in the middle of the road, with a sign pointing to the event.*

I considered that for a second and once I shook off the scary image of my nakedness being exposed, I decided to relax and just surrender to the experience. I visualized every moment of what the big day was going to be. I saw how the registration went, felt the energy in the room, and envisioned a line up of women at the door. Years before when I had my back surgery, I had spent many hours listening to Wayne Dyer's *Manifest Your Destiny*, and now was my chance to practice those visualization techniques. I am happy to report that over 600 women came and celebrated at that event. So, get what I'm saying here about manifesting?

Nancy W., 1954

When I was fifteen I went to the big city with my mother and her friends. They were going to a theater presentation. I begged her to let me go with her. It didn't take a lot of coaxing. We did a bunch of shopping and one of the ladies knew one of those tea shoppes where there was a tea leaf reader. My mom was uneasy about it, but the others thought it would be fun. When we got there they made sure the lady did my reading first because I wasn't married. I was plain, had no boobs, and wanted a boyfriend more than anything. It was all I had on my mind most of the time. I read hundreds of romance novels. My man would have to be dark, handsome, and madly in love with me. As we sat down, drank our teas, then waited for the reader, one of the ladies asked me if I believed in having your fortune told. I didn't know about anything like that. The lady came, told me I was going to have a boy and a girl, mumbled some stuff I couldn't make out, and moved on. I met my first husband when I was 26 years old. We had one son. It wasn't until my son was three I found out he had a daughter from a previous fling. I divorced him after seven years because he was abusive. My second relationship has lasted for 25 years, but we haven't married. I believe that I have had great success as a hair dresser which I love to do. When a woman comes into my salon, I see the style before she sits down. I have to say that I have only disappointed a handful. There are some women that will never be pleased.

This year I sold my salon to travel. I turn 61.

Our inner knowing wants us to be better or bigger; to have more or less of whatever; to be physically healthy; financially sound; standing on a stage; living on a warm, tropical beach; or have a new venture go as smoothly as possible. And it's not like you only have one chance to listen to it. My intuition still nudges me with new ideas and dreams. For instance, I would love to have that personal chef or even a chauffeur. I haven't manifested either of those yet, which I believe is because of my own personal limits and comfort zone. Some of my inner critics definitely turn up the volume when I consider parts of my potential that have yet to be fully realized. I have chosen to be patient with myself, and I encourage you to extend the same kindness and love to yourself, too. You're probably in new territory, and that's not easy.

That first women's show was the first such event I'd ever planned, and I'm guessing you are also dreaming up some things you've never done before. It's exciting and terrifying, but you can trust the power of your imagination. In my imagination I played scenes I had to build, much like an architect would sketch out a high-rise or a whole city. In my mind, the details were real. I deeply imbedded them into the outcome. Although I was afraid and stressed out, I didn't allow fear or doubt to become a part of the visualization.

I would suggest that you've probably learned a lot more than you think about manifesting and success, even if your attempts didn't turn out exceptionally well. Remember, failure is essential and builds our mental toughness and resilience. No matter how embarrassing or destructive events can be to our ego, ladies, I want to emphasize that our ego can take a lot of hits. After we pick ourselves up and brush the dirt from our faces, I say we hit back harder. In the chapter on rebellion, I go into more detail on why it can be healthy to put more positive nos in your life, which can also mean taking a few mental hits. For now we're going to clear up some ideas of what creativity isn't, what role it plays in our lives and culture, and how I relate it to manifesting our forgotten dreams.

Realizing Creativity

When you hear *creativity*, some of you might say to yourselves: I can't even draw a straight line! Consider this your opportunity to expand what you think or have decided about creativity. Here's a definition of creativity that I like: "The ability to transcend traditional ideas, patterns, relationships, or the like, to create meaningful new ideas, from methods, interpretations, etc."[80]

I draw our attention to two words, *transcend* and *meaningful*, as part of human growth and its relationship to being creative. When we are not attending to what's personally meaningful to our core values and greatest strengths, we wander aimlessly. Transcending struggles, finding meaning, and envisioning potential are supremely creative acts, so know that you've been practicing being creative if you've been doing any of the new-to-you exercises in this book.

As for the ability to draw a straight line, well, creativity is not about drawing lines unless it's about boundaries. If we don't have healthy boundaries in our relationships at home or at work, it's time to establish some. You may have to use some creative problem-solving. If you've been accepting the status quo up to now, your immediate circle of family and friends may not comprehend why you think it needs to change. They may not be sensitive to your turning point or crisis. This may be the right time to communicate your needs in a different way that includes the visualization techniques that I used to manifest my first successful tradeshow. If it stresses you out to think about communicating some new strategies and rules you want to bring into your life, doing some mindfulness exercises and making sure that you have an inner safe haven is a start. For some more inspiration, you can turn to Chapter 11 to read about healthy rebellion.

I also suggest that you embrace the fullness of creativity, which is not limited to taking up painting, sculpting, crafting, or writing poetry although all of those can be fantastic outlets for enjoyment and personal growth. It's so much more than that. If you've been looking for patterns in your journaling to construct a better way of dealing with your life, you are engaged in creative practice. You are opening yourself to figuring things out and to gaining insight, and it can be a wild ride. Elizabeth Gilbert, author of *Big Magic: Creative Living Beyond Fear*, writes that, "Creativity is a crushing chore and a glorious mystery. The work wants to be made, and it wants to be made through you."[81]

In this century, being creative might be the most important skill we need to nurture to navigate what lies ahead, economically and otherwise. We are all born with innate creativity. It manifests in the development of certain faculties, the first being our imagination. How many of you played make-believe? Or enjoyed time with your kids or grandkids that involved pretending, like they were the doctor and you were the patient? Did you ever join your mom in the planning and execution of your birthday party, explaining in detail what you expected her to make for you? Even if you didn't have birthdays when you were a kid, you probably used some creative skills to make your son or daughter's birthday wonderful or even spectacular.

Did you ever throw a surprise party for your best friend? It required some complex problem-solving to get her to be there on the right day, at the right location, and the right time. Planning slips us into that part of our brain that's a little bit like a space ride where gravity ends and time is suspended. That's creativity in action.

I bet you've sat down in a quiet state of mind and just wondered. That's creative, too.

I want to emphasize that if creativity as expressed through wonder or curiosity, imagining or planning hasn't been the largest part of your life experience, that's okay. Again, it's not too late!

I want so very much for you to feel that whatever you've missed, whatever you can't imagine right now as being part of your life, whatever moves you as you read the above, that you can prepare to go for it. If the it happens to be a really big step to take, hold it first in your imagination where limitless possibilities exist, where you aren't weighed down by expectations or rules or restrictions. Imagine you have wings of transcendence and feathers of meaningfulness attached to your creativity, and let it soar beyond gravity.

Bettie Y., 1948

The accident made the local news. It involved seven cars, two dead, and six people seriously wounded. I was one of them. Mine was a head and neck injury that left me unconscious for four days. I needed surgery to drain blood that was accumulating in my brain that I had only a 50 percent chance of recovering from. My husband stayed with me while my parents looked after the kids who were in junior high and high school. When I did awaken, my husband was crying. What was devastating was having no idea who he was. It took a week and my cognitive functions returned. So did my memories. What was hard to hear, the doctors said that I might never have use of my right side. I remember lying in bed one night, listening to the steady sounds of the machines I was hooked up to. For years I had been a busy mom, bookkeeper, and volunteer. I hadn't thought about not having the use of all my body, or that what I was doing was satisfying. Lying there, thinking about using my left hand, not having use of my right side, some images began to form. It had been years since I had time to myself. It was sad that it had to be as a recovering accident victim.

Of course I was medicated, but it didn't stop me from lying there wondering about my life, and if I had been missing something. I remembered my grandmother teaching me how to knit. I made a scarf. After that we moved away from my home town only seeing my Grandmother twice before she died of cancer. Overnight my vision for my health, my family, and for my life took a new shape. Maybe my husband was so grateful for me being alive he agreed to everything I proposed for a different life. That was 16 years ago. We raise alpacas, I knit beautiful sweaters, and he runs the online store. The kids have graduated from College. We have one grandchild. Ten years ago I took up photography that has become a nice sideline for income.

This year I turn 67 years old.

⤳⤳

You don't need to read to the end of this chapter or the end of the book to go into those flights of magic and limitless potential. Use them freely, whenever it feels right, including right now. Don't stop yourself from acting on your intuition or experiencing your emotions when they happen. Avoid judging them, and let your inner critic know that you don't need to be protected from your potential anymore. Also, please imagine receiving all the assistance and support you need.

The six most powerful and magical words that we can hear when we're in crisis are, "What can I do to help?" What I offer here is in that spirit of helpfulness and support. What I offer here comes from my own experience and from history that I share with you. We Boomer women were born in the middle of the twentieth century when a rebellious Western society fought for personal freedom, some of it through creative expression. music, cinema, and art filtered into our fashions, lifestyles, and communications. We could be cool or hip, while some were groovy.

In Northern Canada, where I grew up, most of my friends, classmates, and neighbours my age were not worried about having those labels to stand out from each other. In fact, I don't remember anybody needing more than was necessary. Most of us experienced playing outside and not being inside all day in front of a television set, computer, or tablet screen. As I grew up my playmates didn't worry about designer jeans or logos on our T-shirts to break free from the molds that kept us passive and unassuming. We Boomer women grew up before the Internet, where now you can go any time of day to get as many different perspectives and creative solutions as there are trees in the forest.

As we cultivate creativity, we may do well to hearken back to our childhoods and the ways we played then. The Internet can serve us well, but looking for creative solutions on the Internet can actually drag you away from what you need to solve because it can distract and confuse you, not to mention activate your inner critic by reminding you of all the things you might not be. This is the kind of noise that tears us down and interferes with our productivity and growth. If you're not hard-bodied with washboard abs, wrinkle-free, and making a gazillion dollars, does that really matter?

You're here now, still breathing, and feeling anticipation, and that's not noise. Instead, it's a powerful feeling to harness.

Our work here is creativity and how you might use it to manifest your potential in real and joyous ways. So get your journal and pen, and get ready to let loose your creative self. Write, draw, doodle, and colour in this chapter. In fact, you can do that anywhere in this book. This is a tool you should feel free to make your own, to mark up, write in, and discover aspects of the old you who had some forgotten dreams that may be ready to come alive right now. Let's get started.

Ingredients to Gather

Music, Movement, and Mantras

It's hard to create when you're crabby. So if that happens to be you right now, get your body and mind into a state of relaxation. Breathe slowly and deeply. Music is an excellent source for creating a mood and atmosphere conducive to lowering our stress levels and connecting to our inner rhythms, so take a moment to turn on the radio or listen to a favourite album.

Research shows that we are hard-wired for picking up beats and rhythms that tap into and activate our emotions. If you're listening to the kind of music that makes you snap your fingers, tap your toes, or gets you off your chair to really bounce around, let it happen. Nothing needs to be censored or criticized. Release some happy molecules like serotonin. If others are around, try to get a hug or two to increase oxytocin's love and bonding molecules too.

Movement, hugs, listening to music, or getting out to listen to birdsongs are great treats to give ourselves when we need to shift our emotions to optimism. A good mantra can help us clear away crabbiness, too. Try saying this one aloud:

I am creative. I am full of wonder. I am bonding with my dreams.

Creative Experiments

You can find plentiful exercises to tap into your creativity outside of this book. Inside of this book, I'll share with you a few I find especially intriguing and engaging. Creativity expert and best-selling author Michael Michalko offers this very cool *thought experiment*.[82]

This is one of my acrylic paintings that fits well with Michalko's experiment. The lack of color is not important. Imagine walking up a path and coming upon the house in the painting above. As you go, notice the yard and outside details, and take a walk around the house.

Then imagine walking through it, seeing where the kitchen is, what furniture there might be, the bedrooms, bathrooms, and any other features that strike you. Does it have patio doors from the master bedroom? Are there curtains or blinds on the windows? Do you smell any odours or pleasant scents?

Now you see a secret door. You go inside the room. What do you see inside? As you leave the house and head back down the path, turn and give it one more glance. Notice anything else?

Be specific about as many details as you can think of because after you've done the mind exploration you'll draw the details of the outside and inside of the house. This can be done on several pages of your drawing pad or several drawings on one page. Once you're done, give the drawing to a friend and ask her to construct the personality of who might live in the house, based on your drawing. Listen carefully as your friend describes this person, and see what insights you might gain about yourself.

If you are inspired and able, feel free to send me your drawing as a pdf in an email. I would love to see what we could find together.

Imagine that you are about to write a novel that is the story of you.

What would you title the story of your life?

_____

_____

If you have trouble, list some of your favourite book or movie titles, and temporarily borrow one that seems to fit. Start out with the title, then try to write the first line or even the opening paragraph. At what point in time does it seem to make the most sense to begin your story? What key moments would you want to include? What does the main character daydream about?

_____

_____

_____

_____

_____

_____

Our complex brains thrive on newness. When we were kids, most of us loved novelty. It's time to delight your inner child. Promote building some new paths in your brain by trying some new activities, new recipes, or visiting a new place, which doesn't have to be a new city or country. If you haven't done it yet, visit a greenhouse or a park in your own city. Take pictures with your smartphone of things that are paradoxical.

According to Bob Deutsch, in *The 5 Essentials: Using Your Inborn Resources to Create a Fulfilling Life* (2013), contradictions can be combined to "create something genuine and distinctive."[83] Whether I'm looking at fashion or decorating, I love the look of old and new together. Like putting on a beautiful new dress and adding a vintage scarf or brooch. Same goes in our house. I've collected many pieces of old furniture and mixed them in with modern items, and this gives our home a distinct feel that I love.

Something I find paradoxical is:

_____

_____

Ask yourself questions about the paradoxes or contradictions or mysteries you see. An example:

Which one do you think came first?

As adults, it's so easy to forget sometimes that we were kids who had fun. Now we're grown ups, and we have to do grown-up things: worry about problems, our spouses and kids, family, work, co-workers, doing too much or not enough. We've become a stressed bunch who have learned that when we have the choice between having fun and being responsible, we have to—or are expected to—act like grown-ups and be responsible. Too much responsibility can get in the way of creativity.

Do you remember when you were a kid, what being a grown-up meant?
Did it seem more or less fun than its turned out to be?

_____

_____

_____

Whatever your recollections, don't forget to remind your inner critic that you don't need protection for your memories. Maybe your writing could be as a dialogue between the you and your inner critic. Just keep it friendly and fluid.

Manifesting Practice

We're coming to the end of this chapter with one last ingredient to add. I've found that manifesting something is not difficult if I really want it to be part of my life. If you feel that you've had no luck with bringing things into your life, now is an ideal time to determine if you really want it or not.

Pick something that you believe would enhance your life. Let's say it can be love, money, success, abundance, or something more tangible like a car, a diamond ring, or anything you want to name. I could make the list to fit around the earth if I let me have fun! For now, just make it one thing.

Get a picture of that one thing in your mind.

Close your eyes if you feel like it. Get easy and comfortable with the image. By easy I mean be relaxed and in tune with it, or if you have trouble visualizing it, get a physical picture of it to hold in front of you. If it's an emotion, try to visualize what shape it would have. If it doesn't take a particular usable form, let it be a symbol.

Take note of your body. How does it feel? Is your breathing fast or slow? Do you have any ticks, itches, or pains anywhere? Are your feet warm or cold? Where do you have your hands? Are you able to hold the image in your mind without other thoughts intruding? Now ask yourself:

Do I want this?

What happens now? Keep in touch with your body, your feelings, and your subtle reactions. Write down your feelings. Imagine going back to the house picture, and see if what you want is in the secret room.

Does having what you want create a paradox in your mind, a maybe yes and a maybe no, the thing jumbling around and you feeling indecisive? Try a meditation that clears your thinking, and then return to the question.

Give some energy to doodling, word games, or shared creative time with friends, perhaps to do the house drawing experiment. Whatever you do, I hope these activities and exercises allow you to be playful and to remember that whatever you need to open up to creativity is at your fingertips. Pick up your pen and write something. Moving that hand does wonders for our brains.

So does moving on to new concepts and ideas. Meet you in Chapter 8 where we cover some of those anger issues.

Chapter 8
Reactor Factors

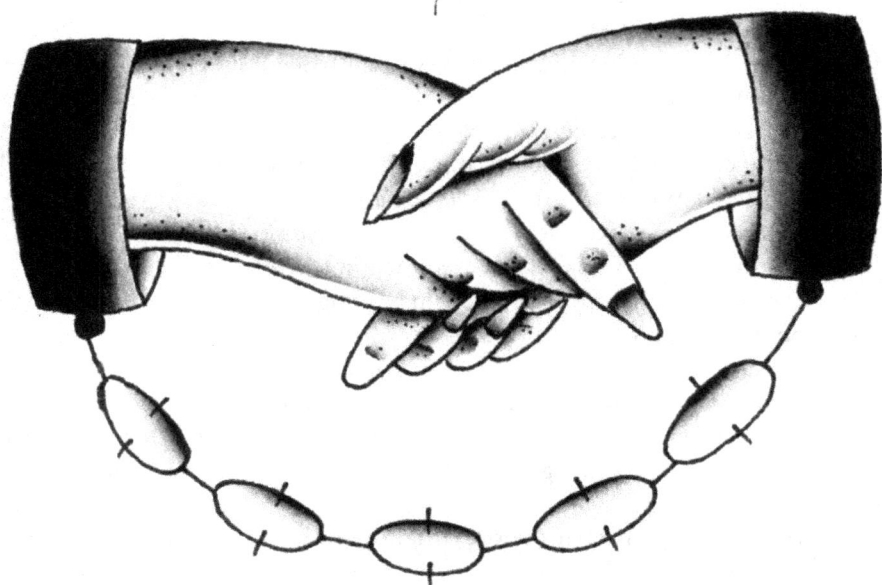

> But how will I eat cake if my head
>
> is over there, and my hands
>
> are over here?
>
> Marie Antoinette

❦

Unlike proactive response, reacting delays success, puts you in a funk, and makes you vulnerable to others' opinions. Marie Antoinette may have literally lost her head during the French Revolution in the 1700s but some of us still lose ours in a figurative way.

When the traffic backs up you sit fuming, wondering why this has to happen now. You'll be so late for that meeting. Your kids don't return your calls, and you blame their thoughtlessness on being part of the coddled, selfie generation. The cake burns in the oven that you told your husband to watch while you ran to the store for candles. You drop the F-bomb as you throw the cake in the garbage instead of scraping off the bottom to save the good part. The list of all the emotional infractions you've endured is pretty long.

So far, we've covered numerous choices we can make for well-being and thriving. Transforming health and exercise routines, listening to intuition, and creatively manifesting our dreams are only a few. We also have a choice when it comes to addressing some of the challenging emotions we experience. Feeling angry or jealous isn't a problem. What's unhealthy is letting anger get the best of us and lashing out, sometimes blaming others for situations beyond anyone's control. What's also unhealthy is when we bury anger and resentment. No matter how invisible we feel to those around us and regardless of how infuriating they or life may be, we often benefit from bringing grounded awareness to anger.

I haven't always been proactive and mature, and I don't expect anyone to be present and unconditionally forgiving 100 percent of the time. Because I've learned how to value and develop self control, I'm pretty slow to fire up when it comes to anger or resentment. Even though it feels counterintuitive to settle ourselves when anger flares up, slowing down can really help.

As an event planner, I have many opportunities to lose my temper when something isn't done right. I've learned that in most instances, a communication breakdown has created the misunderstanding. No matter what happens, taking the time to slow the conversation down and listening to the problem has helped me more than responding with anger. For instance, at a recent event, I was disappointed with some choices made by the set-up provider, but instead of lashing out on the phone, I remained calm, and listened to their concerns. Although I ended up choosing to work with another company, my demeanour allowed me to preserve the business relationship and my dignity.

When we do react inappropriately, especially when that reaction becomes a repeating pattern, it can result in destroying opportunities and relationships.

It's your mom's fault for making you so mad you broke your favourite mug, so now you won't talk to her. There's nothing you can do about your cat pooping in the neighbours' flower patch, so telling them to go to hell was the only solution. You feel victimized, vulnerable, and limited by everyone else. No one has called you toxic, at least not yet, but they have been distancing themselves from you. The crisis in your life has been overwhelming, and a few of your friends have tried their best to be supportive, but all you feel is misunderstood and more depressed than ever, so you don't even answer when they call. You didn't ask for the situations or tragedies you're experiencing. The divorce, financial problems, addictions, sickness, or feuding with neighbours are problems that may only get bigger, depending on how we manage them through our reactions.

In the beginning chapters, I intentionally maintained some distance from the emotions of anger and hatred. We, as Boomer women, have every right to experience these when we have been disrespected, abused, or left to feel powerless. The nature of morality and debate in our society, along with how justice is rendered or not, are only a few of the reasons we women can get so reactive to what seems like a spiritual war against us. Not only 50-plus women, but women of all ages are part of a world in which our rights to personal safety and dignity are pitted against the seeming right of every man to subject us to cruelty, degrading punishment, violence, and rape.

No man, regardless of power or status or bank account, is allowed to hurt us.

I understand that women can also be violent and mentally unstable and are just as criminally responsible for inflicting physical, emotional, and spiritual pain. The Boomer woman whose mother terrorized her with a butcher knife did great damage, her actions as horrifying as any man's.

Should we be angry about violence, whoever perpetrates it? Without a doubt, yes.

Until something fundamental changes in the hearts of all of us, women will continue to experience such violence and the real danger of it. For now, what we can do is continue to grow strong in well-being, keep our faith, work to reach our potential, and protect ourselves.

Sexual violence is a heavy topic, but like anger it has more power over us in the shadows. I feel that we need to be open in our discussions about it, supporting efforts that lead to justice and healing.

Many women don't come forward when they've been raped or sexually violated. They keep it a shameful secret or may hold off taking protective measures for a variety of complicated reasons. Serious mental and emotional symptoms eventually overtake the daily life of someone who has been violated and unable to heal. If this is you, I urge you to get professional help and support as soon as possible. You can find some resources at the end of this book, or please reach out to someone you trust for names of local organizations that can help you.

We discussed stress, trauma, and PTSD in Chapter 2, and now we'll take a deeper look at the challenging emotions that result from stress and trauma, as well as what we can do to manage them.

Learning how to be proactive in the face of intense mentally, emotionally, and spiritually draining crises can be overwhelming. It may even be hard to imagine any other choices than reacting. If your crises or turning points have pushed you into more adaptation than feels humanly possible, be assured that getting pissed off is not the worst thing you can do. It's not. Being asked to be brave, to shift your focus, and to follow a series of thoughts and actions that bring you to balance may initially make you angrier.

If your immediate family and friends are reactive types, you may have even harder work cut out for you. Resentful or jealous parents, children, and spouses can all be sources of angry outbursts that we aren't always able to escape.

The fact that life isn't always fair comes as a hard lesson to those of us who believe in the goodness of humanity. I think we believe in it because we are fundamentally good. We wish for ourselves and our loved ones to grow unharmed, happy, and prosperous. The world, if we had our way, would be one of peace, wonder, and grace. Communication would be so simple and easy because everyone would just understand each other's culture, body signals, and complex messages. We often get angry as a result of missed messages, and we often suffer because our ability to read and identify those with bad or harmful intentions (AKA, our intuition) is not fully developed.

Many women fall for good looks, excellent grooming, charm, and smooth-talking that seems to meet our needs for validation and love, only to discover that we have been lied to and cheated on regularly. Along with having been raised to ignore their intuitions, Boomer women have also been taught to live with less love than they need and deserve. Our stressed-out and mixed up society led us to believe that romance and sex are only about passion and ecstasy, the cures for what ails us as women.

Dorothea V., 1952

I got most of my romantic notions from novels, magazines, then TV and movies. When I graduated from high school, I wasn't a virgin. One of my bestie's got married by a shotgun wedding before we graduated. She's still married and has a pretty good life. What is funny is when we get together and reminisce how dumb we were about love, romance, our bodies, and men. I could write an entire book about the hours we spent on imagining the kind of prince our husbands would be, how romantic he'd be, and what our wedding dresses would look like. I was a normal weight, but I did struggle with body image and never felt good enough. We went to the shopping center and shoplifted makeup. It changed how we felt about ourselves when we put it on. My mother didn't approve of it, so when we went out, we'd head to the nearest bathroom and transform our underage faces to sexy women ready for fun. I stopped going out when one of our group was murdered by a guy she met who we all thought was a Prince Charming. I got a job in the post office after high school, got married, had twin girls who claim I was too over-protective. I have been thinking about what to do as I get ready to retire. I want to do something to help the young girls in our community that have been victims of sexual violence.

It's a problem that seems to be getting bigger and more serious. I never forgot about one of my best friends dying at the hands of a predator.
This year I will be 63 years old.

It's hard not to lose our minds and easy to lose our balance in a world that is unjust and confusing. To discover that we have been lied to, mistreated, and laughed at is justifiably enraging. If we turn to reactivity by focusing on the past and fixating on why something happened, we might miss the opportunities to grow from mastering our current emotions, which function properly when aligned with our core values and a healthy body.

So here we are, asking ourselves, how do we master this moment?

Figuring out the best method of dealing with ourselves, outside of others' reactive or harmful behaviours, is where we should start. We begin with taking care of ourselves, which means feeling our feelings and moving on.

The consensus from therapists, coaches, and self-help literature is that anger is healthy when we acknowledge the feeling that comes from injustice and release it.

Mastering the Factors

Our attention, our money, and our loyalty are in demand from the moment we wake up in the morning to the time we go to bed, and it's exhausting. Our own inner children are tapping us on the shoulder for some love and care, but we must deal with jobs and careers, household chores, and paying our bills, not to mention managing whatever crisis we're in the midst of. Big Business, our families, and the media shake us down like mob bosses for our love, energy, and hard-earned cash, with double compound interest every day we miss a payment. No matter how adult and responsible they are, our kids still need and appreciate an emotional boost to help them out, even if they don't answer our phone calls. Our spouses need our love, respect, and attention as well.

If we assert ourselves in response to any of these competing demands, we are bitches, and if we don't try to hide our agitation and anger by asking for some distance to gain self-control we are nagging bitches. As a young woman, I had no idea that just asking for what I needed was most often the key to getting it. I can't control what others may call me, but I can control how I see myself. Being true to what you're feeling and speaking from a grounded voice to express those feelings can take you from feeling like that bitch to knowing you're communicating clearly about what you need in that moment. This clarity helps everyone.

For example, as a mature woman I've learned that in most male/female communication, men just want women to ask directly for what they want and stop the guessing games. They can't read our minds, so we have to tell them. Sometimes your partner won't be able to give you what you want or need, so ask someone who can help you. Example: my husband doesn't cook, so asking him to cook for me would end in disaster, so instead he takes me out. Win-win!

I know that clearly communicating needs instead of lashing out or bottling up anger may not be an easy habit to develop. If we're still dragging our pasts around with us, we may need professional support and direction to deal effectively with the quiet rage that has been eating at us for decades. Maybe our parents were abusive and are still too toxic to be around. We have the power and right to make choices that protect our safety and well-being. When you encounter those childhood bullies who nearly drove you to suicide in high school, their aggression doesn't have the same impact since you found all that inner strength and wisdom.

Let this next decade be less about what tears you down, and more about what builds your potential and personal enjoyment. You are learning about what you can and should change. You are recognizing your talents, as well as what pushes your buttons to weaken your focus, and it hasn't taken a rocket scientist to point out you're intelligent and ready to participate in being a change leader, if only for your own magical life.

I'm one of those not-rocket-scientists pointing out your wisdom and power. I know you have it. I don't have a university degree or feel the need to go for one. My life experience and leadership skills may not give me the authority to teach at a university, but I am confident that the wisdom and resilience I've gathered, along with my unending curiosity and desire to serve and inspire the 50-plus women that need it, is a practical certification and all I need right now.

The six words that matter the most to me are: What can I do to help? When it comes to managing intense reactions, what I know I can do to help is to ask you to pay attention as reactivity comes up in your life, and to examine what exactly is in your control and who exactly is your concern.

As you build your internal mastery, your first task is to be clear about what factors set you off in a negative direction, knock you off balance, and create more work than is necessary for you.

If you started the work in Chapter 7 and are building a decent relationship with the inner critics that have disrupted your life, the work of this chapter doesn't have to be too intense or consuming. You are now aware of how your inner critic is operating and can actually support you, and you can use that as you create the new recipe of you.

Ingredients to Gather

Mindfulness, Martinis, and Meditation

Research shows that meditation exercise and mindfulness practice are good for our brains, which in turn is good for our emotions and that goes for anger and jealousy. When we are present and allow ourselves to feel these feelings, they are able to pass.

We also must not underestimate the power of fun and relaxation with our friends. Although I don't drink to excess, I do enjoy having an alcoholic beverage now and then, especially while enjoying good company.

Our Fabulous@50 groups do too, and we'd love to see you at one of our martini parties, whatever you have a martini or not. As someone who lived with people with serious addiction issues, one being alcohol, I'm very careful of how much I drink and know it's possible to enjoy an evening with or without it.

Addiction aside, studies indicate that moderate helpings of wine or beer can help with relaxation, contribute to longevity, and in the case of red wine have anti-inflammatory benefits.[84] But what we see time and time again is one study gives us the pros while another condemns the claim, which can bring us back to information overload.

When it comes to choosing what helps you to relax, I most recommend that you have noble intent and mean to do no harm. Essentially, if something does not resonate with you or you know it will harm you or others, put it aside. That's all part of getting clarity, maturity, and reaching our most authentic selves, which are sometimes buried under excess negativity. So here is a meditation to help you honour your physical, mental, emotional, and spiritual bodies to release negative energy.

Breathe into the palm of your hand to ground yourself.
Take in a deep breath through your nose
and exhale. Give yourself a moment or two to let
oxygen in, carbon dioxide out. Note where your
hands are, what your body wants to do right now.
Follow your body's lead. Let the mental chatter
turn into a fuzzy, warm blanket. Cover the part of your
body that needs warmth. Take as long as you need
to feel completely content.

No one else is responsible for your feelings or contentment. You may have noticed as you did this exercise that no one was there to breathe for you. In the same way, no one else can react for you; you alone are responsible for your chosen reactions. If you felt anything negative float away for even a fleeting few seconds, you found a new open space to fill with love and your breath. You were responsible for that, too. Let me repeat:

No one else breathes for you.

I am so sorry if that brings up a bubble of anger or some other negative thought. If it does, practice reading that statement until you can take it in calmly.

No one puts your hand on a wine glass after you've had too many. When you got angry or jealous at your sister for being prettier than you or getting more attention from your parents, it was you who felt it. Maybe your breathing got faster, your face turned red, your eyes teared up, and a dozen accusations and nasty words formed in your mind. If she stood there smirking as you were ignored, you might feel even more justified in wanting to blame her or lash out. Even if you did, it didn't help. Say it aloud.

No one breathes for me. I breathe for myself.

This is the first thing we do to begin life on this planet, and the last thing we will do before we die. Everything along that continuum requires us to be present in this way, every mundane, tragic, joyous, magical, or transformative moment. While we stood in the middle of those experiences that became our past, we breathed. This one vital measure of our existence is often times the most under appreciated as a tool for mastering our emotions, especially intense stress, anger, or any other negative emotions. Yet I believe it is the cure for so much that ails us.

Try answering the following question with the thought that your best answer will get you a free foot massage. (This is me sharing some creative encouragement with you.)

How much do I appreciate being able to breathe freely?

_____

_____

_____

_____

_____

_____

Understanding that holding onto our intense and damaging anger, jealousies, and resentments doesn't serve us and can leave us feeling unbalanced. You know you need to move through and release these intense emotions, but you've also gotten used to holding onto them. You may want a better life, but by holding on you're unable to move forward to it. Know that you have power to change this and regain balance, through mindfulness and adjusting your focus.

By attending to our breathing, learning how to regulate it through focus, and appreciating our ability to control it, we begin to master our emotions. Our bodily mechanisms are connected to our emotions, and according to the Dalai Lama, emotions serve as "basic material to feel pain and experience pleasure".[85] We laugh until we cry, we feel so happy it hurts, and we can feel as powerless from an onslaught of unconditional love as we can from intense hate.

Boomer women are blessed not only with a variety of emotions that we can choose to learn how to feel and manage, but also with the choice to learn, period. How amazing that we can learn as much as we want to improve our lives, grow into our potential, and live with, not without, well-being into our twilight years.

Speaking of which, I prefer that phrase to calling them our aging, elderly, or declining years.

How would you describe your most picturesque moment of twilight, literal or figurative, that you've experienced so far?

_____

_____

_____

By refocusing on the beauty and wonder around us, by staying open to learning, we find that negativity and destructive feelings lessen. We learn to look into our centers where there is pure, conscious energy and, from there, create a life of purpose and passion. That energy is the source of our power. It is the stuff we need to fuel our lives and actions. Realizing that it is what you own, and no one else can take it away, you will build resilient character and master your purpose. Practice saying this:

**I am the master of
my purpose.
I am the master of
my emotions.**

Give this mantra and affirmation your noble intention and honour as you realize your dreams and align your core values with your purpose. It doesn't matter if you don't know what that is at this moment. It may not become evident for some time, regardless of how long you've spent on this planet.

For the present moment, your purpose is to know that you are an essential piece of the human mosaic.

We have reached the end of this chapter and are about to move on to considering legacy. The chapter on legacy is perhaps one of the most important chapters, involving our spiritual essence, the thing we will leave behind when we transition.

Before we do, let's not forget everyday gratitude. Fit it in somewhere in your journal, meditations, and affirmations. In the first chapter, I suggested you list 50 things you're grateful for. It doesn't actually matter how many things you can think of. List even three things right now. One can be that you didn't fly off the handle at anyone today. Or you got the jealous feelings levelled out and now feel more centered. You have less tension in your back or shoulders, a typical area for us to store tightness and knots from too many heavy, negative emotions. If you can, let yourself have a massage. If not, use your visualization skills to imagine receiving one. It may not work at first, but it's a bit more manifesting practice for you, right?

I thank you for being here. Know that I'm working right along with you, staying mindful, mastering my emotions, and manifesting my dreams. You're not alone, so don't forget to get in touch with me, visit the Fabulous@50 website, and get connected.

Reflections of a Boomer Woman

❧

Finishing Gets a Hallelujah

I just listened to a heart-wrenching rendition of Leonard Cohen's "Hallelujah" sung by three pre-teens that was a post on someone's Facebook page. I'm still humming the tune while I sit and contemplate my situation. There's a time, like when I am sitting on the bathroom toilet, that I am given to ruminations of life and what it has meant to me while I am finishing my business. In 29 days, I will be 57 years old. In the fall, I will be attending a post-secondary program, not in Graduate studies as I had planned, but as an Undergraduate because not all my previous coursework is transferable. I am coming off a three month medical leave with no job to return to. There's still three months left before I have to move to a city 16 hours drive from where I am right now.

Where am I right now? I am living in my parents' basement, with my disabled brother and my elderly parents whose deeply ingrained beliefs will never understand mine. Financially, my credit reporting agency has been recommending that I claim bankruptcy. My car sits with a dead battery and no insurance in my parents' driveway. My three adult children are estranged, mean-spirited, and didn't bother to pretend that Mother's Day mattered. Maybe I deserve their coldness. I left them 14 years ago with their father who had the steady job and could provide a stable life with a roof over their heads.

They were surrounded by their childhood friends, and loving family. Our separation came after me suffering a Kundalini crisis the psychiatrist argued was a "psychotic break" and labeled me schizophreniform because he didn't know what else to call it. All my talk of spirituality and God was pretty confusing to him. I was left with recovering while in my parents' care, with no spiritual mentors to guide me.

The realization that I had to find meaning and purpose that would piece me back together was imperative. Finding two books, one on scriptwriting and one on story boarding, forced me from my attempts to be normal and finally do something with all the pictures and stories in my head. Family and my friends whose desire was for security, a mortgage, and Sunday dinners was all that should have mattered to me.

Sadly, I just couldn't come to terms with that definition of happiness. My children and I made a pact that I would win an Oscar as a screenwriter and our reunion after a year or so would celebrate that success. Packing what little I had into a rusted old car and driving to Los Angeles wasn't the stupidest thing I've ever done, not by a long shot. Each year in Hollywood passed with money, success, and glamor getting further away from reality. There is very little want to promote aging, women that lack "hotness", and emerging artists.

In the strangest twist of logic the expectation is to "be somebody" before you are a nobody in Hollywood. An abusive marriage, career burnout, and my younger brother's heart attack had me rethinking what was supposed to be next after 14 years of trying, failing, and trying not to fail. Nearly a year later I have two things to be grateful for; sacred and shattered "Hallelujah" thanks to Leonard Cohen. Only the Lord knows how long I have to finish my business on this Earth. This I believe.

Deborah Elle Smith
cristlentertainment@gmail.com

Chapter 9
Reclaiming Your Legacy

Cakes are special.

Every birthday, every celebration ends

with something sweet, a cake, and people

remember. It's all about the memories.

—Buddy Valastro

As a child growing up in the mid-twentieth century in Northern Canada, I was part of a culture that valued baking skills, stay-at-home motherhood, and family. Most of the birthday cakes were made in home kitchens rather than purchased at local bakeries or grocery stores. Grandparents and parents who had experienced the Great Depression and hard-times respected their money (which was cash), learned how to do more with less, and did what they could to impart those values onto the next generation.

As Boomer women we also spilled into another side of the century, which involved being more driven to succeed, acquire things, and compete for everything. Life became a stressful hustle to and from work and play, which meant spending less time with family for fear of losing our jobs, not for the joy of having them. We paid for purchases with credit cards, made twenty-minute meals while rushing to organize our lives for the next day, and to make sure we had some down time watching favourite TV programs. Our hard-working parents and grandparents watched us learn to multi-task, take on more than they thought was necessary, and become adept people-pleasers. In the midst of all that, our children grew up right learning to be self-sufficient, angry at us for not being there for them, and worried about an uncertain future. Their children have become our hope for a future that remains in the hands of men whose fingers are poised to press the red button of mass destruction.

Is this the legacy we want to leave?

I say no. We Boomer women want and need to offer something better than that. Before we decide what we want our legacy to be, it's important for us to look at the current state of affairs.

So what is our legacy? For me, leaving a legacy will be about love and about the creation of Fabulous@50 and the stories people will tell of a woman (yours truly) who suffered adversity and choose to thrive in her life because of it.

In *Dare to Wear Your Soul on the Outside*, Gloria Burgess writes that through four generations of cohort groups—the Traditionals, the Boomers, the Gen Xers, and Gen Ys—we've been passing on "destructive narratives" of greed, fear, self-gratification through consumerism, and the influence of bias; that is, preferential treatment of the pretty, rich, tech-savvy, or youthful.[86] Big Business and politics don't need to hide their agendas anymore because we know about them.

According to a generational differences chart, our cohort of Baby Boomers is considered to be "greedy, materialistic, and ambitious team-players."[87]

With that in mind, I want to direct our attention to the fact that we live in a patriarchal society, with primarily male leaders in business, politics, and religion, most of which are riddled with corruption. Mainstream society does not teach us to nourish our souls through honouring our world and each other, or that we should make an effort to leave a healthy, clean, and peaceful global village for those who come after us. Instead, we learn to maintain an ideal of opportunities, experiences, and acquisitions that spoil and poison our environment, destroy opposition to tyranny, and fill the pockets of men who expect it.

In the face of this state of affairs, it's easy to feel powerless, and in fact it is incredibly difficult to bring about large scale change. However, we do have a might that should not be underestimated: the power to change ourselves, communicate what matters, and choose what nourishes our well-being.

As a 50-plus Boomer woman, I've lived my life as a people-pleasing, mild, and work-oriented mother, wife, one-time divorcee, and entrepreneur, but those aren't the only ways I identify myself. I am also a creative, hard-working, intelligent, woman, motivated to inspire and support the personal growth of other 50-plus women so that we all may reach levels of well-being beyond satisfactory. Excellence is our birthright, and to me excellence includes safety, a clean world, authentic living, and community. I believe that every generation after us, anywhere within the global village, has a right to all of these things. One of the biggest reasons for this book is to support you in reaching your excellence and building a legacy worth sharing.

Alaine M., 1965

I grew up in the city with a whole family that had a lot of holes in how we communicated. Dad came home from work and we ate the same thing for dinner most every night: roast beef, mashed potatoes, and coleslaw. No kidding. He ate, went to the bedroom, got in his pajamas, and read until he fell asleep. I did feel love from him though and my mom. There was no yelling or name-calling unless you count the time that my dad got mad at my older brother for being disrespectful. What was strange to me was the choice of man I made to live with and did so for twelve years. He was an angry, abusive, drinking, carousing, loud guy. Then one day after a particularly bad night, I woke up, packed my bags and went to live at my parents. I stayed there for four years. I had visions of the man I wanted to be with who manifested in my life with six adult children. Darn it though I am so happy and love my family so much I think I am the luckiest woman in the world. I wake up every day, literally with a smile on my face. After 10 years we act out our affection and love in front of people who keep calling us lovebirds. I think about what I might leave behind as my legacy even though I am only a stepmom, seeing as how I have none of my own. Even if we were to divorce, because our lives aren't over and I know it's possible, I want for the kids to know it's so much better to be with someone who gets excited when they see you. I don't know if that's all of it, but we make each other proud in the things we do for each other and our loved ones. I'm so happy.
This year I turned 50 years old.

Building a Legacy Through Inner Work

I knew that a status quo life was not for me, yet I had no idea what life beyond struggle even looked like. That's why I've read hundreds of books on self development and spent thousands of dollars in personal growth seminars. I also knew that the adversity I have lived through was given to me as a gift, so that I could take it and reuse it to inspire others. This I hope will be my legacy: inspiring, educating and empowering women to push through their adversities and grow.

You might be wondering how a fifty-seven-year-old woman from Northern Canada grew into her awareness that she should or could say something powerful. I am not that big physically, but I have some feistiness in me. At several turning points, I've had to fight for what I needed. When I was only twenty years old, I faced the life-changing tragedy of my first husband dying in an explosion. I remarried after his death to a man who struggled with alcohol, gambling, and his responsibilities. As I've mentioned, I felt like I was left taking care of what felt like 200 percent of everything financial, emotional, and organizational in our family, and that feeling of dissatisfaction led to our divorce. I experienced frightening, major surgery and financial challenge. I struggled and suffered, and for a long time I succumbed to that idea I had in childhood that it was too late for me to take a dance class or anything else.

So how did I find my voice to claim a legacy?

The answer is woven into the pages of this book, particularly in the ingredients I offer at the end of each chapter. I found my voice through persistent mindfulness, facing inner critics, caring for my inner child, self-improvement, continuous learning, and committing to actualizing my dreams. And I'm sharing it all with you so you can also find your voice and claim the legacy you want to leave with your life.

As you have been working through the exercises in this book, I hope that you have been able to see a new you at the end of your crisis, choosing new labels to replace older destructive ones that were given to you. You have been uncovering strengths, interests, old dreams, and self-love, all of which may need a good dusting before they're fully revealed. I've done it myself, and I know that it's more than possible for you too.

At 50-plus our bodies change as we move further from birth and closer to being finished with our earthly objectives, but we still have a lot of years left to fulfill. I and many of the women in my community are blessed with the opportunity to choose the legacy we wish to leave.

What we choose can and should include how to honour our lives and the lives of our loved ones, those who have come before and those yet to be born.

It makes sense that we'd look to solutions from government health organizations and social welfare consultants, but these solutions sometimes point out our weaknesses rather than address what kind of emotional environment we live in. When I had my back surgery, I wasn't sure I would be able to work for awhile, if ever again, so I went to an agency that I thought would help me for the short term. What they offered me was long-term poverty and a victim's mentality.

I left that office determined to get back on my feet without their support.

Our social welfare system seems to be leaving a continuous legacy of poverty and disenfranchisement from generation to generation. They make recommendations that are not entirely practical or helpful that drive many families to live through years of borderline poverty, struggling to re-establish stability and find resolution. I don't know how to change that system. What I do know and offer here is the kind of inner work that helps you to gain insight, build resiliency, and prepare for living to your potential.

Marie S., 1958

My childhood was bad. I was sexually and emotionally abused. I left home when I was fourteen, didn't finish high school but managed to make money. I was a hard worker and eventually started to run and manage kitchens. My first husband left me for another woman. My four kids were still small. They all grew up and left home. I lost my job when the restaurant burned down, then I got really sick with triple pneumonia. I nearly died. I live in a state where it cost my savings for health care. The social worker that was assigned to help me sent me to get food stamps and general relief. It being the first time I was ever on assistance I didn't know my way around. It was so full and busy with people. They sat there while I was going crazy sitting for so long. It took three hours to call my name. The caseworker was rude and made me feel like I was bothering her. I never wanted to go back. I enrolled in a vocational school to learn legal assistant. I still haven't found work with that diploma. It's been fifteen years. I've been working at Walmart as a cashier after they laid me off at K-Mart. Things are bad in the economy. The Walmart managers want to give me a supervisor position that gives me twice the responsibility and only a dollar more an hour. I don't hate the job, I need it. I like the people I work with. Lately, nothing seems to be right. My common-in-law man has been so depressed he hasn't been getting out of the house. I don't know if I love him anymore, I wouldn't leave him. We been together for fourteen years. I'd like to start my own business but I don't know how to start. What makes me sad lots of times is that I won't have nothing to give me kids when I pass. Maybe I won't worry too much about it. I probably still got at least twenty years left.

This year I turn 57 in the fall.

～❧～

What I also offer is my genuine interest in you and your well-being, and I won't know you personally unless you introduce yourself to me. You can email me through the Fabulous@50 website. I want to hear from you, learn about your efforts and whatever failures and successes you've encountered as you engage in the work of this book and experience transformation.

I was able to flourish and identify a legacy as I came to understand who I was on the inside, what I wanted in my life, and how I wanted to achieve it. I accomplished that because I was optimistic, one of the first core strengths of positive psychology.

I put trust in my intuition and faith that life was there to support me through my own efforts, and I allowed myself to give and receive help willingly. I get that for some Boomer women—maybe for you—life is more painful, chaotic, and sad than should be allowed. Yet time after time we all see and hear of incredible recoveries, astounding comebacks, and unexplainable miracles. Absolutely everyone is capable of this kind of transformation. I believe that we've all been blessed with a human, spiritual legacy that got its start in unconditional love, not hate. Whatever your religion or spiritual practice, I offer the belief that a higher power pours love into our hearts from the minute we are created and continues to send love to us even when we are not aware or open to it.

Many 50-plus women haven't been connected to their core selves for decades. What they have learned to honour has been dictated by sets of values that include authority, logic, and aggressiveness at the expense of the feminine qualities of tenderness, cooperation, and nurturing. How we have perceived ourselves often depends on the legacy that was left for us. Our pasts, our cultural consciousness, our ancestry and genetics, the values we were brought up to adhere to—all of these things have led us here.

And here is where we get to create our own legacy. If we are ready and willing to transform and re-experience our lives, we may need to redefine some of our ancestral influences and social expectations in ways that allow us to value ourselves as the heroines of our own fulfillment, a most wonderful legacy to leave for our loved ones to come. Before we choose and identify the legacies we wish to create, in addition to looking at the current state of affairs, we must also come to terms with what got us here.

Honouring and Forgiving the Legacies That Were Left to Us

So what have we learned from the past and the legacies that were left to us? If we've been hurt badly, how do we begin to heal through forgiveness? If we begin to reject traditions passed down from generations, how do we honour that past while forging ahead into the future with a new found spiritual practice?

Let's start with honouring the past. Memorials, celebrations, and acts of respect—visiting a grave site, story telling, or even making a meal to honour your ancestors—allow us to pay homage to what got us here. Without ancestors…well, we wouldn't be here. If you were adopted, you may not have easy access to the link that connects you with a heritage, and you may need to rely heavily on your creative skills from Chapter 7 as you commemorate your past.

We can honour what we were given including the idea that we could have it all: success, wealth, and career, plus a blissful family life—an idea which led many of us to unhappiness.

We can honour the noble intentions of our justice system, a system that happens to have failed many women who have experienced sexual violence.

Raphaela P., 1959

It was one day in English class, our teacher gave us a reading assignment. Before she left the classroom to do some errand she left us with the task of figuring out what the story was about. It described some village where gale force winds blew people around including one fat, obnoxious woman the villagers didn't like. I don't remember the reason. But I thought the writing was funny. I was the only one laughing. My classmates thought it was a serious event and chided me into changing my interpretation. When our teacher came back she asked each one of us what we thought the writer intended. When she came to me, I said, "Gripping." She looked at me stupefied. "What?" I said it again, only this time with a hand gesture, "Gripping." Our teacher stomped her foot into the rug. "What is wrong with you people? It's funny!" That was the power of the group. I never forgot that, because she turned to me in frustration. "Why didn't you stick to your guns?" I studied law, but changed to teaching. I just hope that my kids learn and know that it matters what they feel and to stick to their guns. I also hope that I make a difference.

This year I will be 56 years old.

❦

We can honour our fathers and mothers, parents who may have taught us to be afraid, that we were less than valuable, and that feminine cultural norms and rules were more important than fulfilling our dreams.

Honouring is obviously complicated. So how do we move forward from honouring with dignity and peace? How are we supposed to be healthy and happy women when we've experienced attacks on our bodies, minds, and spirits and then been silenced, shamed, or forgotten?

Well, that brings us to forgiveness, something rooted in compassion and unconditional love. It is as much of our human legacy as war and destruction. We see it time and time again: victims able to forgive the perpetrators of unspeakable acts. And forgiveness has benefits. Releasing those we hold responsible for acts against us serves to return us to health if we can "remember with compassion" according to Fred Luskin, a researcher in forgiveness.[88] That means doing some emotional memory reconstruction, because we are hardwired to remember what threatens as and to hang on to those bad memories.[89]

An example: When my daughter was small, we were on vacation having a fabulous time exploring the town of Kaslo, located in the Kootenay region of British Columbia. Now Amber can be pretty headstrong and insistent, so even though she was only five she wanted to carry my purse. Wanting to reduce conflict on a family vacation, I let her. Later, when we'd left Kaslo and I needed to pay for something, she didn't have the purse anymore. Now an adult, my daughter still clearly remembers her five-year old self feeling like she was going to be in big trouble.

Of course it was my fault for letting a five-year-old carry my purse with all my money and ID, so we calmed her down and drove back to Kaslo.

Thank goodness for kind and honest strangers. A local had found my purse and turned it into the closest business for the owner to find. I was struck by that virtuous behaviour and have fond memories of that place and our trip.

As for Amber, she remembered the bad part of the trip, and not the parts that were fun, exciting, and beautiful. According to neuroscience, the increased activity of fear triggered the part of her brain responsible for memory.[90] The incident was not life-threatening, but it still left a mark. So does that mean we have to be stuck with those kind of markers from our past?

Thankfully, no.

Traumatic or stressful events can be revamped. We can remember with compassion. Martin Seligman noted that it's possible to "build optimism" and rethink how we perceive past events.[91] We can forgive ourselves, and we can forgive others. Most academics and spiritual teachers do agree on one important concept: forgiveness is not forgetting. It is a process that requires courage, perseverance, and love, and the best place to start is with yourself.

It's difficult not to say, "I don't want to do this." The truth is that forgiving is one of the hardest things we do as humans. It can be especially painful to overcome our anger at an injustice in order to do the right thing. It is the right thing to forgive.

When we forgive, we can set down the baggage of the past and free up our hands and hearts to act with the future in mind. We can teach our children and give them powerful gifts to take with them into their lives. I've taught my son and daughter to be assertive, strong, and self-directed.

When we forgive, we can blend our intuition with self-confidence, maximizing our ability to make tough decisions, which aren't always popular ones, especially when they fly in the face of others' expectations. If you have some unpopular decisions to make, know that you have a lot support behind you. Those decisions may be ones that suit your personal transformation or create a new situation or prospect to move you closer to your potential and well-being. No one should have to be forced to give up their health, dignity, and inner joy to fulfill others' expectations. Sometimes we are willing to make personal sacrifices for our families, and if that's the conscious decision you make, there is no shame or shadow in it. Selfless determination is another of our greatest female legacies.

When it comes to the violation of women, we have a lot of unanswered moral questions. Women who have been abused, mistreated, emotionally paralyzed, women whose lives were taken from them and ended—my prayers go out to all of them.

For now, this is my voice speaking to the living. Creating honourable legacies and finding our way to the healing and freedom of forgiveness are our responsibilities and opportunities.

So get your journal and a pen, and get ready for some creative thought experiments.

Ingredients to Gather

Thought Quilt

In my travels, I've met fascinating people. Some are famous, and others are on their way to recognition. Most are humble people who accept my curiosity and highest regard for their stories, experiences, and thoughts. I've met men and women who are out of the Boomer cohort, younger and older, with wisdom, intelligence, and insight the world needs. I watched a recent talk shared via TED, an organization dedicated to ideas worth spreading that showcases such fascinating people.

In the talk, visionary and futurist John Nosta[92] claims that "genius is our birthright, mediocrity is self-imposed." He suggests that genius has never been the sole characteristic of a handful of people, but rather is "thought, transcending and profound."[93] We all have thoughts. In fact, I had one about what to do for this part of our exercises.

I propose you build a thought out quilt, as a legacy quilt, one that preserves your stories and sews them into the fabric of our humanity and spirit, one that inspires visionaries yet to come, one that honours the truth, genius, unconditional love, and grace within you.

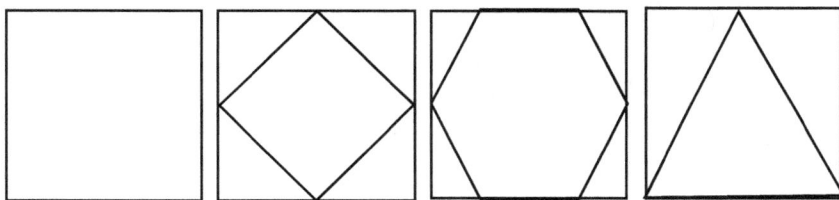

Please entertain your inner child and build one or as many different combinations as you want to design a quilt with as many squares or panels as you feel energized to create. Use the individual shapes above to incorporate into your design, or create whatever you envision as rich and beautiful.[94]

As another option, use some of your favourite mindfulness techniques to simply create a quilt in your mind.

Draw Genius, Love, and Forgiveness into Your Legacy

Breathe calmly and don't forget to ground yourself by first breathing into the palm of your hand. Really feel the warmth of your breath on your palm. Close your eyes. Feel tension leave those hard spots like your shoulders, or your head—in case you might be hard-headed like my daughter, or like me. Sense all the things that are ticking, humming, buzzing, or pulsing. Let fear or sadness lift from your body and mind.

Now, think about a symbol for your genius; you could think of this as your core magic, your identity, or your essence.

What does your genius look like?

_____

_____

_____

_____

Use your genius symbol for the center of the circle below. Draw it or practice your visualization skills. Either way, see it in the center of the circle. Then write the word love, right next to your genius symbol. Take a minute to feel love and genius together. Honour that combination.

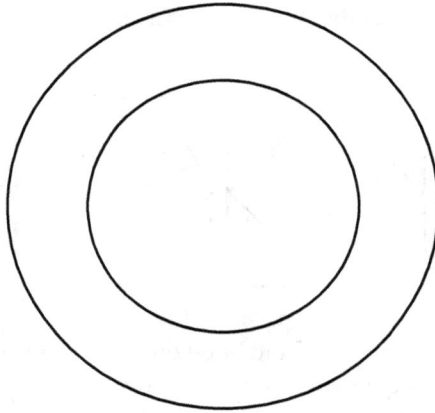

No one can take your love or genius away from you.

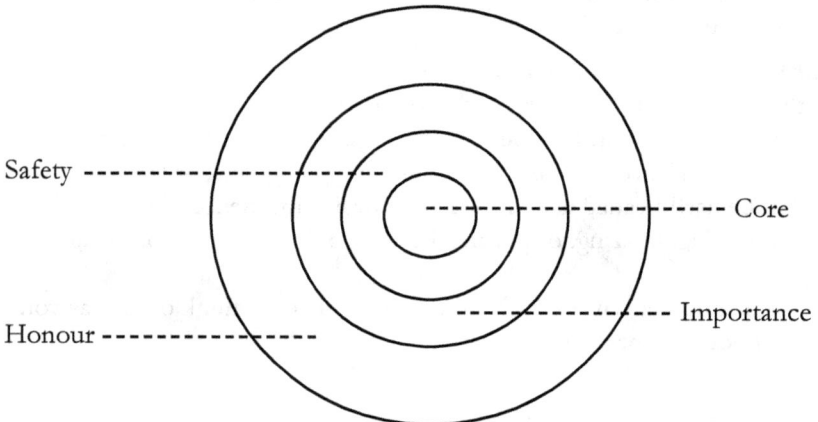

In this exercise you'll be using the diagram above and building a circle of protection around you. First, imagine your core is forgiveness. Then, imagine someone you want to forgive or from whom you want forgiveness. Bring them into the core with you. Bring light into the center. Share your warm breath on the palm of your hand. Forgive yourself. Let them forgive you. Say the mantra:

I am wisdom. I am forgiving. I am forgiven.

The second circle, safety, includes what you have that physically protects you. Can you imagine what it looks like? Is it water or some other liquid? Is it some color of light? Write down what safety looks like to you and who sits in the safety circle with you.

My safety looks like this.

_____

_____

_____

_____

In the third circle, choose something you want to be part of your legacy, something that would give strength to your transformation and well-being.

The legacy piece that gives me strength is:

_____

_____

_____

_____

_____

Like the safety circle, the fourth circle is about protection. This protection, however, is a spiritual shielding of honour, grace, and unconditional love. It is the biggest circle to encompass you, always present and available for you to draw from. Use this time to feel its power surround you.

No matter the past, how you feel right now is what you have to work with. If you haven't gotten comfortable with visualization or creative manifesting, this exercise may be difficult.

If this happens, please be patient with yourself and start slowly by taking time every day to sit in a quiet place and connect with yourself. Shut your eyes and focus on how you would like your life to look. Notice what images and ideas arise.

You have powerful genius inside of you. You have the ability to overcome your toughest physical, mental, and emotional crises and struggles. When you get clarity and truly feel your core that is now filled with love, you begin to understand your magic, your femininity, your well-being, and your meaning, and you are able to move forward. Forgiveness is not forgetting. It is your right thing to do.

So, we move on to Chapter 10. As we do, honour your work so far and give yourself some time to soak in the rays of a new day, the blue sky, and the gentle spirit of Mother Earth. I remind you here of the power of breathing in fresh air and taking yourself out among the plants and growing things. I believe She so wants to continue to nurture us, to calm us, and support our well-being. In fact, I'd say it's Her legacy to us.

Reflections of a Boomer Woman

~

My Food Story

I've been told some people think that as a petite woman of small build I must not have had any problems with food, that since I'm not overweight I probably haven't had any food issues. Nothing could be further from the truth. Let me tell you why it's not all about what you see through a peek into my food story.

My heritage is filled with hard-working farmers and gardeners. Having been raised in this culture, I learned to respect the land. During the summers my sister and I helped with planting and harvesting. I did not realize at the time that this hard work was shaping my respect for food.

In my early married life it was easy to please our tribe of two with simple dishes. Things shifted when our family expanded to three, then four. I became obsessed with providing good meals.

I wish I could say that family meal time in our household was a delightful picture of happy people taking time to savour food while enjoying each other's company. I now see that I held these beliefs: my kids would "die" if I did not nourish them; it was my duty to provide "proper" meals; meals were to include many vegetables; and supper had to be a regimented experience. I am not proud to talk about actions that caused a great deal of tension at the table. Talk about indigestion with every bite!

After my Dad passed away from what I feel was an avoidable disease due to poor eating habits, things only got worse. I unconsciously chose not to care for myself, physically, emotionally, and spiritually. I was a mess. I was stuck in a high-stress corporate career, constantly tired, gained the most weight since being pregnant, had daily migraines and brain fog, cried at the drop of a hat, persisted to take my insecurity about food out on my family – all while trying to come to terms with my Dad's death.

145

After surgery for kidney stones, likely due to dehydration, I had to deal with what I was doing to myself. I knew better. I was an experienced gardener and cook with an interest in nutrition. I began reading again all sorts of material about diets and a healthy lifestyle. Then I had a real breakthrough.

I will not forget the vivid moment, one that seems kind of funny now because it took place in the shower. It was as though my body said, "why do you hate me?!" I was struck with the truth that I was not taking very good care of myself. The love I professed for God could not be so if I did not love myself as one of God's creations. This realization brought real change to my life.

Soon after my breakthrough moment, I got laid off from that stressful job (funny how things work, hey?). While looking for new work I continued reading more and more about food. My passion for nutrition was reignited! I learned how different foods could help my body, so I incorporated them into my diet as much as possible. I also began a regime that included daily exercise, quality supplements and meal planning. My body responded: weight was released, headaches subsided, and brain fog lifted. I also became relaxed about preparing food for my family.

I began to play with recipes out of love, not fear. Gradually the self-imposed burden of feeding my family was released too. I'm happy to say that our dinner times greatly improved!

In my mid-40's I took my love of food to a higher level; with the support of my family I graduated with a natural nutrition diploma. Today, in my early 50's, I am a Certified Holistic Nutritionist, educator, speaker, writer, and business owner. It thrills me to work with like-minded folks who are passionate about field to fork and plant to plate. I enjoy creating meals that use local, natural, and highly nutritious food.

My heritage and love of the land has come full-circle.

You can choose wellbeing no matter how old you are. My road to wellness started with a commitment to look after myself and to create a new food story. I believe in the power of whole-health living, and am stronger than ever as a result.

Will you take time to discover your food story to help grow your health?

Loretta Friedrich, C.H.N. N.N.C.P.
Sprout Natural Nutrition
http://sproutnaturalnutrition.com

Chapter 10
Reassurances and How to Manage Them

Delia was an overbearing cake

with condescending frosting, and frankly,

I was on a diet.

Maggie Stiefvater; Lament: *The Faerie Queen's Deception*

⁓

Reassurance is a genuine need. Not everyone is skilled at meeting that need.

For example, when your piece of cake falls on the floor into a crumbled mess, just as you were anticipating savouring that first bite, using it as the temporary spiritual lift out of your crisis, you may not feel happy. You have to delay your gratification, clean up the mess, and spend the rest of the night with your grumpy self. Depending on how you manage your emotions, your inner critic may be getting lots of chances to pipe up and remind you that *this always happens to you. If you weren't such a klutz!*

How does this always happen to you?

You decide to call your mom.

"Honey," she says, "you didn't need that piece of cake to make you feel better."

You bristle. Just the thing you didn't need to hear.

Reassurance doesn't always help when it's bad advice, lacks real empathy, or seems to be coming from a less than well-intentioned place. Family, friends, and co-workers can miss the mark when it comes to what to say—or not say—to someone in crisis. An ill-timed trite phrase can set a negative tone for the day—or longer if you let it.

So you're 50-plus, mid-crisis, and getting ready for transformation. You still have work to do on your self-confidence, and those small steps you're taking towards goals mean you're moving out of your comfort zone. You also have some unhealthy habits to break. All of this effort leaves you vulnerable but not powerless. Speaking of vulnerability, you know you have some trust and boundary issues to address (see Chapter 11 for more on that). At least a thousand details demand your attention at home and at work. That piece of cake was supposed to be your moment to sink deeply into tranquility and stay there as long as you possibly could.

Just because your tough self needed a break, your problems aren't going to dissolve with each mouthful of cakey goodness. Like many before you, you have no map to lead you through this turning point. Too much is happening internally for logic to be soothing. It isn't good for you isn't going to make you not want that perfect piece of cake. You did want it, and you chose it, right out of that glass bakery case full of sugar redemption. You just weren't planning on what happened next.

You lost your grip on the plate, and the cake dropped to the floor. Now you have the chore of cleaning it up. You won't taste any sweet goodness right at this moment. But the kitchen is still filled with the aroma of the cake, so the reminder is lingering.

You may have spent weeks at working through mindfulness practices, strengthening your alignment with core values, sticking to a budgeting and savings plan, or getting those resumes fine-tuned and ready to send. You've caught up on laundry, which you hate, cleaned out your closet, and made amends with two old friends who had fallen out with you after a jealousy thing.

That cake was your reward for enduring so many mental and emotional heartbreaks and hurts and working on your reinvention. Even though the cake is history, before you go to bed, maybe sharing your low moment might be good enough to make you feel better, so you make the call to your mom. What you get? "You didn't need that piece of cake to make you feel better."

Debra M. S., 1958
I was going back to college after twenty-five years away. I was a freshman and had to take some core courses to get my degree. I remember my heart sinking when I found out I had to take math classes. I hated math when I was a kid. I barely passed it in high school, even though I was good at everything else. I struggled along, just passing the tests. One night when I was having a particularly hard time with some equations, I started to hit myself. Physically I was beating myself up. I cried, called myself names like stupid, dumb, and useless. The next day, I had actually given myself a bruise on my leg. No one could have been more confused than I was. I mean I had an inner critic, but I was old enough, mature enough to realize that what was happening was neither helpful, nor was it coming from me, the inner core. I never did this kind of thing to my own children, not name-calling, or any kind of physical discipline. One night when I was relaxing into an English assignment, the reading brought me back to my childhood when my younger brother was struggling with his math. My mom would stand over him, beating on him with a ruler, and scream all those insults that I was hearing myself say to me as a grown adult. I talked about it with one of my professors. He assured me that it wasn't unusual for old memories to crop up like that. It was good that I had made some peace with it and was able to come to focus on letting go of some of my perfectionism too, to always getting things right the first time. I let myself get the marks I got, and decided to take the class over again. The second time was much better. This year I will enter into a master's program.
I will be 57 years old.

❧

Yes, you did. You had that piece of cake, that glass of wine, and your perfect time to relax in front of the TV to watch that movie you finally rented to feel separated from the troubles in your life and connected to magic, if only for a few hours. You not only needed that savouring moment, but you are also absolutely sure you didn't need a trite consolation that just made you feel ten years old all over again.

You find yourself spinning backwards to the dozens of times you were hurt by insensitivity and careless treatment by the adults in your childhood. For some Boomer women, this can mean remembering serious trauma. For others, not necessarily trauma but still painful memories. Being spanked, laughed at, insulted, or sent to bed with no supper are emotional injuries that don't need to carry the same weight now that we're growing into our adult knowledge and feminine wisdom.

However grounded, healed, or enlightened you are, right at that moment when you most need reassurance, the wrong words that come out of another person's mouth are like the proverbial straight pin to the balloon, and the cannon-sized "*Pop!*" is just another moment to recover from.

When you're in the eye of a crisis, your emotional well-being needs fortifying, and thoughtful reassurance can be so nourishing. I understand the power of words. I have been the perpetrator of platitudes myself, entirely missing the purpose, which was to put that other, hurting mortal creature at ease. Even in those moments of missing the mark, I intended to offer the appropriate sympathy, word of advice, or assurance that things would be fine. Yet I don't always have the right words to alleviate someone else's suffering. Neither does anyone else. In fact, depending on someone else's reassurance for our well-being is a tricky business.

Whatever they say, no matter how well- or ill-intentioned, we must check in with ourselves first, because we do have control over ourselves. Thus far, I've given you numerous tools and exercises to help you build those mental and emotional muscles. So before we go over some ways to deal with well intention that doesn't make us feel well at all, let's do a brief review of what we've covered, plus a few new tips and ideas, so you can tend to your own well-being first.

Grounding/Balancing Yourself

Whatever you've learned so far, from this book or otherwise, about grounding yourself, take the time you need to do it. It's the first and best thing you can do for your own balance and well-being.

One grounding activity I've suggested, something I believe to be better than counting to ten, is to breathe into the palm of your hand. Warmth soothes us, along with the gentleness of air on our skin. It's a pretty simple start to getting yourself under control. Focusing on the act of taking in a deep breath, your fingertips gently touching your cheek, is an act of self-love. Closing your eyes and resting for a short time to bask in the effortless, no-frills delight of your breath on your hand, and your own loving compassion, you can quickly sink through negativity to your groundedness.

Another way to ground yourself is to visualize your inner genius. If you've managed to create your symbol (Chapter 9) try this to take the concept one step further: add the word *feminine* to it. Our femininity is not something we've been trained to celebrate, but it matters to remember and honour it, as a way of honouring ourselves. We are Boomer *women*, sophisticated beings, different from our male cohorts. The Dalai Lama speaks of the feminine-masculine energies.

Receptive, nurturing and creative feminine energy creates a balance with the opposite qualities in masculine energy. We need balance of both feminine and masculine in every stage of our growth.

Louise R., 1950

I hear it all the time that Baby Boomers are a selfish bunch of "A-holes." It's all about our feelings and how much we need to fill the emptiness in our hearts is why we got busy with careers and obsessed about success. I was an only child and never had a real desire to have a man in my life. I dated, I'm not gay, and I just seem to like being alone. They tell me I'm like an aunt that had lived all her life that way. Anyways, one day I was feeling like having some company. I called my mom to see if she would go for tea with me. I genuinely wanted to spend time with her. I could hear her breathe on the other end, "You don't need me to go anywhere with you today. Why don't you find yourself a man?" She launched into a sermon that I listened to politely enough, but couldn't believe what she was carrying on about. I apologized for bothering her. She finally came out with what she wanted: a grandbaby. I had nothing to say or to offer. I said goodbye. I spent that day wondering why I should try to make her happy. I was okay. What I decided to do was get some advice from a co-worker that I liked and had three children. She looked at me and asked, "Do you want to date, get married, do the pregnancy thing, figure out babysitting, be the one that cooks, cleans, and still has to make him happy? Then your mom will be happy?" She turned back to her work. I stood there, frozen, not really processing her distress. I apologized for bothering her. Later I got a dog, then a cat. I am still alone. This year I turn 65 and officially retire from my job.

∽

Alone-time, or a least time without other humans, can be tremendously grounding. Pets can do wonders for lowering stress. I have pets that I adore. My kitties, Lucy and Finn, are great balancers in my home; they get me to stop and relax or sometimes take a nap if needed. But I also wouldn't advise someone that doesn't have any pets, cats, dogs, or goldfish, to immediately go out and set up their lives with the responsibility. As I've encouraged you throughout this book, trust and listen to yourself.

Find what intuitively works for you to be grounded. What being grounded really means is that you have clear thinking, your body is calm (apparent by how you are breathing), and you are connecting with your mind, body, and spirit. Grounding is not protective but receptive. It is a way to be in acceptance rather than rejection.

One other thing that puts you in a positive, receptive mood: after you breathe that warm air into the palm of your hand, remember to smile. In your meditations and mindfulness exercises, smile. Student researcher Ding Li won FameLab 2014 with a presentation that highlighted the discovery of smiling as a positive feedback system built into our brain reward system.[95]

Meaning, we don't need a reason to smile for smiling to go viral in our lives.

Smiling has health benefits too: it can reduce anxiety, lower blood pressure and heart rate, and has a positive effect on the people around the person smiling. More research has determined that "smiling bonds people together."[95] Earlier, if you posed in front of the mirror and had trouble saying that you love you, try again now. Smile first, as whole-heartedly as you can, and see if you don't want to invite that lustrous, noble beauty into your life.

Now, grounded and smiling as whole-heartedly as we can, let's return to how to manage those not-so-reassuring reassurances.

Advice-Reassurance Management

Crises put you in a funk and kept you off balance, stressed-out, and angry for a long while. At 50-plus you've managed to find some balance and made decisions for your future transformation that make you feel humble and grateful, as well as newly confident and proud. Then it happens: advice that's supposed to double as reassurance rolls your way like an ocean wave you thought you could withstand, but the strength of it still knocks you over.

No matter how dear our friendships or close our family relationships, advice either inappropriate or untimely needs careful handling. Welcome to Reassurance Management for Loved Ones 101.

Everyone has experiences and opinions, but that doesn't make them life-skill experts. Each one of us has value, and for the most part our positions on love, kids, marriage, divorce, and what we should do about life issues have merit. What we are not adept at, when we aren't trained or tuned in to it, is how to time, phrase, or deliver advice effectively.

At its most basic level, communication is a process, an exchange of information that includes listening, hearing, and speaking.[96] Researchers don't agree on what percentage of our information exchanges come from verbal or nonverbal cues, but most of us Boomer women have come to understand that we need the communication skill of emotional intelligence, considered a soft skill, to get around in life.104 It may be soft but there's nothing easy about using all six of your senses to read a situation that requires you to be kind, aware, and decisive while sympathizing with someone whose opinion you have to deflect.

At this point I'm not referring to strangers or casual acquaintances that we may never meet again. Not that we shouldn't keep ourselves as civil and respectful as a situation calls for, but this section is about managing challenging communication situations with family and dear friends.

So how do we kindly yet assertively correct or deflect someone we care about, someone who wants to give us his or her best advice? Especially if not following that advice sets us up as responsible for hurt feelings, temporary exile, or some degree of a cold shoulder? We may need the support of our loved ones, but for some people that means giving them blind loyalty in return.

I know one Boomer lady whose Italian mother has angry outbursts when someone in the family doesn't obey her. The seriousness of the mother's explosive tyranny may mean it's clinical, but when this Boomer woman needed some support after deciding to divorce, didn't want to lose her family. Until she got her bearings, she needed a place to stay to figure out a new plan for her and the kids. Her mother, a devout Catholic, told her it was a sin to divorce and spent the six weeks that this poor Boomer woman stayed with her shaking rosary beads at her to pray for forgiveness. If she went back to her husband, her life would be saved. It felt more to this Boomer woman that returning to her husband would mean her mother would be saved.

When faced with the toxicity of advice and reassurance from parents or siblings that feels oppressive, I think it makes the most sense to find a neutral place to recover, if even for a short time—for instance, a walk by yourself. This is imperative to your emotional health and stress levels. Even if your toxic family would give you anything to meet your material needs, the cost to your overall mental and emotional health is far more important to consider.

Still, if your search for higher ground is desperate and immediate, toxic family may be your only option. You may be in a situation where you have a mixed bag of resources in terms of financial or emotional safe places, which may cause you to settle for a less than perfect short-term solution. You may be staying with a toxic friend so you can get a reasonable distance from your immediate crisis. In that case, get to work as soon as you can on building your inner strengths. In the previous chapter you did some spiritual work on honour. Revisit your core of love, and visualize your honour circle in Chapter 9. It is there to surround you with power.

Sunny E., 1962
I wanted to be a dancer. Thing was I never danced because I felt really stupid doing things in front of people. I was shy. I didn't make it to graduate from high school. It was all bad for about ten years. Drugs, prostitution, problems with the law kept me busy getting beat up, in and out of jail, too many times out of an abortion clinic. I wasn't no saint, but I wasn't no devil. I was always thinking about how I was hurting myself, and that I could do better. I met this girl on the street that we ended up being best friends. She used to smile all the time.
Man I never smiled. But when I was around her, I'd start to feel better. One night she got the shit beat out of her for smiling. How crazy is that? I could have been like some of my friends and stayed on the street. She was a kid and deserved better. I kinda felt like maybe we should be someplace else. My boyfriend I was in love with bigtime. He never hit me. When I talked to him about leaving the street, he asked me to marry him. It wasn't the first time it happened to me, but I watched him really hard when he said it so I could get a feeling about whether he meant it. I didn't say yes. I made him believe I just wanted to live together. A month later I moved out, brought the kid with me. She was sixteen at the time. I cleaned myself up, and became a drug counsellor. I use my emotional listening with my clients.

The kid went on to college and became a physical therapist. We spend Christmases together, which is also my birthday.
This year I turn 53 years old.

❧

Honour is actually an important part of a powerful skill for dealing with problematic reassurance, a skill that can also translate extremely well for work or casual situations. This skill? Focused listening. In his book *Mental Traps* (2007) Andre Kukla, describes the problem of "scattered thoughts."[97] Often times in conversation, we're not wholeheartedly focused on or honouring the speaker. Our minds are on other things, especially our own problems. When our thoughts are scattered, we miss important subtleties that could allow us to hear where the advice is coming from emotionally and to know what we as receiver should do with it.

For instance, focused listening may allow you to realize that the advice may not be practical, but it is heartfelt. This can create more ease for you and the speaker, especially if you ultimately disagree. When people feel respected and heard, disagreeing doesn't have to be a problem. To show the speaker you're listening, nod occasionally, smile and use facial expression, make sure your body posture is open and inviting, and encourage the speaker to continue with verbal comments, like yes or uh-huh.

Reflecting back to them—*What I am hearing is, or Sounds like you are saying*—is also a great way to practice your listening skills.

Here you could also tap into the power of smiling, and offer a warm smile while you paraphrase back to the speaker what you heard them say. In a potentially tense situation, regardless of how serious the speaker may be, it can be in the best interest of your own mood to smile with your mouth and eyes to give your brain a happy boost in serotonin.[98] Even over the phone, you can use the smile booster to positively shift the tone of the situation, which can elevate the overall mood of you and the other person.

Speaking of advice, I don't know how well my suggestions in this chapter or in this book work for you. They may meet you in the right way at just the right time. They may not. Whether you are mid-crisis or well on your way to reinvention, I do hope this book directs you to the greater connection and reassurance you want and need. Joining up with Fabulous@50, you will likely find dear friends that may last you a lifetime. Some of the same people I started with remain strong sources I draw from for insight, beverage sharing (coffee or wine), and conversations about everything. I am grateful to have these women in my life, women who know how to take care of themselves and offer focused listening as well as helpful reassurance from time to time.

Okay ladies, get out your journals and pens. It's time to put what we've been exploring here into action and to add a few more ingredients to your recipe for reinvention.

Ingredients to Gather

Smiling

In each chapter I've introduced variations of mindfulness exercises, new mantras, and activities that give you the opportunity to practice and possibly step out of your comfort zone. Earlier in this chapter, we learned that smiling can be a powerful anti-negativity tool. If you aren't smiling right now, give it a shot. Practicing without anything else in your mind besides using your mouth and eyes to create a big grin across your beautiful face is all you have to do. You won't need a mirror. If you want to take a selfie with a smartphone or tablet, that's fine. Go for it. The point is to make smiling and laughing a daily habit for yourself. Try this mantra on for size:

I am a habitual smiler. I am love. I am on higher ground.

Matching, Listening, and Reassuring Yourself

In their book *A Toolkit for Motivation*, Catherine Fuller and Phil Taylor talk about "matching styles of rapport, energy, and pacing" when you communicate with people.[99] This kind of matching facilitates trust and subconsciously tells the other person they are being listened to. Wherever you are in your reinvention, you benefit from improving your communication skills. Learning how to actively listen is one of the best skills you'll ever develop for yourself, and matching can help you focus in on the other person to do just that. So as you go about your day, try and match the energy, pacing, and rapport in your interactions with people.

Throughout your life, people are going to give you advice and feedback. Some of it you will ask for, and some of it will be completely uninvited; some will come from well-intentioned family members or co-workers, some will come from ill-intentioned friends or acquaintances; some of what people offer will be platitudes or trite sentiments that are not particularly helpful, but some of what they share may also have a deeply imbedded insight or golden nugget that can be truly helpful. When you actively listen, you'll be better able to sort out the gems from the rocks.

One thing you might also try is matching during a conversation with yourself. Remember that you are your first noble friend. Ask for whatever reassurance you need. Then offer yourself advice that aligns with your values, your developing goals, and what really lights you up.

Imagine the best advice you could hear right now. What might that be?

In the spirit of reassuring yourself, remember to rely on what you already know works for you. I know that humour always helps me to feel better.

If that's true for you too, an idea: find some time to watch some funny movies or short videos on YouTube.

For instance, there are some screaming goat videos that cracked me up[100] Visit the link in the back of the book if you want to see them. I find animals so delightfully honest with their behaviour, even the dog in last part of the video looks like he wants to say something funny. As a visual person, I like videos and physical humour to lighten my spirits. You might prefer funny books or other activities that loosen you up. Also, you might revisit where you are with positive emotions right now, or consider how you've been kind to yourself. What about allowing your authenticity to shine through?

Today I am doing this for my well-being.:

_____

_____

_____

_____

Last but not least, you can visualize some welcome support in whatever form you think would move you forward.

Remember, you are a lustrous, noble beauty. It's not too late, and you're not alone. So keep learning and staying receptive and loose. Take every opportunity to relax your muscles, stretch, and breathe deeply. You are doing what you need to do.

Next up in Chapter 11, we'll look at what a little bit of rabble rousing can do for your well-being. So get ready to cause some trouble, the best kind.

Reflections of a Boomer Woman

~

The Gift of Adversity

Parents do their best to protect their children from adversity and loss. But sometimes life has other plans. After a brief illness, my mother died very suddenly when I was 17. In 1967, mothers didn't die, at least not in my world. It was my last year of high school. For most of my life, I had lived in my mother's shadow, staying safe and playing it safe. Mom had always wanted me to go to university. I was eager for that higher learning because of my dream to become either a teacher or a social worker. I worked hard to be a good daughter. Although our family wasn't super religious, from the time I had learned about God, I believed He and I had a deal. I would be on my best behavior; He would make sure nothing bad happened to me.

Mom's death changed everything. Too numb with grief to care much about schooling, I failed two crucial final exams and couldn't qualify for university entrance. Dad pleaded with me to go back to school to improve my marks. Leaving my older brother and me in Calgary, he was moving my younger brothers to his business in Saskatchewan.

Anger at what I felt was God's betrayal along with a newfound sense of freedom from Mom's expectations provided the determination to shape my own destiny.

When the worst thing that you could ever imagine happens, nothing else seems as tough. I decided I had had enough of school and started job hunting. It was pretty typical in those days for an 18-year-old to make her own way in the world.

I found an entry level job at an oil company, rented a partly-furnished apartment within walking distance from work and started my new life. My enrolment in the School of Hard Knocks began.

Looking back, I realize that having the worst happen turned out to be the best for me. Don't get me wrong — there were many sad moments because Mom was gone — all the special occasions in life when a mother's presence is so valued.

But that fire of adversity so young propelled me to seek my own destiny, to venture out, to learn and to grow. I marvel now at the twisty, winding path I took, and I'm so grateful for all the gifts I gathered along the way. That first administrative job led to sales, which led to the personal growth arena. In that environment, I found where I belonged — at the front of the room — teaching. Years later, even without a degree, I was hired to teach university classes.

My life hasn't been all roses — I have survived bankruptcy, failed businesses, two divorces, and two bouts of cancer — they don't call it the School of Hard Knocks for no reason! Still, I'm reminded of an old saying, "life happens for you, not to you." I've come to believe that to be true.

All of my life has been perfectly orchestrated so that I could learn to be unapologetically Me — my likes, values, dreams, and desires — whatever is unique as far as my talents, skills and experience. Most times I had little idea of how my decisions would turn out. What I did have, though, was an unshakable faith in my willingness and ability to deal with whatever life threw my way.

A big part of my journey involved my spiritual growth. I began to wonder about my view of God as a sometimes benevolent — sometimes vengeful dude who couldn't really be trusted. A near-death experience in 2007 shattered that illusion once and for all.

What has evolved is an all-encompassing belief in the power of unconditional love of which we are all a part. As I surrender more each day to that love and acceptance, I feel that Universal Spirit that is the birthright of each of us.

While adversity has come and gone, at the end of it all I'm still standing — wiser, richer, and very humbled by the beauty of it all. Like the rainbow after the storm, we are all blessed in this way. I would like to think that my mother is proud of who I turned out to be despite or maybe because of that path of adversity.

As a speaker, Sue Paulson's passion is to inspire others to experience their own magnificence. Her third book, "Magnificent Misery- from Adversity to Ecstasy" is now available. You can reach Sue at www.suepaulson.com.

Chapter 11
Rebellion is Healthy

Love is like a good cake;

you never know when it's coming,

but you'd better eat it when it does!

C. Joybell C.

The world is ready for healthy rebellion. So are Boomer women who have planned the parties; done the shopping; baked the cakes; cleaned up before and after, somehow still ready to make everyone an after-party snack; and looked fantastic through it all. Yes, we're able to do a lot of things the people who surround us often take for granted. You can spend your life waiting around for love (or good cake) to arrive, or instead, as I hope you've learned in these pages, you can own the courage you have to create it for yourself. We Boomer women are a dynamic bunch who have spent decades in the shadows, working damn hard without asking for anything in return, and it's time to use that courage we have for emotional rebellion.

First of all, erase this sequence of words from your vocabulary: *I'm too old.*

Instead, how about being old enough to have perfected so many life and other skills? How about asking yourself, *Too old for what?*

I say not much.

It's not too late to get a tramp stamp tattooed in the small of your back fat. It's not too late to let go of being right all the time or to drop required politeness and pick up helpful honesty. Not too late to rebel your way out of old, unhealthy roles and whatever upsets or degrades you. So, own the courage to step up to the next level of your transformation, which may involve putting up some boundaries. Healthy rebellion may make your family and friends uncomfortable, but in the end it's good for everybody.

In our Fabulous@50 community, we have spotters on standby to help with the weights you're lifting to strengthen your mental and emotional muscles. Or imagine that on either side of you are fellow spiritual soldiers who are really angels, surrounding you, prepared for battle. They have your back because it's time to fight the good fight and win back your core magic. I believe that all people have trust and caring surrounding them when they step out of their comfort zones, and I believe this support comes from God. You might call it the universe or a *higher source*, but whatever you identify with, know you are supported.

The point is, you rebel, you are not alone.

So what is rebellion? It may have been a while since you revolted against anything, so let's review.Rebellion is about courage and revolution, all of which comes naturally to teenagers. Rebelliousness, according to family therapists, is a healthy way to develop independence and establish boundaries[101] Unfortunately, our Boomer cohort of women weren't often encouraged to develop independence or clear, healthy boundaries. Instead, we were conditioned to disregard our emotional needs, depend on men, and forsake our boundaries for everyone else's benefit.

Despite what we did to rebel, most of us were coerced back into roles that made sense to others. Many of us chose motherhood, determined to give the next generation a better life, but it turned out that we had to be prepared to do it without any real support from a patriarchal society. Boomer women who remained single or had no children also worked hard in their chosen roles, sometimes as leaders and businesswomen, but also had to make their ways without respect or acknowledgment.

Despite what we've been told or how we've been ignored, I maintain that Boomer women are naturally courageous. We have it built into our DNA. Anthropologists suggest that our female ancestors were not just gatherers, but also hunters who shared those responsibilities with men before farming and settlement predominated.[102] Of course no one seems to know for sure or to agree. What we do know is that we must carry on, clean house in our minds and hearts, get fit, and head full-on to our birthright, which is well-being and life on purpose.

In *Real Magic*, Wayne Dyer tells us that "everything in the universe has a purpose," and the internal process to achievement requires realignment.[103] So basically, you have a purpose, and it takes realignment to get there. I will add that realignment can require rebellion, and that how you rebel depends not so much on where you've come from, but where you want to go.

Through the power of forgiveness, I'm able to leave my past in its rightful place of honour and focus instead on the legacy I want to leave. If you've been through the exercises in Chapter 9 and played with building a "thought" quilt, you may have gained insight and clarity as to your own legacy and how it means you must realign with your core magic and authentic self.

Tabitha B., 1947

My family was a bunch of fine artists, orchestral and performance musicians and intellectuals. My friends from college enjoyed Jimmy Hendrix and Janis Joplin. I was expected to be like my family, graduate with a degree that would make me a classical artist or musician, find a husband with the same interests and sensibilities, have two children, a huge house, and attend our family gatherings in formal wear, prepared to perform or discuss my latest works. My third year, I rebelled. I had been a quiet teen, studious and obedient. Literally, I broke out of the mold of my family expectations that made them insist I go to a psychiatrist. It was like a kind of madness. I want to say when my parents sat me down and gave me the "We will not support your experiment to question us so your cut off" speech, I was shaken. I knew it was about discovery and expansion. It had drugs in the mix, sex, and a hippie commune. I stayed a vegan, eventually became a yoga instructor, and have been a community leader and activist in greening the environment and ocean. My family and I get together every Thanksgiving. I bring my favourite salads and tofu dish while they scarf down the murdered turkey and duck. My oldest brother is an accomplished cellist with two daughters who are following in the family footsteps. My son on the other hand lives in Mali working on a village project to improve agricultural irrigation. There's no judgement on my part.

161

One of my spiritual teachers showed me the harm I did to my spirit if I followed that part of my mind. I love them all. That's not just the hippie or the pot talking. This year I turn 68 years old.

⪦⪧

As you reflect on your past and begin to plan for the future, you may find yourself drawing on the experience and legacy of some long-lost relatives who happened to be rebels. Of course, it's not a requirement to have a cast of colourful characters in your family history. You can be the first in your lineage to start a rebellion of your very own. Your rebellion doesn't have to be against society as an organized assembly of thousands to march and chant against injustice and inhumanity. It just needs to be against whatever doesn't serve you in your commitment to thriving and well-being.

Throughout this book, I've taken a stand on some issues I feel we have to have a voice in as Boomer women. My dip into rebelliousness is not leading a group into Parliament, but instead making calls to organizations and businesses to ask why they have ignored our Boomer women's segment in fashion and preferences. I will face anyone who wants to criticize my chosen battle. With confidence, I contend that Boomer women are a dynamic and complex group who have a key role to play in these economically, scientifically, and technologically unprecedented times. We have more information than ever to consider. We have unique opportunities to explore our emotional lives, particularly in light of significant challenges and affronts to women. We have unique wisdom and lived experience to contribute to the world. At the same time, we Boomer women must still go about our daily lives. We still have to get up, bathe, get dressed, go to work or find employment, drive, eat, read, communicate, listen, and plan what's next.

No one who might be busy judging our cohort or me will jump in to help us with house cleaning, paying our bills, or arranging our schedules to take a night course. If I want any of those things to happen, I need to be the one who makes them happen. So if I want to be my best, have my hair done, purchase a new dress with matching shoes and a purse, I'm allowed. If I want to go out in sweatpants without lipstick, I'm allowed, too. How many rag magazines catch celebrity women with their casual looks, sans make-up and hair dos, with some awful caption using words like *ugly* or *Imagine seeing this in the morning?* I have to ask, is that coming from an average guy, twenty-five pounds overweight, without washboard abs, and with a receding hairline? I don't gamble, but I might put my money on any member of the paparazzi not being their freshest either first thing in the morning.

The point is, I choose not to worry about what other people think or want of me, and you don't need to either. It took me into my forties to break out of the mold that kept me invisible, being what others wanted me to be, and trying to fit in where I wasn't sure if I belonged. The more I separated from judgment and negativity, the more I was able to find compassion and peace. Some women don't start breaking molds until they're in their fifties, as they realize that they need new boundaries, some new rules, and some well-chosen rebellions to win back their lives. Whenever you start, remember it's not too late to pick your own battles and choose your focus.

Doing so is an important part of realizing your authentic power. What you focus on, like the signal-to-noise ratios from Chapter 3 and where you put your energy, can either make your way clearer or not. We do know this, but our conditioning has made it difficult to see where we begin and the crap that doesn't belong to us ends. Still, I say we should strive to choose our own focus, while not losing sight of the practical matters in our lives.

For instance, my bank won't take buttons for a mortgage payment. It's hard to win over a client for a graphics contract if they can't get close enough to see my portfolio because I've chosen not to shower and brush my teeth before the meeting. I think that's being real. I could choose to rebel at my next presentation with my hair in shades of purple, pink, and green strands and me wearing tiger-striped spandex leggings, four-inch spike heels, and a tube top, showing off my new tramp stamp.

I'm honestly not saying to stop yourself if that's what you want to do to show your rebellious side. Just make sure that how you rebel isn't one more example of you trying to do something the "right" way.

Ask yourself: *Does this align with my authentic self, get me what I want, and lead toward self-healing and my well-being?* Ask it out loud, and several times if you have to.

Rebellion does not only include external actions that go against the grain of your family or society. It's also about questioning the boundaries and myths that chain you to mediocrity, that don't feel right on the inside.

We can and should question if we are doing our best, sometimes use others' success as an example to measure our own, and strive for better physical and emotional health. This process of rebellion and reinvention isn't about doing a little bit and getting a lot back. It's hard, healthy work, and it will change life as you, and the people you love, know it.

Kathy A., 1960

I've been married twice. I am planning a third marriage with a guy that I've dated for four years. This time I approached the relationship much differently than I had before with the first two. I can't say that I am all grown up yet. I went through a phase about six years ago where I dropped all the worry issues about weight and made it about my health instead. I stopped trying to get my adult son a job and spend some money on myself now. I get manicures, take a new class about something that interests me every six months and cancelled my subscription to two celebrity magazines. I got a nose piercing and have tattoos on both arms. I've worked most of my adult life in customer service. This year I plan to try my hand at a business I've wanted to start for decades, a small restaurant. What surprised me was how my parents thought it was such a bad thing to try to do. Gosh, the naysaying and overprotectiveness was pretty thick.

I respect my parents, but I did something for me by tuning into my "self" and gave myself permission to succeed or fail accordingly. I wasn't going to be using their money or my new husband's. It was entirely my own doing and responsibility. It wasn't overnight I came to being self-assured. I've learned what battles I want to fight. Before I never fought any. On my birthday this year, I will open my cafe.

I turn 55 years old.

Rebellion is healthy for two reasons: it wakes everyone up, and when done in alignment with your core values, it establishes new energy in your life and in the lives of people around you—family, friends, coworkers, bosses, clients, or support workers.

Rebellion is also personal. The kind of courageous action you need to rise above your circumstances depends on you and your circumstances. It also depends on your own efforts. No one else can do the work for you. If you've found yourself in crisis and have been blaming everyone and everything else, you've missed the point. No one else breathes for you.

If you need grounding, don't forget to try using the breath into your palm exercise. Combine that with taking a break, and doing some releasing and visualizing. Take these times as you need and are able to take them.

Rebel against those thoughts that make you too busy and overwhelmed, too stressed out, or ignore your tiredness and frustration. In fact, even if you have a looming deadline, can't take the rest of the week off, or have too many things in the fire to leave undone, take a brief holiday anyway, an idea we'll return to in the "Ingredients" section of this chapter.

Right now, get a feeling for where you are and where you have been when it comes to boundaries, limitations, and the skills you've been cultivating in minimizing weaknesses and fears and building on your strengths. Believe me, even a new small set of these skills are like gold in your arsenal of rabble-rousing and stellar ingredients for a delicious new recipe of you. Now you just keep building these skills to your advantage.

When you're grounded, self-aware, and skill-building, it's much easier to know what you want to say yes to, as well as no.

Saying No

When did you first say that? It's hard for most of us to remember, but it was likely the second word our infant selves used, right after *mama or dada*. Anyone with kids remembers the baby's refusal to take those mushed peas, looking you straight in the eye as she dumped her food dish on the floor for the sixth time, or the baby-turned-teenager, storming out of the living room over a fight about you never understanding her. Of course she hates you for all of it, either what you did or didn't do.

Whether you raised kids or not, have you ever surrendered to someone else's drama to keep the peace?

Changed your no to a yes to make things easier for everyone else? Are you always the one apologizing and feeling guilty? When someone needs something, do you drop what you're doing to help them? Even if you love what you found to wear, if someone says that it looks awful, do you crater to their opinion?

You might be most familiar with no these days in terms of saying no to yourself.

There's a show called *Say Yes to the Dress*. It's a reality show that starts with a bride-to-be discussing her budget and vision for the perfect wedding dress. Based on that discussion, the concierge dressers take the bride to a fitting room and choose some gowns for her to try on. You're probably wondering where I'm going with this. Stay with me.

Weddings are big events. In fact, a wedding is the most stressful event besides childbirth that is considered positive and so falls into the eustress category. Weddings can involve any or all of the trimmings, from a church ceremony, to flowers, to a reception, to a honeymoon. And let's not forget the cake! All of that means planning, detail management, budgeting, and lots of feelings as a woman prepares to make a major commitment. Whether that woman is you, your daughter or grand-daughter, sister or best friend, you can find yourself handling just as many responsibilities and emotional highs and lows.

Here's my point about the television program. It sheds light on how we women navigate choosing something that we will make us feel beautiful, confident, and committed.

Some might say it's just a dress, and marriage is so volatile, etcetera, but I see that choosing a dress symbolizes something elemental in our lives. Saying yes to something important. Preparing for something in the future, for which we anticipate success. Imagining a life full with promise and happiness. Imagining someone we love light up to see us when we come towards them. Committing to dates and times, sending invitations, hoping the weather holds out, the caterer gets the food right, the photographer gets all the best pictures, and Grandma will be healthy enough to make the ceremony. It's a risky business. Choosing a dress is about preparing for a future you have no control over.

Sound familiar in terms of any choices in your life right now?

Back to that dressing room for a moment. The bride is full of questions. How does the dress look on her? What are the reactions of the people who see her in it? If it's important to have everyone agree, how does she handle the charged reactions if they're different than hers? As I've watched the program, I notice most of the brides-to-be need approval from the people they bring. Is it giving up your power if you let someone or a group decide what to wear, especially for something like your wedding dress?

You might think back on your own life. If you had a wedding decades ago, what was it like? I heard of one Boomer woman who wanted to have a big wedding, but feared it would turn into one fight after the other with her controlling mother. The Boomer woman was certain she'd have no say in her own special day. So she said no to the big wedding and yes to eloping.

Weddings aside, maybe you're familiar with toxic relationships that forced you to keep your innermost wants in check. Or other circumstances in which you put your own desires on the back burner. Do you ever wonder about what your life would have been like if you would have said no instead of yes?

Lizette O., 1958

When my wedding was being planned, I really wanted to have my mother's dress to wear. I was a lot bigger than she was though. So I decided that it was better to go for a fitting at a dress shop. We lived on a farm in a small community that was a few hours' drive. We decided to make a weekend of it and piled six of us into a station wagon and went to get my dress. Talk about a horrendous experience. We tried to do it in one day. Every thing I tried on was a no from my mom. She is normally very quiet. She never says anything to my dad even if she disagrees. I liked all the dresses I had tried on. There was one that I really liked, but my mom just pursed her lips, crossed her arms, and uncharacteristically stood her ground. I was getting mad but she insisted that we come back one more weekend. I couldn't believe it. But we came back one more weekend. Then it happened. I loved this dress. What was she going to say? I walked out afraid of her reaction. She burst into tears. Then we were all crying, even the lady who was helping us. I celebrate 38 years with my husband this year. I turn 57 years old.

If you're getting a divorce, having to face bankruptcy, being forced to relocate, or learning that you have to finally speak up for yourself or life is going to spiral out of your control, again, now is not the time to get squeamish about healthy rebellion, or to dwell on regret. Regret is how we feel about something in the past, remorse over something we said or did, and ideally, we've forgiven ourselves and moved through anger, guilt, or shame to honouring those results. Regret is not a factor in lives that are transforming and on the way to well-being.

You are a courageous woman strengthening your authentic self, and you know what you need to do and when you need to say no. This is about trusting your intuition. When you see those brides-to-be look at themselves in the mirror, when they are moved by their own images, and smiles drift soulfully across their faces, or tears stream down, you know they've made their decisions. You can use that same intuitive knowing to determine the rightness or wrongness of important decisions, the questions that sometimes force you into the kind of no zone that moves you forward.

Just as the bride experiences alignment with her expectations, with her loved ones, with her budget, with her vision, and offers a satisfied yes to the dress, when you are in alignment with your true self, you can come up with an equally confident answer. Regardless of your crisis, you can say no to the stress that no longer empowers you, contributes to your meaning, honours your values, or gives you the love you deserve.

You can also learn to watch other people's nos and to recognize when a no might do us the greatest service. Some of us have loved ones and dear friends who really want something for us that is more magical than we've imagined or allowed. Watch for those uncharacteristic moments from your loved ones. When they reach into a no that surprises you, take a step back and stay open. Ask them some questions to clarify what they're feeling. Remember that wholehearted communication takes skill and effort.

Now get your journal and pen ready for some more ingredients. Or feel free to say no to ingredients for right now, go have a rebellious piece of cake, and come back exactly when you want to. This is your party, after all.

Ingredients to Gather

No Practice and Boundary Setting

We Boomer women often do one part of communication exceptionally well. In fact, we are not only skilled at this, we wouldn't be able to live without it. What is this amazing skill?

Talk. Talk. Talk.

Oh yes, ladies. We talk, and talk, and talk some more. For me and many women I know, we need to talk to dump out all the words that are stirring around in our heads. Unfortunately, this can also look like we are just talking, but for me, it's part of my thinking process.

Still, when we talk without paying attention, we can lose authority, assertiveness, and energy, and those are the exact things that can help us get where we want to be. As we forge ahead in our reinventions, we might take a cue from actors who rehearse their lines. Before you're confronted by situations that demand your rebellion, practice in a mirror, or even tape yourself speaking aloud and listen to what you sound like. Breathe into your palm first. Remind yourself what you own.

Try saying this, with authority and confidence:

I am centered. I am love. I live a recharged life.

Speaking your truth, expressing your needs, and keeping your emotional balance can be challenging if a situation has escalated to name-calling and blame. Setting boundaries with dignity takes courage and balance. In his book *The Power of the Positive No*, author, anthropologist, and crisis-mediator William Ury details an interesting, three-step plan to get to your no and leave everyone with their dignity intact.[104]

Before you try Ury's plan, described below, see what your no feels and sounds like. Recall that when we were kids or when our kids were growing up, when the word came out emphatically or firmly, no was definitive. We can listen for and learn to deliver the same definitive no in our current decision making. As you practice, keep your awareness on your body. Does your head move side to side?

Does the word stick in your throat?

In actual communication, that can be a signal that everyone needs to step back and wait.

If you are being pressured, state simply and clearly:

"I am not making a decision right now."

Sometimes we struggle with no because we want to be liked and accepted. If you've done some work on that inner critic voice, and it shows up at times when you do want to assert yourself, it's a good time to dismiss yourself from commitments and do more inner work.

Or if you can't step away and your crisis demands quick thinking and a clear decision, if it has to be no, try William Ury's three-part technique of a "positive no."[105]

1. Yes!

2. No.

3. Yes?

The first part is to describe clearly what you do want or intend, what you say yes to. For example, "I want to have my cake and eat it too." Avoiding hostility in your tone works best. Take in a deep, relaxed breath as you prepare. Smile with your eyes and mouth first, if a smile feels right. Remember, a genuine smile can help to dissolve some intensity of emotions, for yourself and the person or people you are addressing. You may even get them to relax.

The second step is to state your no as a limit, i.e. "I will not take your advice and limit my choices because you feel it is best for me." Ury feels that this asserts your power.[106] If you've found yourself calm at the center, that your breath is easy, and there is no stiffness in your body, this is your authentic self ready for action. You might want to look deeply into the person's eyes to make them feel your assurance and trust. It's not a must. Follow your body's lead.

The third step, getting to the yes? is to offer a proposition that can further the relationship with the other party or parties.[107] In the cake example, you might say, "Might I propose that we discuss what other options you could agree to for next time? For now, please join me while I have this cake and eat it, too."

I used this technique recently in a business situation, and the result ended favourably, with no harsh words or lost relationships. I started with my yes, which was based on the relationship I had with these people, then followed with the no to the agreement we had made, and then said yes to other ways we could work together. Despite my fear that it could end in a dramatic, angry movie scene, I was delighted to discover that my honesty allowed for greater emotional connection and healing for everyone in the room. If you determine to practice this along with learning to trust your intuitions and body reactions, you may find that saying no not only asserts your position to get what you want, you build healthier relationships with people.

Ury reminds us to treat everyone with respect, listen to understand, ask questions to clarify the stance of the other party, and to recognize their humanity.[108]

We sometimes forget that our opportunities to develop meaningful relationships come from modeling for others how to be respectful.

It's easy to default into old defensive reactions, but part of re-experiencing life is communicating in new, healthier ways, including asking to begin again, being willing to say "I'm sorry," and finding more heartfelt ways to express what you want, set your limits, or offer a winning resolution.

Gratitude and Holidays

Even rebellious women remember to say thank you. As you practice saying no, I encourage you to continue practicing gratitude as well. It works wonders.

I am grateful for these things in my life.

_____

_____

_____

_____

_____

_____

_____

_____

_____

_____

_____

_____

_____

_____

_____

Don't worry, I didn't forget about what I said earlier about having that holiday. This is a visualization exercise that you can do at home or in your car. It doesn't take long. It's a short holiday. Ground yourself and get calm. Then begin.

Where I go is warm, safe, and beautiful.
The air is fresh. I can breathe so easily.
I hold my drink in my hand. It's my favourite.
Mmm. Wonderful. Delicious. I am savouring
this experience. I am so relaxed. I am going
to come back here soon.

Go back there for a holiday as many times a day as you need to. Add some details that make it even more delightful. For instance, I take myself to Cabo, one of my favourite vacation destinations, on a regular basis.

I visualize myself walking out of my condo, down the path to beach.

It's quiet, as all the guests are getting ready for dinner. I find a nice spot on the beach and watch the big red sun sink down into the ocean.

I smell the fresh air, feel the breeze, hear the waves crashing on the beach, and feel the warmth of the sand under me.

Wow. You've done even more work that is really getting you stronger and more balanced. I can almost see your smile, and the twinkle in your eyes. You are beautiful and ready.

So we're moving on to Chapter 12. It's time for a professional reboot.

Reflections of a Boomer Woman

My Badass Life

I was born in the last month of the last year of the baby boom in Canada, which means I just celebrated my 50th birthday. As a gift, my sister paid for me to have a tattoo that says "Live Inspired" indelibly inked on the inside of my forearm. It's an elegant font, and there is a ladybird at the end of it, so I absolutely love it. The script is heavy and black, and catches my eye frequently.

Somehow, having a tattoo has made me feel like a bit of a badass, and something inside of me likes this expression of badassery even more than I thought I would. I mean, I expected something out of it, but not as much as I got.

Years ago, when I was in my early 20's, my mom said that my language left a lot to be desired. She found my propensity for cursing wasn't very lady like, and she didn't like it when I swore. I remember replying that as a member of the army, swearing was something I came by a lot (which was also saying something considering how much of it I had heard at home). Besides, it's not as if I let off a litany of curses for just anything. There was always a purpose to it, although I did temper the cursing quite a bit as I moved on in my career, had kids of my own, and tried to make a positive impact in the world.

I didn't let go of cussing entirely, however, and still operated under the rule that a well-

placed curse word (even a fake swear word) sprinkled into an otherwise stellar string of vocabulary, could be very appropriate. I liken this to a scene from *A Christmas Story* where Mr. Parker can let loose with a whole string of gibberish yet you know precisely what he is saying. "You wart mundane noodle! You shotten shifter paskabah! You snort tonguer!"

I've been cursing more frequently since I got my tattoo, I have to admit. It's actually making me feel more confident. I stand a bit taller. I'm dressing better so that I can show off my tattoo and look good doing it.

Most people would not suspect I've been a badass in training for the first 50 years of my life, but now that I've turned it on, I think they get it. People who've known me a long time might have even been waiting for this.

You see, a long time ago, before I decided to buck the family history and attend university, I invested a semester in myself as a high school dropout. I thought I'd had enough of schooling, and that I knew everything I needed to know. Then I realized that in order to study anything to the extent I wanted to, I needed my diploma and so back to school I went. I studied a lot: music, teaching, business, counselling, culinary arts.

I've worked with lots of people who were down on their luck and needed a leg up, but I think for the ones who missed it, what was missing was a bit of attitude. A commitment to their own badassery.

As someone who is now a part-time badass, I am connecting with more people right now than I have in the last several years.

I am more committed to my own business, and to helping people get more of what they want out of life than ever. We're going to achieve it through some badassery, and probably a little cussing! If you're ready to take charge and make some changes, just let me know.

Dr. Pam Robertson
Conundrum Buster | Coach | Part-time Badass
www.ladybirdfiles.com
780-232-0083 pamrobertson@live.ca

Chapter 12
Reboots for Careers

Fenworth nodded. "Yes, yes. Urgent, deadly, insidious.

The world is in peril and we must rise against evil."

The old wizard released the general and patted

him on the shoulder. "Tea and cake first,

don't you think?"

Donita K. Paul, DragonQuest

⁓⧼⧽⁓

Before your tea and cake and all that business of saving the world, you've been saving yourself.

You've prepared for re-experiences by digging deeply into your core values, found a whole new way to look at your inner critics as defenders, and learned how to say no so that both sides win. Finally, some resolutions have presented themselves that make the crisis in your Boomer life digestible and contribute to your well-being. Even though you may have no attachment to wizards or dragons, you understand the mystical nature of your journey and what you have overcome. You are transcending judgments and rules that have kept you small, invisible, and ineffective. For a 50-plus woman in the process of designing her destiny to suit her refreshed body, mind, and spirit, there is definitely time for tea and cake.

While delighting in the flavour of cake you've chosen and the warmth of a healing tea, you can give thought to the next order of business: your new career. You understand you may have to relocate, give in to the inner call to quit that old job and start you own business, or jump in with both feet to attend college, reinvent the job you already have to suit the reinvented you, or finally get that degree. You might need to consider a long list of things like what to do about your ill mother, if you can stand to be so far away from your grandchildren, and whether you have the excitement necessary for embarking on a whole new career.

So, there's research to do. But where to start? This might require a lot of thinking outside of the box; that is, creative thinking about family, finances, and energy. As for energy, that's where taking care of your health and well-being comes in to give you strength to continue aligning with your core self and cultivating a positive outlook.

Imagine that everything you do from this point on fits into the you that's emerged from the work you've done in your journal as well as applied to your daily life. You are ready for re-experience.

Although you are ready, the world may not think it's ready for you—yet. What the world also may not know is that your healthy rebellion, your courage, and lustrous noble self—your re experience—will actually be of great benefit to everyone else. They'll learn.

For now, know that you may face the stigma and prejudice of being "old," the bind for women at 50-plus.

No matter how we might think of fifty as the new forty, or know that we Boomer women are actually just now ready for engaged and dynamic lives, hiring managers and corporations can see our age as problematic. Unless you come with a recommendation for the job, or with a stellar career portfolio, the likelihood of being a top contender or candidate among the younger competitors is doubtful, but not impossible. According to Stats Canada, "The majority of the Baby Boomers [are] still in the labour force," and reports indicate that the start-up markets and careers for 50 + workers have increased from 2009 to the present.[109, 110]

No matter what, skill, talent, and persistence still trump age. If you've been active in networking, volunteering, and keeping on top of trends and technology, you stand a better than average chance of successfully navigating labour markets. If you haven't, remember, it's not too late. Never ever think that you can't re-educate, rebuild, or find a new way to make use of skills you acquired over your lifetime.

Bonita J., 1964

I'm a single parent of a 17-year-old. I am staying with my widowed mother. I don't like my living situation. I plan to move in two years after my son graduates from college. I don't have a good job. It's a clerical job at a hospital. If I could I would move out now, but I don't have the money. I am looking for training in a new career field, but I don't know where to start. All I know is that I can barely survive on what I make now. My hours were cut twice and any more cuts I might have to start going to food banks. I don't have the kind of energy I had when I was younger. Is that bad? Sometimes I struggle with depression and trying to get a clear picture of what my future will be. Things are getting hard. I made some calls the other day to trade schools and private colleges. They seem like they all have something good to offer but it's not about getting a job anymore. It's about doing something that means something to me, that I would love to get up every day to be involved doing. I don't know what that is. My son said maybe I should go to his college. That would be strange. I think so. He doesn't, and maybe I should go find out. I just want to know what to do with my life.

I turned 51 this year.

As you reconnect with your authentic self, you may only just now be discovering needs that haven't been met since childhood and desires you'd forgotten you had. The Boomer housewife who never worked out of the home and suddenly finds her house too quiet, her husband too disengaged with her interests, and herself yearning to do something to make her own money, has some decisions to make. Any restless Boomer women ready for reinvention can feel overwhelmed with the choices they can or must make. Philanthropy, volunteering, mentoring, or turning avocations into skills that you can teach are possibilities for a new career path. Other Boomer women need some real solutions to potential relocation needs, financial dilemmas, and troubling uncertainty. So who can help?

Although it might not make sense, the best advice is not always available from career counsellors and consultants, who can be insensitive to your plight and only offer patronizing counsel. In some government centers here in Canada, I know Boomer women who have reported being treated as if they were more of a nuisance than human beings. Of course I can't speak to how our government workers treat all clients who come in for advice or support. Personally, I've managed to find other ways to transform low periods in my work life, through reinvention, adaptation, and relying on incredible friendships, networks, and communities, including Fabulous@50. The way you transform your work life is, of course, up to you and your own core magic and genius.

Yes, you can find support, one way or the other, but ultimately I recommend that you leave your career reboot into your own two hands. The process and practices I've laid out in this book are not always easy or comfortable. Learning mindfulness and challenging negative thoughts help us to use everything we've experienced, including failures, in service to our goals. Failing at meeting challenges isn't the worst thing that can happen. In fact, for most of us, those lessons build our mental toughness and spiritual character to rise up as shiny, dynamic women who are ready for anything, including new careers. In this chapter, I invite you to imagine a new work life or career path that will lead you to prosperity and contentment. I invite you to trust yourself, and to dream.

As you dream and reboot, know that you don't have to have your life planned down to the second. I cringe when I see someone working on a dream board but filling it with painstaking details and minutia. Details matter and you'll get there eventually. However, this chapter is about broader strokes, and dream boards, as far as I'm concerned, contain broad-strokes outlines for the future. Right now, I invite you to focus on uncovering meaningful work that brings you greater well-being. The best way to get started is to tune into your own feelings.

Crissie N., 1963

As bad as it sounds, I would get upset when someone took up a hobby and started to make money. It's pretty sorry to admit that I was jealous and petty when someone showed talent and promise in something artsy. I would quietly put myself down, and gloom around my house like I had no reason to live. I was a drama queen, but I didn't think I had any talent. Eventually, I got over myself. My husband and I were getting a divorce. The kids were going to stay with him for the summers. I took that first summer to do classes for pottery and glass blowing. I liked the crafts, but I wasn't sure that I loved them. I stayed with my regular job for the next year as a child care worker. Then I found out I had breast cancer. After recovering from the double mastectomy, I was at home alone while the kids were with their dad, and listening to a record that reminded me about when I was a teenager. I used to daydream about acting. There was nothing for me to lose if I did something about it. I joined a drama group, then volunteered to be a stage manager for our local theater. I started writing plays for kids.

Imagine my surprise when I found out that you could get paid for writing plays. My life changed dramatically, literally. Now I go across the country to schools with a troupe that acts out my plays We have discussions with the kids on some controversial topics. It is the most awesome thing I never imagined. My youngest has joined the troupe as an actor. I turned 52 years old. I've been cancer free 15 years.

In *Real Magic,* Wayne Dyer writes, "When you know and feel the miracle that you are, you begin to know and feel that nothing is impossible for you."[111] When your choices make sense to you and are aligned with your core self, no one can steer you off course. Miracles grow out of the belief that you are worthy, the trust that you can handle any issues, positive and negative, and the knowledge that love is defining the course of your life.

You may still have your job as a cashier, or for the first time you may be about to go out and pound the pavement in search of work. I say that if you've been doing your inner work, something has shifted in you. It may be a small shift, perhaps even imperceptible to others, but there is a resolve that wasn't there before. You're finally able to look in the mirror and really love that person staring back at you. Myths have been dispelled and what resonates with you intuitively calms and invigorates you at the same time.

Your brain may feel quieted from old, wild thoughts of disaster and your heart zone warm and centered. As you reboot your career and reinvent yourself, trust your feelings and trust what shows up in your body—there's lots of helpful information there for you. Check in with your body for all those tight spots, cold feet, facial twitches, or breathing changes. Take a minute to be grateful, move your limbs, and smile. Feel a new sense of flow, the willingness to allow well-being into your life, and the savouring of life's gifts.

Good. Now let's return to a familiar question, this time about that career: Now what?

The simple answer is: now it's time to use some incredible skills you already have to figure out your own reboot.

Curiosity, Intuition, and Empathy

Are you naturally curious? Do questions about people or situations bubble up to your consciousness, make you ponder, inquire, and desire to learn more about them? If you haven't already zoomed ahead, are you wondering right now what I might provide in the rest of this chapter?

Can you feel into situations and anticipate with accuracy what people want before they even describe it and through a series of compassionate questions get to the bottom of those wants?

When you've read the stories of women scattered throughout these chapters, have you felt a sense of understanding and emotional connection, even if the circumstances or situations were unfamiliar to you?

You might think that empathy, as the "vicarious experience of others' thoughts, feelings, and attitudes" isn't an important skill because you as a Boomer woman have had that all your life.[112] You might still be unsure about the value of your intuition, something you've also had your whole life, but may just be accessing now. You might think that your inner-childlike curiosity isn't all that valuable; you might have even learned that it was dangerous to cats and women. Yet according to scholars like Todd Kashdan, empathy, curiosity, and intuition rank as top skills in leadership and management, not to mention everyday life.

Kashdan, author of *Curious? Discover the Missing Ingredient to a Fulfilling Life*, writes that curiosity fuels our ability to communicate with our environment and others in a way that engages "interest and meaning."[113] While empathy drives our ability to reflect on another person's experiences and feelings, curiosity opens the ability to find novelty and possibilities within those two elements.[114] Kashdan explains that we grow exponentially if we remain open to exploration, discovery, and spontaneous experience.[115] When we ask ourselves why someone makes the choices they make and stay open to what we might uncover, we grow. We could ask ourselves why does someone who is smart, talented, and funny work at jobs that don't embrace or enhance her skills. I hear this answer a lot: *We need people to fill positions where they can.* To me, this often seems to be at a high personal cost. If we are encouraged to actively be our own human resources department and direct our investigations to jobs or careers that fulfill us, the world may just work better for everyone.

When we're at turning points and caught in the middle of crises and traumas, we may not feel energetic enough to tap into curiosity, empathy, and intuition. If we're depressed and not getting much support, or have been letting the noise of fear-based media messages and our negative inner critic get the best of our free thinking time, it may be hard to pull out of a spiritual nosedive. Even after all the work you've done up to here, you may still not feel certain when it comes to the new career path that you anticipate but can't envision how to get to. Although it might take a little energy, curiosity can be of service here.

Kashdan feels strongly that by reclaiming our natural instinct to be "curious explorers,"[116] we can connect more profoundly to what we don't know about something, and thus open up to learning about it and to new insights that expand our brains and contribute to our well-being. Shifting how you think about events, people, or beliefs and staying open to possibilities will indicate how you approach a new career. Asking yourself new questions about the how, why, when, and what of a career change or educational opportunity can put you on track for the deliciously unexpected.

Charlotte P., 1951

I have always been curious. It used to get me in trouble when I was a kid. Growing up in a strict religious household, I was often spanked for being too frank and outspoken about what I didn't understand. I wanted to know how babies were made, where they came from. Why did some take nine months after a marriage, but others took less time? I would get spanked, sent to my room, and have to do penance of some sort, like clean our family restaurant's toilets or scrub floors then go to church every afternoon and pray for forgiveness. I got pretty adept at cleaning. It wasn't expected to be successful, or run the business, or make it through high school. I almost became a nun. What stopped me was one day, I was walking home from school. I was attacked from behind, dragged behind a bush, and raped. The man was found, tried, and did his jail time. I got pregnant. I turned 14 and had the baby that my parents made me give up for adoption. This should have stopped my curiosity. Instead, I asked if I could volunteer at the hospital. They agreed. I asked so many questions the nurses would send me to different stations. I eventually got to work on the maternity floor. I got my nursing degree but after 12 years, I went for my master's in psychology and worked exclusively with unwed mothers for another 10 years. I found myself asking questions again. Something deeper was calling me, but I wasn't used to trusting my intuition. I gave into it when I also knew that I had to find my baby. I retrained as a midwife. It took 11 years to find my daughter. I will be a midwife as long as I am on this planet.

I am 64 years old.

❧

Of course, anyone who needs assurance about their finances or living arrangements may not want to deal with risk and ambiguity. That's okay. There's nothing wrong with wanting to be safe or not having the energy to get busy with exploration of a career. I'll say it again: being safe and getting well physically are your first priorities. When we are healthier, we have better access to our intuitive, curious, and empathic selves.

So if you need a break, please take one and take care of yourself.

If not, it's time to collect some new ingredients for your recipe and to practice your own curiosity, empathy, and intuition. Beyond what I offer here, know that you can find an abundance of online and other resources and tools to sharpen your resume, or tests to figure out your competencies and preferences. Let your intuition guide you to other resources you need for your own career reboot.

My intention is to help you get started with a creative and imaginative approach, so that you can craft meaning and joy into your career and life. So get your journal and pen, and get ready for some fun.

Ingredients to Gather

New Possibilities and Old Disappointments

Maintain the practice of mindfulness. Ground yourself using the palm-breathing technique or another one that works for you. Wherever you are now, get a feel for the environment you work in—home, home office, office building, or shop—and imagine what else you might like to be part of it. Would it involve working on your laptop from your bed? Will there be coffee, or tea, or cake on hand for breaks? If you are dreaming about a return to school, what is the class setting like? Imagine the career you want has already manifested and you are in your new workspace.

Also, remember that smooth sailing without any storms won't keep you sharp.[117] It's not as though leaving your current work circumstances will mean you're free from negativity or challenge ever after, but as part of your re-experience you can certainly learn new ways for navigating trouble. So go ahead and release any pre-conceived notions that you are seeking the "perfect" career or job. What we are moving towards is integrating what we know with something we didn't know or imagine before. Try the following:

Close your eyes. Breathe deeply. Feel yourself tense up. Ball up your fists. Clench your jaw. Squeeze your eyes tightly. Feel like you want to scream but fight to stay quiet. While you experience the tension, imagine your customers, co-workers, employees, fellow students, and your own voice as you get through your toughest moment at work or school. Release the tension. Breathe through your nose. Exhale through your mouth.

Did anything pop into your consciousness?

_____

_____

_____

Even if nothing entered your mind with this exercise, take a minute or two to write about something you imagine might be disappointing about a new career or job. Then take it to the next level, and imagine how you could handle this disappointment in a new way.

I know that regret and disappointment are in the same vein but in the case of regret, it's about personal choice. On the other hand, disappointment usually results from what happens to us. Disappointing things are like the rainstorm that ruined your wedding day, not getting that hoped-for promotion, or losing a 4H contest when you were sixteen. Regret is not accepting the marriage proposal or not having risked entering the contest in the first place.

If only fifty people had shown up to my first Fabulous@50 tradeshow, that would have been disappointing, but I would have lived with massive regret if I hadn't even tried to create the event. Still, I'm familiar with disappointments, and I've found wisdom in those experiences. Taking a look at our past disappointments can be useful as we learn new ways to be in the world. Disappointments test our resilience and values, and it's possible for us to emerge from them with more wisdom and courage.

So gently allow yourself to reflect a little on disappointment.

What is something I am still disappointed about that happened years ago?

_____

_____

_____

_____

If a few more disappointments cropped up into your conscious memory, write them down, but remember not to include anything that was something you decided (i.e. a regret). Then pick one of those disappointments, and ask yourself a new question:

How does this disappointment really look to you now, years later?

Research shows that we add and subtract details from past events simply because that's how memory works.[118] We can end up with quite creative, distorted recollections that differ from others' who were present at the same events. We each get some of the past right and some of it wrong. The point is, the past is in the past. So in this case of the first disappointment you recalled, if it were to happen to someone else, what advice would you give them?

This is the advice I would give them.

_____

_____

_____

_____

_____

Life is full of hurts and injustices, so we get lots of opportunities to practice responding to them. After my first event in 2009, I was devastated with disappointment at not making any money on the tradeshow. I was proud of the fact the show was well-attended but felt let down that I'd worked for over nine months and had nothing but the experience to show for my time and efforts. This was a turning point for me. I dug deep, put on my big girl panties, and raised my prices.

The search for a new job or career path can be full of disappointing twists and turns. Tension, struggle, and disappointment are normal parts of our work lives. Whether our work is raising children and running a household, running an office, or running a cash register, we know this troubling trio. We also have a more helpful threesome at our disposal. The skill trio that can circumvent the intensity of tension, struggle, and disappointment?

Curiosity, empathy, and intuition.

These skills engage all of our senses, and in combination, make us, as women, extraordinarily strong, so let's spend a little more time with each of them.

Curiosity and Decluttering

If you haven't felt your curiosity for awhile, let's start with this mantra:

I am curious. I am playful. I am naturally energized.

Remember to engage those smile muscles too. Your brain fires up and will make you feel better. As your brain does its job to make you more optimistic, try this exercise on for size.

> *If you haven't cleaned up some corners of your home, like a closet or basement, give yourself permission to groan. After you get over your discomfort or reluctance, smile, breathe deep, do some decluttering, and see if you find something that was forgotten, lost, or misplaced.*

This serves a two-fold purpose: you get prepped for re-experience and you get surprised.

If it's been a long time since you cleaned, took stock of what you had, and discarded what you didn't need anymore, you'll probably find yourself energized by the results of it. This chapter is about rebooting, which is an act of shutting things down in order to restart them again. As part of the preparation for re-experience, decluttering allows you to do just that. To delete, change, or update old programs and make space for new ones, all so that you can squarely meet your realigned self.

The second purpose of going through that file cabinet, box of papers, closet, backroom, or basement is to be surprised, to realize or find something you didn't expect. Some of this project might seem more of a noise-to-signal problem that would be easier to leave for another time, but trust that if you turn it into an expedition of discovery it won't feel like lost time.

Also, trust that I empathize with you on this. I've had to make several purges over the course of my lifetime, and I know what can surface. Once, I found it so hard to let go of that silly book I made out of a bar of soap in grade five for my grandmother. When I saw it, I instantly remembered how grateful she was for the simple things in life, how inspired I was by her gratitude for what others might see as insignificant. That soap book was a surprise reminder of the importance of gratitude.

Another time during a purge, I found a set of pearl earrings in a chest I kept in our basement. They had been hidden there by my first husband, and I believe he was going to give them to me for our first wedding anniversary. He died ten days before the date. Finding those earrings brought back a lot of sadness, but it also brought sweetness as I thought about how excited he must have been planning that surprise for me. It just happened later than he'd planned.

If you are launching yourself into a new career, job, or educational experience, I want to emphasize that the lightness you will feel when you deal with that clutter is worth it. You need all of the energy you can get to re-experience your life, so why would you want to hang onto anything that drains you or holds you back? Call in a noble friend, or a bunch of them, to help. Give away what you don't need, or better yet, have some fun and make something out of those clothes or old furniture and books with a lot of glue. No one is the boss here but you.

If you want to fire up those curiosity neural networks, don't restrict yourself in asking questions. As you go, ask them all, even the ones you think are stupid or pointless. If you don't ask, you're limiting your possibilities.

Get curious. Ask questions. Think about the answers. Ask more questions.

Hard Work, Empathy, and Intuition
I ask a lot more of myself than I do of others, and I can be quite the taskmaster of me.

I mentioned that workout regimen that leaves me hurting for a day or two after. I'm definitely not crazy about the discomfort, and you might be saying to yourself, *Why do something to hurt yourself, Dianna?*

Because I understand that I won't strengthen muscles I don't push a little further and harder once they get used to a certain amount of resistance. I hold myself to a high standard when it comes to empowering my body, mind, and soul, and I invite you to join me. This doesn't mean to throw compassion out the window. You can work hard and be kind to yourself.

If you've followed along and tried even one or two things in this book, I already know you have a strong spirit. You may have more to do, but when consistently taken, small steps make a big difference. At some point, you'll step out of the comfort zone and into the workout zone and be stunned at how far you've come. You are one powerful woman.

Right now, get back into a grounded state. Use whatever technique works for you, the one that's becoming easier to use and get you to a calm state of mind. Say this mantra out loud:

I am a feeling, sensitive, vital, and gifted woman.

In her book, *The Spiritual Power of Empathy* (2014), Cindy Dale describes empathy as "a vital pathway for continually transforming our physical experiences into spiritual lessons."[119] I agree that we can't have one without the other. Our embodied, tangible lives are tied to something bigger, and we can use our curiosity, empathy, and intuition to ask questions, come to deeper understanding of ourselves and others, and learn spiritual lessons. In that spirit, try this thought experiment.

The center of this picture is the moon. Send it compassion and love. Know that all actions lead to knowledge and meaningful work. When it is next a full moon, imagine that the entire side of the planet that sees it experiences the energy of your love and compassion for the next thirty days.

I chose this picture of the moon because it's something we all have access to, and something that inspires me. When I look up at the moon shining in the night sky, I remember that I'm part of something bigger, and that just like anyone else looking up I can soak in moonbeams of love and compassion. If this thought experiment misses for you intuitively, that is, it doesn't feel right somehow, jot down what's going on, and then answer this question.

I know I am connected to my intuition when:

_____

_____

_____

Some research in predictions has shown that things like increased heart rate and sweating palms are present when test subjects use their intuition. Kelly Turner describes a test that involved a rigged deck of cards beside a safe deck that test subjects were to draw from.[120] The decks were stacked so as to "provide big wins followed by big losses."[121] Starting after drawing the tenth card, the test subjects' palms began to sweat, on average, two to three seconds before they would draw from the rigged deck. Turner explains that the subjects who ignored these body reactions averaged drawing five times more cards from the rigged deck than those who didn't ignore their bodies before they could describe what differences they found in the two decks.[122]

These test results point to the notion that our bodies know how to warn us when something is off, better than our rational brains do. It takes some work to become aware of and attuned to your body's subtle messages, which is why throughout this book I've emphasized the importance and value of doing so. If we've been conditioned to repeatedly ignore our gut instincts—about choices, people, and situations—we have in effect been working against our own bodies, minds, and spirits. We've all heard of someone who has averted tragedy because she trusted her intuition and changed course from a planned activity, like not boarding a flight or taking a different route home, or of someone who ignored his intuition, suffered as a result, and was still lucky enough to live to tell the tale.

We each have our own work to do as we tune into mind-body signals and learn to tell the difference between what our slow, rational brain is saying after the faster, instinctual brain chimes in.[123] The takeaway here is that it's about you. If your body is always a little achy in the left ankle an hour before it rains, maybe it's time to learn to bring an umbrella with you.

Since we all have intuition, empathy, and curiosity to varying degrees, how else can we use them in service to a career reboot? Try this mantra out loud:

I am curious. I am empathic. I am intuitive.

These skills are not soft, misty-eyed dribble that some men (and women) would dismiss in favour of analysis, performance, facts, and numbers. They are powerful tools.

We Boomer women are well-equipped, and we have no use for labels and stereotypes that degrade our efforts to find meaning in our lives and work. So, with confidence in your own mega-skills, try any of these tips and ideas as you discover your steps to that new career path, job, or school:

Interview yourself. Ask interesting questions.

- *Dress up like you would for your new job. Ask yourself how it feels.*
- *Go to a place that intuitively feels like your office or school.*
- *Before you go to bed, put in a dream request to get clarity on your career.*
- *Look through your journal to find some hints about your life purpose.*
- *Feel your bodily reactions to a list of different occupations or colleges.*
- *Use the mirror technique to smile at your image. Do you see confidence? What else?*
- *Have a play meeting with noble friends. Experiment with being their boss for an afternoon.*
- *Sit in front of your computer. Ground yourself. Hit the first key that comes to mind. Follow your intuition along the path of clicks, and see where it takes you. Allow counterintuitive ideas to filter in.*
- *Take a minute holiday. Then plan a real holiday that you deserve. Let it be wild.*
- *After each exercise, set up a new interview with yourself. Ask more questions.*

185

You get the idea. What I hope you can do is allow yourself to have some fun. You can and will need to take yourself seriously later.

As you dream and play, ignore the voices that say we think we're better than anybody else, we have our heads in the clouds, or who are we trying to fool? No one breathes for you.

Take a deep breath for yourself, and realize that disappointments have made you aware of some of the important things you want in life, things you're willing to work for. As you wind your way down the path to meaningful and purposeful work, remember to gift yourself, which is exactly the subject of the next chapter.

I packed this chapter full because I sincerely wish for you to find what matters to you and adds to your well-being. Remember you can work hard and be kind to yourself.

It's time to move on, so get ready to reward yourself for all your hard work.

Noise was my Chocolate: what's yours?

I distinctly remember a time when I was proud of the fact that I could multitask in the nosiest of situations. I would pride myself for being able to read a book while the TV was blaring, my children were playing rambunctiously down the hall and the dog was barking while chasing the hissing cats. Sounds peaceful right?

How was this so? How could I filter all that was going on around me - to read and digest what I was reading?

I think the better question, is why. Why was I doing this? You see, I had become a master at managing noise. In fact the more the better. For years I would never be alone in silence with my thoughts. To ensure that I didn't have to be alone and in silence, I would simply add noise. If the house was quiet I would turn the radio and the TV on to fill the void and busy my mind.

Some who knew me when I was younger, working in a call center, might say that was why I was able to multitask so well. After all, working in a call center does take a certain amount of discipline and focus. Being able to tune others out is definitely a benefit and required to complete tasks. While working in the call center I worked with a team of seventy other people each shift. Their cubicles surrounding mine on either side; and although the cubicles were manufactured to reduce sound, I am here to tell you, mine was sound generating. The call center is not where I learned to manage and harness noise.

No, the call center had nothing to do with my ability to manage noise – nothing at all.

I used noise, as a coping mechanism. If my mind was being bombarded with noise – I wasn't afraid. Afraid of being found, discovered and therefore, I felt safer. I was actually afraid to be alone and in silence. Noise was my best friend, my go to, my comfort food – if you will.

Much as someone might use chocolate, chocolate ice cream, cake or potato chips to distract ones self. I used noise.

Noise allowed me to focus on the task at hand rather than the fear (real or imagined) or past sadness. I'm not sure when or how noise became my coping mechanism, I'm not even really sure, I knew back then that I used noise as a frock.

For decades, the last thing in the world I wanted was to be alone in silence with my thoughts. I took measures to ensure this was so — if the house was quiet I would turn on the radios and the TV — to avoid the silence.

Often when I overheard others speak about meditation and silence and how much they loved it, I couldn't understand what the draw was. Sure, I too like Yoga and Pilates — I especially liked bending myself into a human pretzel but then the instructors would spoil it — with the need for us to be silent. What was this need to be silent about? You know what they say about an idle mind?

Why did we need to go inside and reflect? After all, I was doing my darnedest to keep my frocks on and make sure no one knew anything. Silence was no where near golden for me; instead, it was frightening and threatening.

An interesting thing happened when I began writing Frock Off: Living Undisguised in 2007, silence became less a threat and more a comforting friend. I wrote in silence and during that time I began to realize I used noise to protect me as a frock.

Gradually I began to crave the peace and release silence offered. I found myself seeking ways to get quiet to just BE.

Over time the frock I once donned about silence faded away. It wasn't overnight, it would take years. Just like the frock of weight, when we use food to cope, it takes time to shed the pounds we accumulate in protection. It took time to shed my irrational belief that silence was deadly; and to replace that ill-serving frock, with the fabulous frock that silence is a gift, a time to reconnect with our heart, our purpose and our soul.

This past weekend I was sitting in silence in the early morning hours and I flashed back to a time when I would have had to fill the silence with noise. Yet here I was sitting in complete glorious, fabulously, yummy, frock-alicious silence. I celebrated with a cup of tea and rejoiced that this frock of fear that once required me to fill silence was gone forever.

Jo Dibblee
Founder, Author and Speaker
Frock Off Inc.
www.frock-off.com

Chapter 13

Re-Gifting Yourself

When someone asks you if you

want cake or pie, why not say

you want cake and pie?

—Lisa Loeb

❧

We Boomer women are notorious for giving and gifting to everyone without expecting anything in return.

See if you recognize yourself in any of these scenarios:

- Even if you would love that last piece of cake because it's your favourite and you arranged the perfect party, if someone asks for a second piece, you give it up without hesitation.
- Receiving a compliment feels excruciatingly uncomfortable no matter how well deserved. When the attention turns to you, you cringe or turn beet red.
- You live your life so often on the defensive that even when someone offers kindness, genuine praise, or recognition for your work, you snap back with meanness.
- You've contributed massive volunteer hours at school events, baked and donated the results, and supplied anything else that's needed. You've gladly handed out money when you had it. You still work tirelessly to give back to your community and to causes you believe in, and you don't expect anything in return, not even a compliment. That's not why you do it anyway. It's all noble service. So why do you feel so empty?
- Your husband and children, family and friends are first priority. You don't really need anything for yourself. Besides, that would be selfish.
- You work yourself to the point of exhaustion for a party or event or meal, then when it's all over, minimize any compliments you receive. You brush them off with an, "Oh, it was nothing."
- When you were a little girl, you were taught to believe you had little or no worth, and you learned to downplay your successes, blend into the background, and remain invisible until called upon. As an adult…well, you find that old habits are hard to break.
- Praise? If in the midst of your crisis, you can get out of bed in the morning, find quiet time and just get to a point where you feel okay, that will be plenty, thank you very much.

Whether any of the above ring true for you or not, I want something different for you. I want you to thrive. I want you to learn to genuinely accept rewards and praise. To allow yourself gifts that reflect the energy, quality, and hard work you put into achieving goals.

This chapter is about you getting that big beautiful cake I described at the beginning of this book, just for you, and not only learning to say thank you very much but also learning to enjoy it. This chapter is about receiving, recognition, and rewards, all for you.

Receive

It's time to stop minimizing what we offer or shying away from compliments like they're poison ivy. What you offer is not nothing. You planned, arranged, cooked, cleaned, sweat, charmed, and one way or the other, made it all happen, whatever it happens to be today. Want to know what I call a Boomer woman who shuns recognition for anything she does, makes sure that everyone else is happy first, and drops whatever she was doing to give herself empty all over again?

Gift-challenged.

I want you to be gift receiving geniuses. I want you to learn how to prioritize yourself and to say no when you need to. Feel free to review Chapter 11 if you're feeling like a little healthy rebellion is in order.

As a Boomer woman, you may have trouble with placing value on your time and efforts, thinking of yourself as special, and especially saying no to requests that put you in a bind. I would offer that if you can't say no because it means saying yes to something that's important to you, then you can at least learn how to take something back for your hard work. For starters, take the compliments that you earn with dignity. Treat them as natural consequences of the efforts you made. Those around you, your children especially, will learn how to follow your example. If we don't value ourselves and we belittle our own work, our daughters, our granddaughters, will pick up on that, and that becomes the legacy we leave for them.

Self-deprecation when it comes to achievements reflects larger societal expectations of how women are supposed to entertain rewards for efforts, of what it means to be a "good woman." Society says it's admirable if you're a woman who isn't conspicuous with your power, capabilities, or feminine wisdom. I say those are the exact ways women nourish this world and our power, capabilities, and wisdom should be celebrated and honoured by others and by us.

We Boomer women are mentally tough and spiritually powerful, and this maturity must not be hidden by fear. We must respect our changing bodies, minds, and souls as wondrous gifts. After decades of denying our authentic selves, we need to realize that giving is not only a selfless act, and that giving doesn't have to mean we never get anything.

We can have the cake and the pie, and we certainly can give and receive.

Recognition

Let's talk about accepting honour, praise, and recognition, which can mean everything from ceremonies, plaques, and monetary awards to simple encouragement and the reassurance of a warm hug from someone who sees you're on the right path and wants you to know you're supported.

In earlier chapters, I've mentioned that not everyone wants you to change. You'll probably find that those who are uncomfortable with you changing will be even more uncomfortable if you're rewarded for it. They're happy to help you, but the help is conditional. You can't rock the boat too much.

If you do, they might have to wake up too and not everyone wants to do that. If you find yourself in this situation, it's time to seek out some noble friends who are willing to recognize and celebrate you and your success.

The community of Fabulous@50 exists to empower women and their success. Women have often been conditioned to believe that when someone wins, someone else has to lose, or when someone else is celebrated, someone else has to feel small. None of that is true. I believe in win-win. It's the only way that makes any sense because we can see how far the win-lose strategies have gotten the world.

As the saying goes, hard work pays off. Or at least it should. When you put your wholehearted effort into something, why would you need to be so humble that you can't accept recognition for it? Required female self-loathing is a false construct that no longer serves the global village. Our effort, our value, our womanhood is not nothing. Boomer women must learn new ways to see and value themselves, and to fight for their right to be recognized.

Terri Rose B., 1961

I had always wanted to be a filmmaker. I worked fulltime. Money was tight. My boyfriend wasn't working, and I was pulling all the weight financially. He wanted to be an actor. I wanted to make films. It worked for that reason, but I'm not sure he loved me. What mattered is that when I did find money to make the first film, he did everything to provide anything I needed by way of help. As long as I had the money. Distribution is the toughest part of movie making. I thought about it, found a lady to help with it, and created a film festival. It was a three-day event.I pretty much did everything. The other lady did what I told her, but I had kept most of the stuff to do myself. My boyfriend had found a job by then so he wasn't available. At the end of it, on the third day after I had clean up left,someone came by to say that they heard that it sucked. I looked at them. I had nothing to say. That was the only thing I heard about it. That was 13 years ago. I am not trying to be a filmmaker anymore. I have a decent business that is a rental agency for parties and catering. I am single.
This year I will be turning 54 years old.

~⧢~

As hard as the battle is to ensure we women are gifted back with honours and awards, it's still a worthy fight. Some years back I was blown away by being selected for the YWCA Women of Distinction Award in the Turning Point category.[124]

If anyone had told me twelve years before that this was going to happen to *me*, Dianna, I would have laughed, waved it off, and said, "Not in a million years."

Being the center of attention is not something I'm comfortable with. Even now, after a few wonderful, magical moments of accepting recognition for working with fundraisers and for building the Fabulous@50 community to empower women, I'm still learning to receive these honours with grace and dignity instead of disregard.

Why do I still work at it? Because doing so aligns me with my core values.

At that YWCA awards event, I felt humbled by the women next to me, but I also felt proud of having done something helpful—something that reflects my core magic—to get there. That evening I took the opportunity to meet with the recipient of the Lois E. Hole Award, Margaret-Ann Amour, also named one of Canada's most powerful women in 2010.[125] A distinguished scientist and advocate for creating more opportunities for women to enter the science, technology, and engineering fields, at 70-plus years strong Amour remains steadfast in her commitment.[126]

I was deeply honoured by the opportunity to speak with her, and I told her I wished she could have been a mentor to me when I was a young woman. I had the feeling that with the right guidance, I could have done so much more.

Amour graciously responded, "Dear, you did the best you could with what you had." I was moved to tears with that acknowledgment. She had said exactly the words I needed to hear, and her words rang true for me.

That's the truth for all of us. It's the truth for our parents, our ancestors before them, and on down the line. That why I feel that ultimately, all we can do is honour them, forgive them, and love them. They did the best with what they had physically, mentally, emotionally, and spiritually.

So can you. Doing the best you can with what you have means that you can choose to celebrate, learn, embrace, enhance, and delight in your magic, transformation, and well-being.

We also need to learn that we don't always have to wait for others to recognize us. It's okay to ask for the acknowledgment we want and need.

How many of you Boomer women are uncomfortable asking for something for yourselves? Does your mouth get dry when you finally get up the nerve to ask for a raise? You have your perfect opportunity, a meeting with the boss. You have in mind to ask for a $2.00 an hour raise. The file folder you hold has all the background to support your arguments for how well you've handled the increase in workload during the last six months.

He shakes his head. The budget can't take a hit like that. All he can offer is a fifty cent increase, but only after another six months.

Sometimes we won't get the answer or acknowledgment we want, but I say the asking is the most important part. It takes courage to finally express our wants. It takes courage to break through guilt or the fear of being labelled a bitch and to assert ourselves anyway.

I am here to encourage you to release the conditioning that has made us yes-women who have yet to reward ourselves.

The question now is how do we make sure that this new phase of manifesting our dreams, goals, and wishes comes with more than a few perks?

Anita F., 1957

My family is huge on both sides. Everyone is having kids, getting married, anniversaries, and there have been funerals too. It seems that they all looked to me for organizing any party or event. I was a stay-at-homer. I have seven of my own kids that are all big eaters and huge fans of my baking. So is my husband. I never had a want or need that was more important than my family. When my husband got sick with heart disease and nearly died, we needed to tone down all that baking, sweets, and savoury food that was no good for him. Now I was pretty heavy myself. I hadn't thought about my own health until it became time to change. A lot things had to go from our fridge and from our lifestyles. He had to change his job too. It meant less money for us. I had to rethink everything that I was spending, that included all the volunteer work I was doing at the nursing home. I was pretty sure that I wanted to spend some years with my loving husband doing things we had put off for decades because we spent everything on our families. You know, I thought they would have understood what we should do for ourselves. Some of them still don't talk to me after four years. This year we are going to Niagara Falls. I am 58 years old this year.

We've taken an honest look at ourselves: where we've come from, where we are, and where we're going. We've worked on new recipes for cakes we'll actually enjoy, eating and being. We've done the exercises, and some of them were hard. A review of our journals has revealed insights and patterns that we can use in service to our re-experiences. We are courageous, whip-smart, determined, and beautiful.

We are ready to be treated handsomely.

Reward Systems

It's hard to pat yourself on your own back, unless of course you are that flexible.

Some 50-plus women may be that in-shape and others of us might not. Some of us have worked exercise into our regular routines and changed the way we nourish ourselves with food and some of us have not.

There is no right or wrong way to achieve your goals for well-being or otherwise. We all have full plates. Most of us are still working. The majority of us have aging parents with needs, and some of us will have the added responsibility as guardians of young grandchildren in our homes.

Due to hormonal fluctuation, our bodies are changing and challenging. I want to repeat that most of us have also done the best we could with what we had. Rightly so, many of us don't actually feel responsible when we see commentary that Boomers are responsible for the world being so messed up.[127]

For any who want to lay blame, point fingers, and rally fault-finding missions that don't address what we can do to improve, change, and transform a few things that matter to us collectively and individually, I respectfully suggest that you practice some mindfulness techniques and get back to me.

Way too much energy gets wasted, and we Boomer women need it. I say we also need some blessed assistance to get through our crises. And a few heart-warming rewards. There is nothing self-indulgent or foolish about treating ourselves. We need to adopt healthy reward systems that motivate and lovingly build us up, and below you'll find plenty of ingredients to serve that purpose.

This is the easy part of what has been a long journey. If you've been doing the work earnestly and are proud of what you've accomplished, then get to it. Even if you haven't, even if your accomplishments feel small or imperfect, please, still give yourself a pat on the back for what you have done. If you don't already have one in place, it's time to develop a regular reward system for yourself, and to make it thoughtful and thorough. Grabbing the first crumb is a start, but remember you deserve a piece of cake and a piece of pie.

Ingredients to Gather

Below are three categories, with starter ideas for gifts and treats, to get you started with your own reward system. Add your own rewards, ask for some ideas, surf the net, and get curious about different ways to delight your new you. Remember mindfulness to get you grounded, and try the smile technique to get that neural happiness flow ignited and yourself ready for reward.

REWARDS FOR THE BODY

Practice twerking.

(If you don't know what this is, watch a you tube video.

When you do, your laughter might be the real reward.)

Go for a walk, but try walking like a model on the catwalk.

Take a nap.

(All that twerking and cat walking is exhausting!)

Go to the park and swing on a swing.

What's your body reward?

_____

_____

_____

_____

REWARDS FOR THE MIND

Write yourself a love letter.

(Or copy some beautiful poetry and imagine you authored it to you.)

Develop a rewards program for yourself.

(Make it as fun and creative as you can.)

Speak your mind.

(It doesn't have to be to anyone but your cell phone or a plant.)

Renew an old hobby.

What's your mind reward?

_____

_____

_____

_____

_____

_____

_____

REWARDS FOR THE SOUL

Create a kindness jar.

(Every time you are kind to yourself or others,

make a note and drop it in the jar.)

Invite friends to have a hug-fest.

(Afterwards, everyone can share a recent kindness;

add those to your jar.)

Activate your healing powers.

(Breathe a warm breath into the palm of your hand,

listen to what your body needs, and act on that.)

Stay one whole day in your pyjamas, don't make the bed, and eat cake.

(Self-explanatory).

What's your soul reward?

_____

_____

_____

_____

_____

_____

_____

_____

_____

_____

I hope these ideas surprised you and brought a smile to your face. I do realize that rewards may not heal or lessen the urgency of your crisis. From experience, I also know that moments in which I gift myself do release some tension and open a space for love.

If like me, you like movies, you might add a few suggestions to your rewards list from the book *Positive Psychology at the Movies 2* (2014). *One is Field of Dreams* and the other is *Groundhog Day*.[128] *In Field of Dreams*, you encounter the story of someone building something that no one else believes in because they can't see it, and having to keep working at getting it right regardless, all of which is what most transformational work is about. What I love about both of these movies is that they end on a positive note.

Wherever your life may be on the stress continuum, I encourage you to do what you can to lift your mood. You can find truly simple ways to get a little lift, and while I won't say it's not hard work, learning to smile your way out of a minute or two of misery puts you on the path of mastering the rest with grace.

We're about to move on to the final chapter in this book, and I'm so excited for you. It's time for us to tie up some loose ends, and it's time for you to get ready for the world to see and celebrate you. You are ready for success, magic,

Reflections of a Boomer Woman

❧

A Taste for Adventure

If you had told me 8 years ago that I would be a successful owner of a wine and spirits store in Edmonton, I would have laughed at you.

8 years ago, I was happily living in Vancouver. I moved to the west coast from Montreal when I was 19 and enjoyed a wonderful, long career in the travel industry, working for CP Air and Cathay Pacific Airways in the golden years of airlines, followed by management positions with international tour operators. I have travelled the world for pleasure and work, sat on boards in the industry and enjoyed teaching part time at the Canadian Tourism College.

8 years ago, contracts Grant and I had were starting to shrink as were a lot of opportunities in the travel business. I re-trained in interior design and started up a small business while keeping a few travel contracts. When Grant was preparing a business plan to sell a store in Edmonton for someone, I didn't take much notice.

After weeks of analyzing data, researching etc. he came to me and said "We love wine, perhaps we should look at this business." Right, Grant, it's in Edmonton.

In January 2007, he convinced me to fly to Edmonton and check out the store. We arrived on a sunny -35c day in our thin, unlined leather coats. We were shocked when we saw the state of the store at West Edmonton Mall. It was filthy, had no stock, was not inviting at all. We met with the mall leasers before heading home.

Seeing the place got my creative juices flowing along with the excitement entrepreneurs get when starting up something new. We low-balled an offer, got rejected, countered, but before we had time to consider the next offer, we received a call to say the owner was being evicted from the mall!

In February 2007, Don Ghermezian called. Said he knew we were interested in the store and if we could put a "damn good " liquor store in, we could sign up a lease.

The next few months were a blur. Licences, renovators, selling a home, etc. We drove to Edmonton like the Beverley Hillbillies, lived in the Holiday Inn while renovating and setting up the store while looking for somewhere permanent to live. We opened July 1 2007.

We've worked extremely hard to create a strong, independent business in a tricky industry. Margins are small, chain stores abound.

Many doubted our decision to open in one of the world's largest shopping malls, where we learned locals don't like to go, but our research determined we could be a destination store in a destination mall. We've chosen to carry specialty products, unique accessories and wines in an attractive environment. We work as marketers not just retailers. We listen to our customers and stock items chain stores choose not to. We've grown a good local customer base through our email newsletters, social media and offer reserved parking outside Entrance 58 at the mall for added convenience for our shoppers.

We proudly won Liquor Retailer of the Year in 2009, I have educated myself achieving Level ll Sommelier designation and am a Certified French Wine Scholar. We have 5 knowledgeable people working with us. We teach Wine classes, host tastings and events as well as support local businesses and charities with their social requirements. We are now combining our travel passion with wine and doing wine tours, the first one a Viking River Cruise to Bordeaux in 2014, Okanagan in 2015 and South Africa Winelands and Wildlife planned for September 2016.

It's not easy moving to a new city, starting a new business, and making new friends in mid-life, but Grant and I are happy we took the leap. Edmonton is a welcoming environment in which to do this even though I still do miss the west coast.

Alison Phillips
President/ Co-Owner Aligra Wine & Spirits
www.aligrawineandspirits.com

Chapter 14
Recharged and Ready to Rock

Is it better to be feared or loved?

Loved, because people associate with you because they want to,

not because they need to. We need to eat beets, but we want to eat cake.

Be the cake of the world.

Jarod Kintz, *Xazaqazax*

❧

This moment is just for you.

You've worked hard. You've looked honestly at your life and asked, how can this be better? In response you've slowed down enough to reconsider what you thought you knew and learned how to savour and re-experience the best of your life.

Words of inner and outer critics can't change your mind, stop your heart, or deny your spirit. When you ask yourself, Now what? you're confident that it's not too late for you to realize your forgotten dreams. Fear, anger and confusion give way to something new. Hopefulness. Determination. And did I see a smile there, brightening up your neural pathways?

You know you're not alone. You have a noble friend or two or more at your side, and you're ready to attend some parties, have some fun, and enjoy your feminine self.

Here at your magical turning point you are fully awake, recharged, and ready. Some of you are ready to save the world and some of you to finally save yourselves. Both are cause for celebration. So celebrate in whatever style you choose; trust yourself to know what you enjoy, and then let yourself enjoy it.

As we started this adventure together, I shared with you how food was love in the home where I grew up, how even when I visited as an adult, I always found something delicious to nibble on and left with a package of treats for later. I hope this book has been like that and continues to be so for you—a place you can come to enjoy tasty bites of information and inspiration, and a place you can leave with treats to savour later when the time is right.

So as you reach the end of this book, congratulations! I'm here to give you a virtual hug and step away from the spotlight. It's all yours.

The flavour of cake that you imagined yourself at the beginning of your journey may have changed. You may no longer feel like an angel food but are now a thicker-textured white cake, marbled with chocolate. Or you may have no room left for sugary flavours made from refined flours. You may feel more like a honey-sweetened, gluten-free red velvet cupcake, or a brown rice cake, helping you to bypass the bloated gut and low-energy reactions you get when you eat the sweet treats you used to love. That may be a big shift for you.

Take heart that once you establish healthy daily routines for diet, exercise, and mental rejuvenation, things get easier.

Recognizing the physical energy drains of some foods you eat, as well as of the relationships that don't serve your greater good, and making a conscious effort to transform in a way that fits and works for you, contribute to your recharging.

Many of the issues I've addressed in this book came from my own experiences that needed deeper investigation, from stress to myths to forgiveness to legacy and healthy rebellion. I also included tools and skills that have been invaluable to me, like intuition. At times, I've moved through crises with nothing but the power and wisdom of my own inner voice to guide me. I hope these pages have reinforced your own trust in your internal guidance system, one that communicates in ways that are unique to you and don't always rely on logic. The symbols and images that bubble up in your consciousness may be ancient, but they are also particular to you in the present moment. Courageous, lustrous, heroic you.

Unfortunately, most of us weren't schooled to recognize the hero's journey outside of and within ourselves, a journey that's repeated itself through all of human history. According to the late Joseph Campbell, the leading scholar on mythology and anthropology in the twentieth century, "The hero is the one who comes to participate in life courageously and decently."[129] Campbell did not distinguish the hero as male or female because we all share the history of humankind and the collective memories from the first storytellers. You as a Boomer woman are your own hero. You've battled and toiled to find your way back from crisis, tragedy, or the stress and challenge of big changes.

Because I know each of our journeys are different, I've done what I could to suspend my judgments here. Throughout this book, I've done my best to share some of the endless variations of circumstances and choices in Boomer women's lives. The Boomer woman with financial stability will not experience the same stresses as a Boomer woman in poverty. However, both can reach turning points, have tough decisions to make, and experience the symptoms and effects of stress. It's easy to play the comparison, blame, or victim games, but these do not lead to thriving.

So, we could live in envy, jealousy, and regret, or we can live the last bit of it like we are in a Magic Mike XXL movie, filled with sexy dancing men not afraid of pleasing mature and fearless Boomer women. Now that we're recharged and ready to rock, let's not undervalue our sexuality and the expression of it by being prudish and conservative. My hope is that Boomer women like me are over the extremes of censorship and realize the real battle is for a civilized, ethical, and compassionate world. I know I'm mixing male strippers in with ethics and compassion, but hear me out.

Teresa W., 1951
My sister and I grew up in the same household always fighting. I realize that sisters can do that. She was younger, angrier, and found a life with drugs, violent men, and living on the edge got her more attention than being happily married with a growing family like I had. She used to bring a lot of drama with her on holidays that included screaming at me that I always thought I was better than her.

This year she is turning 62, but honestly she looks twenty years older from the last time I saw her at our 86-year-old dad's house. She is legally blind, walks with a cane, and lives alone. She was asking him for money. When I walked in she started to scream at my dad that I was always his favourite and left. I was in customer service jobs. My husband was a welder. We did alright. Our kids and grandkids keep us happy. We have come by our retirement honestly, I feel. My sister hates me, but I never hated her. I never knew how to help her. On my birthday, my husband it taking me fishing to our favourite lake. This year I turned 64.

❧

It's hard to follow a perfectly straight path through the wide spectrum of options, choices, and decisions that can lead to a productive, creative, and satisfying life. We wonderful creatures made of sweet, yummy goodness deserve to be curious explorers and experience life with all the fun, sensuousness, and companionship available to us. We still have decades left to live. Are we going to live them restrained and repressed in isolation? If you've come this far with me, I don't think so.

I have some serious points to make, but I also charge myself with the responsibility to temper my existence with humour, the occasional outrageous fun, and the willingness to play devilish pranks on social conventions. I challenge you to join me.

Yes, we will continue to experience challenge, struggle, and even crises, but we can also commit to joy and to remembering that we are part of a world that relies on us to be our best selves.

In *Beyond Religion* (2011), the Dalai Lama encourages our pursuit of happiness and contentment within the context of ethical awareness and the cultivation of inner values that do not undermine our interdependence.[130] It took me many years to grasp the concept of being interdependent. I was that woman…you know, the one who stubbornly could do everything by herself. Not any more. Working together for the good of anything, makes so much more sense to me, than slugging it out alone. The Dalai Lama makes his case for building a "sustainable and universal approach to ethics, inner values, and personal integrity" where he talks about "transcending religion."[131]

Do I want to take up that banner with him? Not really. I know what I believe, and God is in it. At this point in my life I'm comfortable with that and have no desire to debate secular or non-secular issues. Neither do I want to be known only as a woman holding up some five-dollar bills and screaming for hard-bodied male dancers to come over to my table for a lap dance. Still, if that's what I happen to choose to spend my money on, I'm grown and capable and not looking for approval.

Come on. Boomer women are a complex bunch!

Rosanna D., 1964

It left scars on bodies, deeply wounded spirits of our mothers, fathers, and grandparents. Residential school was an open secret that no one talked about in our communities for decades, a silence that cut deep into families—including mine. It was only four years ago that I first heard my mother's residential school story. She was five years old when she was taken and held in Catholic-run schools until she was a young woman. Never to see her parents again, she was stripped of everything that made her Cree. My mother suffered abuse, neglect, and faced starvation before being discarded in a world she was ill-equipped for. Still, she survived. She told her story. A stranger to me before, I now understand why as a child, my mother could not hug me and say, "I love you," why she drank so much, and why she would often cry. I am a journalist and activist. I have yet to formulate what I expect for the future of my daughter and grandchildren. I am a Canadian, an Indian woman, and a global citizen. The struggle to be heard, understood, and have equal justice is exhausting. But I will keep on. I don't spend all my days immersed in my social commitment. I eat, drink, dance, and enjoy what I can with the time I have to do it. I love my mom. I cry for her. I maintain that one day, things will right themselves.

This year I turn 51.

For example, I live in one of Canada's wealthier provinces. I have overcome financial struggles through hard work and learning how to ask for the help and expertise of others. At the same time, I'm familiar with the struggles of our Native population and their losses of culture and identity in the decades they experienced Residential schools after colonization.[132] My heart breaks for the plight of traumatized Aboriginal children, forced from their homes and families. What kind of legacy are we leaving them? The scars and trauma that many still carry inside, particularly those who are now Boomer women, demand my attention and compassion.

Fabulous@50 offers so much for every woman. There are no barriers to becoming part of this community that serves empowerment through connection to other 50-plus women. Despite the horrors of the past, I want the spirit of living with joy, compassion, and wonder to be the present and future of Boomer women. I contend that no matter how deeply we are wounded, if we are still breathing we can choose how to live out the next year or years we have being productive, outrageous, fun loving, sensuous, wise, strong, noble, and compassionate.

Yes, we can be all those things, even if marketers aren't using those descriptors for our cohort of Boomers as often as they should. I say they better start looking at what those words mean to create the best products and services that satisfy Boomer women, because we are ready to rock.

By rock, I mean celebrate!

You've come so far. If you've honoured your processes by hearing your own story, learned a few things that have shifted you to a more positive outlook, and made changes in service to your health and wholeness, it's onward to well-being. You may have a few more hurdles to overcome, but you've staged a comeback. Focusing on building positive relationships, vitality, and purpose into your work, and play, leads to renewal and satisfaction. You are refreshed.

That doesn't necessarily mean you're brimming with energy to run a marathon or even go after that cleaning chore you meant to get to once you finished Chapter 12. You know what you need to do, and you know how to listen to your intuition, which will alert you when it's time to do those things. Throughout this book, I know I've probably offered just as many reminders as new ideas to you, and I know that this book is just the tip of the iceberg in terms of opportunities for personal growth. I encourage you to follow your inner knowing and find whatever fantastic workshops, seminars, books, and trainings speak to your heart. So many possibilities are available to you.

At the end of the day or the end of this book, if all you're ready to do is settle back into your routine of being in a funk, a little bit angry at everything, and stuffing your loneliness with an extra helping of strawberry yogurt, cocoa puffs, and chocolate chips mixed together and washed down with a Diet Pepsi, go back to the beginning of this chapter and reread the opening quote from Jarod Kintz. Then ask yourself this: *Do I want to be the cake of the world or a beet?*

Sure, both are good. I eat beets, beet greens, turnips, Brussels sprouts, and all kinds of cake—just not at the same time. (That's celebrating my choices and avoiding an upset stomach). The point is, when you have a choice, like you do right now at your magical turning point, do you want to choose fear or love? I urge you to choose love.

If you're depressed and not feeling especially pretty, brave, or ready to put out the extra energy to celebrate your small successes, because you still have doubt, the crisis is not over, and some results of your efforts are not yet clear, I ask you, instead of Now what? a new question: So what?

We started this book together, you and I, as spiritual warriors. I shared with you my own tragedy, illness, divorce, and financial crisis and how I spent decades learning about myself. What propelled me forward? I put faith and trust in my intuition, resilience, and optimism, as well as some awesome family and friends for support. Even if I didn't want to, many times, I did it anyway. Getting out of your own funk will require concentrated effort to pick a day this week, or this weekend, get dressed to the nines, find a few noble friends, and rock the house.

It could be your house. Have some friends over for a poker game, or a twerking contest, even if you've never done either. Have some fun! Life can crush us if we let it. We'll always have hard work to do, crises are not one-time affairs, injustice is everywhere, and some days are going to be bad no matter how hard we try to make them good. That's the package deal that comes with this Earth cruise experience.

We are Boomer women, 50-plus dynamos who have survived numerous attempts to silence our voices, but they can't keep us quiet any longer. Crisis has made us that much more resilient, wiser, and prepared to say no to what holds us back and yes to all we are and can be.

I know will never stop learning. I will keep my mind open to new ideas.

In the last month of working on this book, I asked myself: *Have I done enough? How can it be better?* Since you're reading it I obviously didn't let that stop me. Instead, I'm committed to continuing to learn and grow and to share what I learn with you. The legacy I want to leave keeps me moving and thinking ahead, and I hope the same for you.

I will push myself to master things about myself that I know can be re-experienced because I see things differently now than I did five, ten, twenty or thirty years ago. I make mistakes. I have met and continue to meet accomplished and talented Boomer women who I feel humbled standing beside. Notice that I feel humbled, but that also doesn't stop me from acting on my dreams and living my purpose.

Anyone of my noble friends will tell you that I started Fabulous@50 because I saw a need, and I wanted to help women. I want to see anyone who is willing, who truly wants it for herself, to live her dreams, wishes, and goals, with the kind of power that is our birthright as women. There is so much yet to do and experience. We're just getting warmed up! So get your journal and pen; I have a few more ingredients to share.

Ingredients to Gather

A Musical Celebration and a Challenge to Reach Out

We each have a unique set of needs, values, wants, goals, and personal preferences, that affect how we live and how we like to celebrate. Some of us like rock n' roll, country-western, jazz, or an eclectic mix of pop, folk, urban, and metal. To enjoy music, we can listen, dance, play an instrument, or sing along as in karaoke. Here is an exercise that you can do to ground yourself, no matter how messed up or churning you feel inside.

Get online and go to this link:

https://www.youtube.com/watch?v=4FZbcoWrUsw

In the spirit of allowing you to be a curious explorer, I won't give away the name of the song or the artist. Just use the above link—type it in exactly as you see it in your search bar—and have a listen. Okay, I will give this much of a hint, in the form of a question: Who lets love open a door?

Here's a special offer for you who have come this far: find the name of the song and the singer, email me, and you'll receive a gift for being a good sport.[133]

If you don't feel like going online or can't for some reason, write out the lyrics of one your favourite songs in your journal, starting the lyrics before you listen to the song. Of course, I suggest a song that you find uplifting and positive, one that makes you want to jump up and dance. Say the words aloud.

Then if you have the song handy, play it for yourself. Take as much time as you want to write your feelings, thoughts, dreams that pop up afterwards.

If you felt like dancing when you played the song, did you dance?

Or did you crater to some lethargic wimpiness? Did the song end up being sadder than you remembered it? If it was, take some time to listen to the one I suggested above. It comes straight out of our earlier adulthood, 1980.

I hope you enjoyed it, and of course I won't know unless you reach out and contact me at love@fabulouat50.com. I challenge you not just to enjoy a musical celebration, but also to reach out and engage, with me and others who are ready to be your noble friends.

Trust that you can overcome so much when you participate. Find ways to be involved with others. Yes, there are ways to give back to your community with volunteer activities and those are important, but I'm also encouraging you to let loose, celebrate your new you with other Boomer women, and possibly share some delightful nostalgia.

Some of the music from our day was pretty damn good. What do we hear when we shop at the malls? It's rock music that was written when we were younger. No matter how hard things have been, honestly, make yourself get up and have a dance to a piece of music that lifts you up.

One of my Boomer women remembers the song "Ballroom Blitz" when she and her friends would get together for parties. If that song doesn't fire a room up, I don't know what would. For me it's the song "What a Feeling" from the movie *Flashdance*. It's a song of empowerment and about a woman coming into her own. I actually have so many songs like this, I could dance all day!

Music is healing in so many ways. Even if you don't usually listen to music, try making it part of your reward and recharge. In the "Resources" section, I've also included some links to healing music for meditation and relaxation.

Take Inventory

With all of the reflection and work you've done, now is a great time to do an inventory of what you feel recharged and ready for.

This is what I am ready to take on:

_____

_____

_____

_____

_____

Whatever you identify as the things you are ready to tackle, remember to break them down into steps. Pick one thing you're ready for, and try breaking it down here:

_____

_____

_____

You might also make your inventory one of curiosity exploration rather than a list of actions.[134] You could play with the image above to come up with three questions that open up possibilities. For instance, *How might I become part of a theatre group? Or ask about whatever sparks your particular curiosity.*

I recently met a gentleman who was a nude model. I was very curious as to how he got into the profession and why. I asked him dozens of questions and he gave me the pros and the cons of this unusual career. Whether I ever go any further with it or not, it really opened my mind up to another possibility. Remember, resorting to curiosity may be one of the most helpful techniques to break out of a pattern of thoughts that may not be helpful. You could always use it to explore what inspired the writer of your favourite song. Even if you've heard them explain why, imagine another reason for it. Make believe a scenario that turns the song into a whole other experience when you listen to it again.

If you're stuck with your inventory, ask yourself some questions to get back to that core magic that's been in you all along.

What haven't I done for a long time I used to have fun doing?

_____

_____

_____

_____

_____

_____

You might revisit a past activity that was a little wild or maybe risqué. If you had a problem with addictions, and you've beaten that, congratulate yourself. No need to repeat those behaviours. Instead, find an activity you did when you were a very young child, remember the positive feeling you had when you did that activity, and let it sink in. Perhaps you liked to toboggan or climb trees. Let it be anything that wasn't about substance taking, because those experiences are not natural activations of our neural networks.

However, the research shows that a smile can trigger our brains into a positive loop as easily as a helping of dark chocolate or a run around the block.[135] The reality is that some pretty simple things are all it takes to get us in a positive mood and ready for fun. So start simple. Ground yourself with the palm-breathing technique. Smile at yourself in the mirror. Break up your sitting time with rhythmic movements. Turn off the television when it's fear-mongering news. Make a friend of the inner critic who may have always been there to protect you. These small actions can make a huge difference in your level of optimism and awareness, and your preparedness to rock.

If I had only one thing to celebrate today, it would be this.

_____

_____

_____

_____

Celebration and gratitude are fantastic companions, who actually have a lot in common. Finding many ways to be grateful is a celebration of our human spirit and a belief in human goodness. I know I've invited you to use your pen and journal often throughout this book. I want to add: don't worry about having to write things down; you can just as easily say them out loud. Writing just happens to be a wonderful way to stay brain-healthy. It's not a have to to keep your journal or write things down, it's a can do healthy habit. I trust you can find plenty of others to add to your own ingredient list!

Is there something that still nags at me?

_____

_____

_____

_____

_____

_____

_____

_____

Whatever it is, the issue that cropped up, would it stop you from celebrating? If you answer yes, follow your intuition to whatever you need to deal with it, maybe by reviewing a previous chapter in this book, maybe otherwise.

If you can answer no, then I would drop it into a curious exploration pile for later and busy yourself with making plans for a party. Speaking of which, I really would love to hear from you. Maybe we can make some kind of arrangements to celebrate at a Fabulous@50 event. Please consider getting in touch to discuss possibilities for all kinds of ideas, creativity, and projects. I'm always up for talking about celebrations, overcoming, turning points, and all the things that led me to write this book.

Be the Baker

This is the final chapter but not the final curtain for you who are—ready to expand, rise up, and detach from crisis or trauma in a healthy, liberating kind of way. I've invited you to borrow my recipe, and I've offered you ingredients, but in the end you are the baker, and you get to decide what goes into the recipe for you.

As Boomer women, we know that we are responsible for balancing and re-experiencing our lives. No one owns the air we take into our bodies. While we deal with everything, we continue to breathe, and our breath and core values belong to us. We'll still have to handle the mess of daily life, but we've also become aware that we deserve to celebrate all of it—our successes, failures, missed opportunities, and our magic.

You have lots of years left to shine, break free from the mold, find a new purpose, and to age with dignity, grace, and well-being.

When we began I told you that I wrote this book for my grandmother and for any and all women who have felt isolated and inadequate, in any way. My greatest hope is that you reach these final pages knowing you are not alone and feeling as incredible and powerful as you are.

May this book continue to be a buoyant message of endless possibilities and hope for your bright future and may it be one you pass along to other women who need balance and support, other women who are crying out: _Now what?_

It has been an absolute pleasure to share this book with you, and to be a part of your _magical turning point_ and your bold new steps into a fabulous and freshly re-experienced life.

Notes and Definitions

Chapter 1

1. N.a., April, 2015, www.proflowers.com The Origin of Birthday Cake and Candles, http://www.proflowers.com/blog/origin-of-birthday-cake-and-birthday-candles

2. Friedman, M., June, 2010, Marketers Should Not Ignore the She-Conomy, http://emsincorporated.com, http://emsincorporated.com/marketers-ignore-sheconomy-women-key-buying-decisions-home-work/

3. Sekharan, V., March, 2015, Infographic, Canadian Women in Poverty, http://www.homelesshub.ca/blog/infographic-canadian-women-poverty

4. Boomer Generational Chart pdf., http://www.wmfc.org/uploads/GenerationalDifferencesChart.pdf

5. Erma Bombeck was an American journalist and writer that took up women's rights and advocacy in the 1970's. The website dedicated to her life and achievements, www.ermamuseum.org was the source used. N.a., n.d., http://ermamuseum.org/life/default.asp.

6. Emily Murphy, as a Canadian magistrate and activist heralded reform for women's rights but with racist overtones and serious repercussions for mentally ill patients who were subjected to forced sterilizations. Sources were drawn from: http://www.biographyonline.net/women/emily-murphy.html, http://www.lsuc.on.ca/WorkArea/DownloadAsset.aspx?id=2147484356, http://www.map-inc.org/drugnews/v05/n213/a01.html

Chapter 2

7. Cortisol levels and stress: several websites contain the information about effects of stress and symptoms. As a person with several decades of health-conscious living and personal training derived from various trainers, coaches, and specialists knowledge often comes through these sources. Refer to www.medicine.net or www.todaysdietician.com for additional information on the topic.

8. Rubin Wainrib, Barbara. Healing Crisis and Trauma with Mind, Body, and Spirit. New York: Springer Publications, 2006. Print. (Pg. 1)

9. Hans Selye, Eustress and Distress, flight, fight or paralysis; Selye was one of the first to name the pattern of chemical reactions in the body. Refer to the website: Rosch, Paul J., Birth of Stress: Reminiscenses of Hans Selye, and the Birth of "Stress" and Kupriyanov, Roman, and Renad Zhdanov. The Eustress Concept: Problems and Outlooks. World Journal of Medical Sciences 11 (2): 179-185, 2014, http://www.idosi.org/wjms/11(2)14/6.pdf. N.d. Web.

10. Cortisol, norephinephrine, adrenalin, and chronic disease: refer to www.medicine.net or www.todaysdietician.com for additional information on the topic that explains more about adrenal fatigue and the relationship to stress.

11. N.a., n.d., What is Brain Fog? http://www.wisegeek.org/what-is-brain-fog.htm There are a multitude of causes and cures for this condition that makes us feel fuzzy-headed and unable to focus. For women it can be hormonal, stress-related, and may also signal illness. It's highly recommended to speak with your physician about the problem if you find yourself suffering with the health condition.

12. Girdano, Daniel, Dorothy E. Dusek, George S. Everly Jr. Controlling Stress and Tension (9th Edition). Cummings. 2012. Print. (p. 231)

13. http://homeless.samhsa.gov/ResourceFiles/hrc_factsheet.pdf

14. Girdano, 2012, (p. 231)

15. Levine, Peter A. Waking the Tiger: Healing Trauma: The Innate Capacity to Transform Overwhelming Experiences. Berkeley, CA: North Atlantic, 1997. Print. (p. 127)

16. Tedeschi and Calhoun; referred to in Levine's work, these two researchers began their work in the early '90's with a published article dated July 9th, 1996 addressing the phenomenon of PTSD. http://www.ncbi.nlm.nih.gov/pubmed/8827649

17. Levine, 1997, (p. 133-138)

18. Seligman, Martin E. P., Flourish. North Sydney, N.S.W.: Random House Australia, 2011. Print. Dr. Seligman continues his work from the position as director of the Positive Psychology Center located at the University of Pennsylvania. Further research on the subject can begin at www.positivepsychology.com where you can find access to the authentic happiness portal with more questionnaires and tools for measurement and study Dr. Seligman uses for ongoing research.

19. Circadian rhythm covers our unique 24-hour cycle of responses to waking, sleeping, and body functions. For more information you can use this site and it's links to get up to speed on this important function; The Circadian Rhythms Fact Sheet, http://www.nigms.nih.gov/Education/Pages/Factsheet_CircadianRhythms.aspx

Chapter 3

20. Greek myths and superstitions; refer to http://www.faliraki-info.com/susie/superstitions/greek-traditions.htm. This site is a directory that lists alphabetically a few of the superstitions that are still present in Greek villages and a few protective cures are practiced throughout the globe where the influence has reached.

21. Numerology and names; visit http://www.paulsadowski.com/Numbers.asp . His website has a free resource to use to figure out your numbers if there is an interest in this facet of esoteric, divinatory art. There are several other sites when you search numerology and names.

22. Caulfield, Timothy A. The Cure for Everything: Untangling Twisted Messages about Health, Fitness, and Happiness. Boston: Beacon, 2012. Print. (N.p.)

23 Achor, Shawn. Before Happiness: The 5 Hidden Keys to Achieving Success, Spreading Happiness, and Sustaining Positive Change. 2013. E-Book. (p. 129)

24. Dr. Caulfield uses a quote in his book "get your facts first, then you can distort them as much as I please" and attributes them to Mark Twain, however on the site http://www.twainquotes.com/Facts.html, the words are attributed to Rudyard Kipling in From Sea to Shining Sea.

25. Gary O'Donovan and Rob Shave that concluded: "The public erroneously believes that moderate activity offers greater health benefits than vigorous activity. Refer to article, "British Adults' Views on the Health Benefits of Moderate and Rigorous Activity." Preventive Medicine 45 (2007): 432-35. (Caulfield (2012), References)

26. Caulfield, 2012, (N.p.)

27. Worthington, Jr., E., "Forgiveness and Reconciliation: Theory and Application". Google Books. https://books.google.ca/books?id=HiZTZifesZoC&dq=isbn:1135450951. May 13, 2013. Web. ...the hope (the will) of faith (understanding): Definitions taken from Dr. Everett Worthington, Jr. and his work on forgiveness. As a Professor with Virginia Commonwealth University, he offers counseling resources on his website http://www.psychology.vcu.edu/people/worthington.shtml with a link to http://forgiveself.com/ that includes a recent publication his book, "Moving Forward: Six Steps to Forgiving Yourself & Breaking Free from the Past." (2013)

28. Serotonin: for further information refer to: N.a., June, 2015. What is Serotonin? What does Serotonin Do? http://www.medicalnewstoday.com/articles/232248.php

29. Lyubomirsky, Sonja. The Myths of Happiness: What Should Make You Happy but Doesn't, What Shouldn't Make You Happy but Does. New York: Penguin, 2013. Print.

30. Achor, 2013, (p. 5)

31. Ibid. (p. 124)

32. Krieger, James. The Pitfalls of Body Fat "Measurement", The Final Chapter www.weightology.net. http://weightology.net/weightologyweekly/?page_id=283. N.d. Web.

33. Hydrodensitometry: definition as the "weighing of an object immersed in water and the measurement of the water displaced."

" http://connection.ebscohost.com/c/reference-entries/21231212/hydrodensitometry. Skin callipers: instrument used to determine lean body mass; http://www.medicinenet.com/script/main/art.asp?articlekey=25893, BIA stands for Bioelectrical impedance analysis; DEXA stands for dual energy X-ray absorptiometry. Both are used to gather information about body composition. The caution is to research what these really mean to your lifestyle regimen. If there are more costs related to having them done, what you will do with the information?

34. Achor, 2013, (p. 124)

35. Ibid.

36. Rubin Wainrib, 2006, (p. 28)

Chapter 4

37. Montuori, Alfonso, Creative Inquiry: Confronting the challenges of scholarship in the 21st century. Futures, Volume 44, Issue 1, February 2012, Abstract, http://www.sciencedirect.com/science/article/pii/S0016328711002205

38. Neil Armstrong – First Moon Landing 1969 https://www.youtube.com/watch?v=cwZb2mqId0A

39. Kreiser, J., September, 2012, 1972 Summit Series shaped modern hockey. Summit Series 40th Anniversary. http://www.nhl.com/ice/news.htm?id=640724

40. These are the names of our celebrity women from the 70's and 80's. Check out www.famouscanadians.org for more names but these women do round out the headlines of that timeframe. Note that Margaret Trudeau is not listed at that site however she can be found on IMDb and the web.

41. Hutterite Colonies – This religious group migrated to Northern Alberta and the Prairie Provinces after World War 1 from Eastern Europe to find a better way of life. For more information about the Colonies, their beliefs and lifestyle visit the website, www.hutterites.org.

42. N.a., n.d, The Oil Sands Story (1960's, 1970's, & 1980's)

http://www.suncor.com/en/about/744.aspx

43. Dyer, Wayne W. Real Magic: Creating Miracles in Everyday Life. New York, NY: HarperCollins, 1992. Print.

44. Dyer, Wayne W. Excuses Begone! How to Change Lifelong, Self-Defeating Thinking Habits. Carlsbad, CA: Hay House, 2009. Print. (P. 232)

Chapter 5

45. Seligman, 2011,

46. Dyer, Real Magic, 1992, (p. 236)

47. Neweduk, J., June, 2015, Shrivelling Vaginas? Fabulous at 50 Blog. http://www.fabulousat50.com/Blog@50/TabId/244/PostId/165/shrivelling-vaginas.aspx

48. Dyer, Real Magic, 1992, (p. 234)

49. Garrett, M., February, 2014, Complexity of Our Brain, https://www.psychologytoday.com/basics/neuroscience. On this same website is the definition of Neuroscience as the aim to bridge psychology and biology.

50. N.a., n.d, Madonna, www.madonna.com. If you want to familiarize yourself with how this famous musician has transformed herself over the years this site gives the background for her looks and life as a Boomer turned 57 in 2015.

52. Dyer, Real Magic, 1992, (pgs. 116-117)

Chapter 6

53. Fabulous at 50 Blog: Lean Into Your Life. http://www.fabulousat50.com/Blog@50/TabId/244/PostId/63/Lean-Into-Your-Life.aspx

54. Earley, Jay, and Bonnie Weiss. Freedom from Your Inner Critic: A Self-therapy Approach. 2013. Print.

55. Earley, Weiss, 2013, (n.p., books.google.ca)

56. Ibid.

57. Richard Schwartz, Ph.D., Internal Family Systems Therapy, IFS. Marriage and Family Therapist. http://selfleadership.org/about-richard-schwartz.html

58. Dr. Earley and Bonnie Weiss have their website: www.selftherapyjourney.com

This site has many different tools and resources that are accessible and interesting. It's worth a visit if you want to learn much more about their techniques for self-discovery.

59. Earley, Weiss, 2013, (n.p., books.google.ca)

60. Ibid.

61. Ibid.

62. Ibid.

77. Dyer, Wayne W. Wishes Fulfilled: Mastering the Art of Manifesting. Carlsbad, CA: Hay House, 2012. Print.

Chapter 7

78. Neuroplasticity – The definition according to this site is the ability to form new neural connections follows the current research. This site contains an extensive resource of easy to understand health concepts with images and more links to investigate. http://www.medicinenet.com/script/main/art.asp?articlekey=40362

79. Dyer, "Wishes Fulfilled" (2012) , "Real Magic"(1992). Both books discuss the methods for manifesting and are excellent reading for his material on his philosophy and inspirational teachings.

80. Millions of definitions on creativity can be found in an Internet search. However, this site was found later that may be interesting to visit; www.thesecondprinciple.com. It showcases the work of retired Professor Leslie Owen Wilson, Ed.D. and offers a reading list and links, that even though it is targeted to the educational professional, anyone interested in creativity and multiple intelligence might want to follow up on his recommendations.

81. Gilbert,"Big Magic: Creative Living Beyond Fear" (2015)

82. Michalko, M., n.d., "Thought Experiments." www.creativethinking.net. http://creativethinking.net/the-imaginary-house/#sthash.WYl5R9nN.dpbs. Web.

83. Deutsch, Bob, and Lou Aronica. The 5 Essentials: Using Your Inborn Resources to Create a Fulfilling Life. 2013. Print. (p. 77)

Chapter 8

84. N.a., n.d., Red wine and reversatrol: Good for you're your heart? http://www.mayoclinic.org/diseases-conditions/heart-disease/in-depth/red-wine/ART-20048281

85. Bstan-dzin-rgya-mtsho. (The Dalai Lama) Beyond Religion: Ethics for a Whole World. Boston: Houghton Mifflin Harcourt, 2011. Print. (p. 22)

Chapter 9

86. Burgess, Gloria. Dare to Wear Your Soul on the Outside: Live Your Legacy Now. San Francisco: Jossey-Bass, 2008. Print.

87. N.a., n.d., http://www.wmfc.org/uploads/GenerationalDifferencesChart.pdf

88. Luskin, F., Forgive for Good: A Proven Prescription for Health and Happiness. Harper San Francisco. 2002. Print.

89. Worthington, 2013.

90. Warner, J. Bad Memories Easier To Remember, http://www.webmd.com/brain/news/20070829/bad-memories-easier-to-remember. August, 2007. Web.

91. Seligman, 2011, (p. 91)

92. Nosta, J., Genius is our birthright and mediocrity is self-imposed. www.ted.com, https://www.youtube.com/watch?v=lrdlczkk1Nc. September, 2014. Web.

93. Nosta, 2014.

94. http://www.quilterscache.com/images21/house6x7.gif

Chapter 10

94. Li, Ding, March, 2014. FameLab Hong Kong, 2014 – winner – Li Ding "Smile" https://www.youtube.com/watch?v=_PIubAxEqoo

95. Furnham, A. The Surprising Psychology of the Smiling, https://www.psychologytoday.com/blog/sideways-view/201410/the-surprising-psychology-smiling. October, 2014. Web.

96 Hackman, M. Z., Johnson, C. Leadership: A Common Perspective. Waveland Press Inc. 2000. Print.

97. Kukla, André. Mental Traps: Stupid Things That Sane People Do to Mess up Their Minds. New York: McGraw-Hill, 2007. Print.

98. Furnham. 2014.

99. Fuller, Catherine, and Phil Taylor. A Toolkit for Motivational Skills: Encouraging and Supporting Change in Individuals. Chichester. West Sussex, England: John Wiley & Sons, 2008. Print. (p. 105-109)

100. N.a., February, 2013. Funny Goats Screaming Like Humans. You Tube Video. https://www.youtube.com/watch?v=nlYlNF30bVg

Chapter 11

101. Peters, Brad. July, 2012. In Search of Meaning (Part 2/3): Rebellion. Modern Psychologist. http://modernpsychologist.ca/in-search-of-meaning-part-23-rebellion/

102. Devlin, Hannah. May, 2015. Early men and women wre equal, say scientists. Anthropology. http://www.theguardian.com/science/2015/may/14/early-men-women-equal-scientists

103. Dyer, Real Magic, 1992, (p. 8)

104. Ury, William. The Power of a Positive No: How to Say No and Still Get to Yes. New York: Bantam, 2007. Print.

105. www.willliamury.com. Ury's site offers some sample excerpts to read of his books along with tools for negotiating and self-help with tip sheets and additional links to resources.

106. Ury, 2007, (p. 121)

107. Ibid. (p. 225)

108. Ibid.

Chapter 12

109. N.a., n.d., http://www.statcan.gc.ca/

110. Smolkin, C. February, 2013. Older Canadians Workers Find Success in Second Careers, www.thestar.com. http://www.thestar.com/business/personal_finance/2013/02/24/older_canadians_leverage_experience_to_work_longer.html

111. Dyer, "Real Magic", 1992, (p. 223)

112. http://dictionary.reference.com/browse/empathy

113. Kashdan, Todd B. Curious? Discover the Missing Ingredient to a Fulfilling Life. New York: William Morrow, 2009. Print.

114. Kashdan, 2009.

115. Ibid.

116. Idid. (p. 7)

117. Seligman, 2011.

118. books.google.ca (p. 137): Wyer, Robert S., Roger C. Shank, and Robert P. Abelson. Knowledge and Memory: The Real Story. Hillsdale, NJ: Lawrence Erlbaum Associates. 1995. Print.

119. Dale, Cyndi. The Spiritual Power of Empathy: Develop Your Intuitive Gifts for Compassionate Connection. Llewellyn Publications. 2014. Print. (p. 4)

120. Turner, Kelly. May, 2014. "The Science Behind Intuition." Psychology Today https://www.psychologytoday.com/blog/radical-remission/201405/the-science-behind-intuition

121. Turner, 2014.

122. Ibid.

123. Ibid.

Chapter 13

124. www.ywca.org. The organization is spread across Canada and the US and is devoted to eliminating issues that disempower women. Pay a visit to read their latest efforts and support programs.

125. For more information on Dr. Margaret-Ann Amour and her efforts visit the website: http://www.winsett.ca/team

126. N.a., December, 2010. Margaret-Ann Amour named one of Canada's Top 100 Most Powerful Women. University of Alberta News and Events. https://uofa.ualberta.ca/news-and-events/news-articles/2010/12/margaretannarmournamedoneofcanadastop100mostpowerfulwomen

127. Marks, Gene. December, 2013. This Is Why The Baby Boomers Are the Worst Generation Ever. The Blog. http://www.huffingtonpost.com/gene-marks/this-is-why-the-baby-boom_b_4441735.html

128. "Field of Dreams" (1989), "Groundhog Day" (1993) for more on the films: www.imdb.com

Chapter 14

129. Campbell, Joseph, and Bill D. Moyers. The Power of Myth. New York: Doubleday, 1988. Print. (p.)

130. The Dalai Lama, 2011, (p. 13-16)

131. Ibid. (p. 12)

132. Hanson, Erin, n.d. The Residential School System. The University of British Columbia. http://indigenousfoundations.arts.ubc.ca/home/government-policy/the-residential-school-system.html

133. To claim the gift offer write to the email address: info@fabulousat50.com .

Specify in the subject to: gift offer 2015. There will be a limited time offer that is yet to be determined. Visit the site www.fabulousat50.com for information.

134. Kashdan, 2009.

135. Widrich, Leo, April, 2013. The Science of Smiling: A Guide to The World's Most Powerful Gesture . Buffersocial. https://blog.bufferapp.com/the-science-of-smiling-a-guide-to-humans-most-powerful-gesture. Dr. Paula M. Neidenthal is a Professor with the University of Wisconsin, Department of Psychology. She is the researcher of emotion processes and her study was used in the reference of this material. Her website; http://niedenthal.socialpsychology.org/

Final Notes

The first quote attributed to SSu-k'ung T'u on the Art of Savouring in the introduction was excerpted from: Richards, Ruth. Everyday Creativity and New Views of Human Nature: Psychological, Social, and Spiritual Perspectives. Washington, DC: American Psychological Association, 2007. Print.

Resources -

HEALTH RESOURCES
Canadian Cancer Society
Canadian Celiac Association
Canadian Cystic Fibrosis Fdn
Canadian Diabetes Association
Canadian Liver Foundation
Canadian Mental Health
Canadian National Institute for the Blind
Heart & Stroke Foundation
Huntington's Disease Resouce Centre
Kidney Foundation of Canada
Menopause Canada
Menopause Clinic - Grey Nuns Hospital
Mesothelioma Group
Osteoporosis Canada
Ovarian Cancer Canada
Parkinsons Society of Alberta
Schizophrenia Society of Canada
Spinal Cord Injury Canada
The Society of Obstetrics and
Gynaecology of Canada
The Support Network

COMMUNITIES
aginghipsters.com
Boomster.com
BabyBoomers.com
CafeBabyBoomers.com
BoomerGrandparents.com
Fabulousat50.com
LifeAfter50.com
www.boomerbabesrock.com
www.boomerwomenspeak.com
www.carp.ca

DATING
christian-dating-service-plus.com-
SeniorMatch.com
www.datingforseniors.com
BoomerMatchUp.com
eHarmony.com

ENTERTAINMENT
BabyBoomer-Magazine.com
www.fabulousat50.com
baby-boomers-life.com

FINANCIAL
retirementrevised.com
ccdr.ca
SmartMoney.com
www.fool.com
ProtectYourNestEggInRetirement.com
GuardingYourWealth.com
boomersretirement.blogspot.ca
money.cnn.com
kiplinger.com
TheSimpleDollar.com

HEALTH
ThirdAge.com

HOUSEHOLD
About.com
eHow.com
Mahalo.com
TheSimpleDollar.com
PriceProtectr.com

JOBS
Monster.com
craigslist.ca

LIFESTYLE
boomernet.com

LONG-TERM CARE
nihseniorhealth.gov

BLOGS
www.thirdage.com
aboomerslifeafter50.blogspot.com
www.boomerwomenspeak.com
feistysideoffifty.com
boomerwomanblog.blogsp
baby-boomers-life.com
ot.com
www.nabbw.com/blog
www.womentravelblog.com
www.vibrantnation.com
www.boomerdivanation.org
www.blogher.com/3-tips-boomer-women
www.boomerwatch.ca
www.sharpseniors.com/blogs

MAGAZINES

babyboomer-magazine.com
Be Fabulous! EMagazine
www.fabulousat50.com
www.everythingzoomer.com

NEWS

www.msnbc.msn.com

MEDITATION MUSIC

https://youtu.be/5PIBMLvcAzc
https://youtu.be/
luRkeDCoxZ4?list=RDpZ7XIWgseJ0
https://youtu.be/U-dIEm3fiPQ
https://youtu.be/8e9GllPbg2A

TRAVEL

aarp.org
craigslist.ca
homeexchange50plus.com
www.hotelclub.com/Canada
www.boomeropia.com
BabyBoomerTrips.com

COMMUNITIES

BoomerWomenSpeak.com
www.nabbw.com

DOCUMENTARIES

Your Second Fifty: http://ysfdocumentary.com

COACHES
SEMINARS/COURSES

www.tonyrobbins.com/events
www.stonecirclecoaching.com
www.thecreatorscode.com
www.staceyberger.ca
https://brendonburchard.com
http://mymsuccess.com
www.themasteryworkshops.com

OTHER

Akashic Records - www.maureenstgermain.com
Debbie Dachinger - Radio Mastery Training
http://debbidachinger.com
http://mybestsellerbook.com
Tina and Neil Thrussell
www.bestucanb.ca

BUSINESS/INFLUENCE

Teresa de Grosbois
www.wildfireacademy.com/mastering-influence
Terry Levine, Phd
www.BusinessConsultantInstitute.com

COSMO CLUB COACHES

Shirley Borrelli - Confidence/Image
Dr. Diana Galbraith - Healthtalks
Zandra Bell - Goddess Girlfriend
Jaden Sterling - Wealth Mastery
Dr. Pam Robertson - Business
Rae-Ann Wood Schatz - Personal Development
Patricia Gibb - Natural Weight Loss
Laurel Vespi - Awaken to the Possibilities
Dr. Rose Backman - The Unstoppable Woman
Sharon Carne - Sound Wellness
Katrina Sawa - Small Biz Start Up & Marketing
Liza Copeland - Dating Coach
Debra Kasowski - Personal/Business Coach
Bonita Lehman - Emotional Intelligence
Stacey Berger - Dream Builder
Loretta Friedrich - Holistic Nutritionist

**Please visit http://www.fabulousat50.com/
Membership/Coaches.aspx for more
information on these coaches.**

Index

221

Meet Dianna Bowes - Author

Dianna is a shining example of how to get the most out of life as a "seasoned" woman. At a time when most of us look to relax in front of the TV, she is out in our Alberta communities creating a dynasty! And in her "spare time," she turns her time and talents to family and friends, graphic design, painting, biking, cross-country skiing and fulfilling a host of volunteer commitments.

Though Dianna is now a successful entrepreneur and inspiration to many, she had to overcome many barriers to get there. Raised by grandparents in a dysfunctional family, Dianna was shy and lacking in self-confidence as a child and young adult.

She married at 20, but tragically her new husband was killed in a explosion within a year. She remarried a few years later and was blessed with two children who are the light of her life. But the marriage was rocky and further eroded Dianna's self-esteem. A serious health problem (tumour on her vertebrae) in her 40s brought things to a head and the marriage ended. Rather than wallow in despair, Bowes decided to take control of her life. She recreated herself into the woman she always wanted to be by focusing on personal development and coaching. When her 50th birthday was approaching, she started Fabulous@50 (a community for seasoned woman) and has never looked back. Now confident and poised, Bowes is dedicated to helping other women through their life changes and challenges. Bowes has won numerous awards for her work: a 2014 Leader of Tomorrow Award from Business in Edmonton, 2011 YWCA Woman of Distinction Award (Turning Point category) The 2014 New York Stevie Awards in two categories: Women Helping Women (Bronze) and Best Event (Gold). 2015 New York Stevie Award - Top Canadian Entrepreneur (Bronze).

To contact Dianna - dianna@fabulousat50.com   Please visit us at www.fabulousat50.com

Deborah L. Smith - Writer

Deborah L. Smith, a Boomer-Zoomer woman and Metis, spent 13 years in Los Angeles, CA, as an aspiring screenwriter. The turn in her career focus was meeting up with a Film Cooperative of young filmmakers in 2003 that needed help with their projects. She became an independent producer putting her writing aside to work with these wild, undisciplined creatives. She managed to further her education, ending her stay in the U.S. with an Associate Degree in Cinema, a Bachelors'-in-progress majoring in Communications, a TV Studio Technician Certificate, and a Certificate in Producing and Writing from Los Angeles Film School.

Currently she plans to attend Simon Fraser University in Burnaby, British Columbia in the fall eventually leading to her MFA in Multidisciplinary Studies that will include Writing, Native Studies and Film. She has turned a fresh eye to return to writing having completed two screenplays, a 20,000 word novella she is readying for publication and working on magazine articles.